THEY ALSO SERVE

THEY ALSO SERVE: the experiences of a
Cathedral chorister's chaperone,
is by Christine Hawkins.

First published in July 2021

© Christine Hawkins July 2021

Christine also asserts the moral right
to be identified as the author.

Cover photograph © Alan Edington 2014.

Published by
Christine Hawkins,
Morpeth, Northumberland

ISBN: 978-09-54205-92-8

THEY ALSO SERVE

The experiences of a Cathedral chorister's chaperone.

by

Christine Hawkins.

Acknowledgements

I am grateful to so many people.

To my granddaughter Jessica for all the ways she has enriched my life.

To the Directors of Music at Newcastle Cathedral – Michael Stoddart and his assistant James Norrey, and later Ian Roberts and his assistant Kris Thomsett – who have given my granddaughter a sound musical education tempered with lots of fun.

To the Cathedral Music Assistants – Hannah Davidson, Amy Leach and Emily Stolting, who have given her pastoral care over the years.

To the Cathedral verging staff, especially Gordon Scott and Alan Edington, for kindly tolerance and occasional cups of coffee, and for keeping the Cathedral so clean, warm and cheerful. To Alan for the cover photo.

To the Royal School of Church Music for so many opportunities, especially to Andrew Reid for encouragement and Sarah King at their Head Office for seamless organisation, and to Mandy Walker and many other kind ladies who gave pastoral care and chaperonage on residential courses in far-flung locations.

To Steven Johnson, former Head of Chantry Middle School, Morpeth, who allowed Jessica to leave school very early on choir days, and the staff of King Edward VI School who also allowed considerable time off to meet special choir commitments. I think secretly they felt it was an honour to have a Cathedral chorister in their school, and they were quite right!

An active choir life requires a lot of travel, and I am grateful to Roger for driving us while he could and for enduring so much frustration in the search for parking spaces, and then to so many unknown taxi drivers, bus drivers and train drivers who whisked us safely and comfortably all over the country. I am truly grateful for my free bus pass and my Senior Railcard.

And of course to many, many choristers who have cheered my waiting hours with beautiful singing. May they sing for ever!

Christine Hawkins, July 2021

Beautiful!" She had taken extra lessons in keyboard, violin and recorder at different times, though had not excelled at any of them. It was singing she specially liked. At her last All Saints Christmas carol concert, held at St James's Church, she was asked to sing a solo first verse of *Silent Night*. It went very well, and lots of people congratulated her on it afterwards. "You want to get that voiced trained!" a number of them said to us, as though we were in dereliction of duty by not having done so already. While we were sure they meant it kindly, we were not of the opinion that her voice needed to be trained. We, and she herself, were very happy with it as it was. At Chantry Jessica joined the school choir for a few months, but rapidly became disenchanted with both the choir and the music lessons because the teacher was bossy and shouted a lot. Lessons had to be endured, but choir did not and she gave it up.

Around this time Jessica expressed the wish to learn to play the piano, and we fixed up for her to have lessons with Mrs Pat Hills who we knew slightly from joint church activities between Morpeth Methodist Church and St George's URC. Mrs Hills said confidently, "I'll teach her to read music!" and she did. While Jessica did not seem to progress very rapidly in playing the piano, her ability to read music developed strongly and was to stand her in good stead.

On Saturday, September 15th, we set off for St Nicholas's Cathedral in the late morning. It was a thirteen mile drive to Newcastle, and when we got there we had to find a parking space, not easy on a Saturday when the world was doing its shopping.

St Nicholas's Cathedral is not far from the centre of the city, in what is sometimes called the Mediaeval Quarter which it shares with the Castle. It is on the corner of Mosley Street and St Nicholas Street, and is presided over at the north side by a statue of Queen Victoria. It has hardly any land around it. It's an attractive building with a lantern tower which was, in former days, used as a beacon for shipping. We entered by the north door and immediately found ourselves in a cool, dim, quiet oasis. The contrast between the bustle of the city and the calm of the Cathedral was impressive.

The "Day" was in fact only two and a half hours, and began at 1.30. We were directed to a little group of chairs round a grand piano in the south transept, and sat down to wait to see what would happen. We were the only parents in sight, but we did not plan to leave Jessica till we, and she, knew what was happening. A few children had gathered, but there was no formal welcome. I rather got the impression that this was the first "Be a Chorister for a Day" and they hadn't got their act together. A nice big girl came and sat next to Jessica and chatted a bit, and told the younger children near her in a loud whisper that they ought to socialise, but they didn't. We later learnt that this was Celia Stoddart, the youngest of the four daughters of Michael Stoddart, the Director of Music. Sheets of paper were passed round for details to be filled in, and when we had filled them in we decided our absence might be appreciated all round and we removed ourselves. We did not go far. We had promised Jessica we would stay somewhere in the Cathedral all the time, and we did. From our pew in the nave we could see the children singing for someone who played the piano, and Mr Stoddart seemed to be bouncing around with a camera photographing everyone. We supposed this was so he could later study the video and decide who was singing heartily and who was not, and therefore who was likely to be useful to him.

Thus began years of sitting around waiting for choir rehearsals to end.

We tucked ourselves into a pew and made the best of it. Sometimes we read our own books, sometimes we read the literature off the Welcome Table, and Roger spent quite a bit of time studying the stone memorial inscriptions on the walls. Happily it was a warm day. Almost as soon as we had left Jessica the group had disappeared up the south aisle to the Song School (as we later found it to be). Later still they trooped back to the west end and disappeared again. We thought they must have been taken out of the Cathedral and were slightly concerned, but it transpired they had been taken up the tower and out onto the roof at the bottom of the spire, from where they had a great view of the city below them. I would not have liked that at all, but Jessica found it great fun. Happily no one fell to their deaths, either from the roof or on the worn stone staircase. I gathered later that there had been no refreshments, surely an essential for such occasions, but someone had sent a tin of cheese scones and there was a tap where you could get water if you wanted any. Jessica didn't. Soon after 3 o'clock the Verger began to distribute printed orders of service. Apparently we were all to take part in a special service devised for the occasion. We had heard some of it being practised. About 3.30 the organ played and the choir trooped in wearing robes. Established choristers wore white cassocks with red tabards (girls) and red cassocks with white surplices (boys). Jessica and one or two other little cadets just wore the white cassocks. She looked very dignified as she processed in. She exchanged a little smile with us, but later told us off for smiling at such a solemn moment. The choir were arranged in the choir stalls, and the handful of parents gathered in the front pews. Some of them looked a bit embarrassed and didn't know what to do. We knew, because although we are not Anglicans we have attended quite a few services in Cathedrals over the years and we also read the instructions which were very clear. It was a pleasant little service which included the main elements of Choral Evensong. After this the children went to disrobe and then came back to their parents who were waiting for them. Mr Stoddart had our details, and would be getting in touch with us all during the coming week. Jessica said she had loved it all, and really wanted to join the choir.

We had been afraid of this. To us it seemed an impossible idea. We could take her to the Cathedral on Sundays, but there would be rehearsals and other services that would be sure to be at times she couldn't manage. Morpeth was thirteen miles from Newcastle. We said we thought there was little chance of it, but we would wait and see what Mr Stoddart said when he contacted us. So we waited, but Jessica could think of little else.

At last on the following Wednesday a detailed email arrived shortly before Jessica was due home from school. Mr Stoddart would be happy to audition any child who would like to join the choir. Being a chorister involved both morning and evening services on about three Sundays a month, with after-school rehearsal and then Choral Evensong on Mondays and Thursdays. On weeknights choristers should be in their places ready to sing at 4.30, which of course meant getting to the Cathedral at about 4.20 to be ready. School ended at 3.25, so how could it be done? Rehearsals continued after evensong till 6.30. How much evening would be left for poor Jessica to eat and unwind? And it would cost quite a bit in petrol and parking. When Jessica came in from school we had not had much time to mull it over but we were quite sure it was out of the question.

She read the email and had to agree with our decision, but she wept. It was not the weeping of a child who has been thwarted in a short-term wish, but the weeping of grief at what was greatly to be desired but could never be. We sympathised. Poor Jessica had had so much frustration and disruption in her short life, and we very much wished we could gratify her in this, but we didn't see how we could. We promised her that after she had gone to bed that night we would review the situation and see if there was anything to be done. We were not very sanguine, but she seemed greatly cheered.

Later we talked it over. Sundays were no problem, though we would have to find something to do with ourselves between Eucharist and Evensong, but the weeknights were difficult. It would mean us being ready in the Morpeth Rugby Club carpark to meet her out of school, and driving as fast as was consistent with safety to Newcastle. Roger could drop us off and look for somewhere to park. The cost of petrol and possibly parking was greater than the cost of going on the bus, which was free for me and Roger, but it was really important to have the car to get to the Cathedral in time and get her home earlier to go to bed. Tea would be a rushed job, either eaten in the car at 3.30 when she would not be hungry, or after she got home and had little time left to digest it. But it clearly could be done, and we thought we ought to give it a try. We went up to her bedroom and told her this, and she was so thrilled.

I emailed Mr Stoddart and said Jessica would love to be auditioned, and what was the next step? He replied that she should try to be there by 4.15 on the next choir night and he would audition her then. I promised that we would do our best to get her there in time.

I never knew if any other children were recruited from that day, but recruitment was always difficult because hardly any children lived within walking distance of the Cathedral. Most seemed to come from Newcastle High, Gosforth High, Royal Grammar School and Dame Allan's. One or two parents ferried a bunch from their child's school, or in some cases an older girl bussed and walked younger girls. As I was to learn, they were nearly all fee-paying pupils.

Mr Stoddart had expressed it as highly desirable, if not essential, that every chorister should play an instrument. Indeed many of them were proficient in several. By then

Jessica had just started her piano lessons with Mrs Hills so she met the requirements.

On the arranged night we met her from school as planned. The school cloakrooms were like bedlam at going-home time, and it took a long time for her to fight her way through, especially if she wanted the loo as well. Very often she did not appear until 3.45 or even 3.50, while we sat in the carpark and sweated with anxiety. Meanwhile the school-run traffic was building up between Morpeth and the city. If we got away in good time we had a fairly easy run, but if we were kept waiting the traffic could get really heavy. It was particularly busy on the urban motorway as we entered the city. We were never late, but it was often a near thing. Roger believed it was best to go back into Morpeth to join the A1, but eventually I prevailed upon him to turn right out of the school drive and take the rural route by what we always called the pill factory, joining the main road at the Golf Course, and it worked much better.

When we went through the Cathedral to the Song School door at the top of the south aisle we found it locked. It was opened by a keypad, but of course we didn't know the number. Gordon Scott, the Head Verger, was passing, and he took pity on us. He told us that the number was "the long, hot summer", but that didn't mean much to me. I was older than most people there and I remembered quite a few long hot summers, but I would have been hard put to date any of them. This door turned out to be 19** (I had better not be more specific in case they still use that number). Other doors, I learnt in due course, were numbered in memory of the founding of (a certain notable institution) and the death of (a certain notable person), but I never knew the Vestry number because that was closely guarded. And in any case I never had any business in there.

Mr Stoddart met us in the back hall and took us up to the Song School on the second floor. It was accessed by a

Mr Stoddart, with whom we soon came to be on "Michael" terms, had an assistant called James Norrey. He joined the staff about the same time as Jessica. He was young and handsome, but sadly had acquired some bad habits. He always rushed outside at the end to light up, and would talk about how he was on his way to the pub. But he treated the girls well and they liked him. He usually took one practice a week. Sometimes when he was not there to play the organ Michael Haynes, the Assistant Organist, would play.

We had not been there long before the organ died. It was past repairing, and it was decided to retire it and borrow one for the immediate future, then to buy a cheap one for the short-term future, with a view to having the old one rebuilt. The "new" borrowed one had its console in the Quire near the crossing, and it was nice to see it being played. Over months new bits of casing were installed at the side of the old organ, which I gathered were either to hide work that was being done or to house the new speakers. It was all a mystery to me. Then we had another organ that I gather was bought, but it is still only a temporary measure till the old organ can be rebuilt. Now we have two consoles in the original organ loft, which must be quite a cramped space, and we can no longer see the organist. In my opinion it is not a very melodious sounding instrument, but who am I?

Time went by and we got used to our new routine. The main disadvantage was that poor Jessica got no unwinding time on choir nights. At first she also had Guides at our own church on Mondays and we did our best to get her there in good time for that too, but eventually that was traded for steel-pan lessons which took place at another time. As for food, we often stopped to get her some supper from the Great North Chippy in Gosforth, phoning ahead to ask them to put chicken nuggets in the fryer. We worried in case she was overdoing it. She generally had difficulty getting up in the morning, but with good reason after choir nights. I had never realised how hard choristers work!

Eventually, to our relief, the work on the lighting came to an end and we were able to wait in comfort in the nave again. Maintaining a Cathedral is rather like the painting of the Forth Bridge – there is always some work needs to be ongoing. But whereas the Forth Bridge has plenty of money for paint etc, a Cathedral has little and has to take time off to raise funds. At that point the funds needing to be raised were for the clearing out of the pews from the nave and underfloor heating being installed. That took longer. When that work is finally started and finished there will be fundraising for the rebuilding of the organ. Will that be in our time, I wonder? An artist's impression of the organ project that I saw in the Thomlinson Room shows the original organ mounted over the crossing.

The Thomlinson Room? That used to be a library but has been refurbished for the choir to do general purpose things in, like changing their robes and hanging them in cupboards. It is directly below the room that is properly called The Song School. It's quite modern and pleasant with a big table where, among other things, girls who have managed to bring anything to eat can eat it, or can do a bit of their homework. Meetings are sometimes held in there. I think it was in early 2015 that the Song School roof started to leak, and had to be covered and stripped and repaired. For months that part of the building was covered in scaffolding and netting, and rehearsals took place in the Thomlinson Room.

When we first started the choir was in pretty good shape but losing members. Michael, who had started the girls' choir with his own four daughters, had just lost his second daughter to university and only had Emily and Celia, and of the Dean's children only Bella and Georgie remained, and Georgie was also off to university. The Head Chorister was Rachel Dodds, and she was on the brink of university too. Although girls could stay in the trebles till they were eighteen, many of them were taken out by their parents to concentrate on exams. Boys were very thin on the ground, and Michael had great difficulty recruiting any. For a long time he kept the two choirs separate, but when it was the boys' turn to sing he invited the girls to volunteer to come and sing with them to encourage them.

Jessica liked the girls in the choir and enjoyed being with them. She liked Michael and James, and everything was generally good. She was very sorry in the summer of 2015 when James decided to leave to go to London. He hadn't got a job to go to, but said he wanted to be where the opportunities were. He was a sad loss to the Cathedral.

The clergy we regularly saw when we first went were the Dean, Chris Dalliston, Father Kevin Hunt who was Canon for Liturgy and Music, and Father Steven Harvey who came the same autumn as we did. They were all nice. Kevin and Steven were single, but the Dean had a family. His wife Michelle was also a priest. Gordon was assisted by Alan Edington, and earlier by another Alan (Walton) who retired. Alan was replaced by a lady called Tracy McKeever who was divorced and now in a civil partnership with an ex-nun. Tracy had a very interesting story, but alas her language was not always suitable for a Cathedral. She worked very hard but did not always hit it off with her male colleagues who I think may have resented the notion that their work could be done by a woman. During her time there she often came and had a chat with us.

Only once did I have the pleasure of bumping into the people who kept the place clean. I returned to the Cathedral about 7 o'clock one morning, after having seen some of the choir off on the train to a sports day, and I heard hearty Gospel singing in the toilets. It was a cheerful black lady who was cleaning. She apologised for disturbing me, but she made my day. I forget what it was she was singing, but it was not from *Hymns Ancient and Modern*. More like Sankey and Moody. I suppose the cleaning staff left before the end of the morning, so I would be unlikely to see them often.

In the Lantern Café, where I had sometimes worked as a volunteer twenty years before, there were three or four permanent staff. One was a manageress who I rarely saw, and the others, I was told, were volunteers, though I wondered what kind of volunteers they were. On occasions when my waiting included daytime café hours, which it very occasionally did, I felt I ought to do my snacking in there, but I was annoyed to be asked to pay 15p a sachet for vinegar. I don't think I have ever in my life been asked to pay extra for vinegar when I was having chips. Other condiments, such as tomato sauce and brown sauce, were also available in sachets for 15p, but there was little selection and sometimes they had run out. I asked for mustard to accompany my all-day breakfast sausage, but they did not have mustard. If there was special catering required for an event in the afternoon the café would either close early to the public or seriously reduce its services. I don't remember any apology ever being made for this. But if I was lucky enough to get food it was generally good, and I tried to remember to take my own vinegar. On one occasion I took vinegar, mustard, tomato sauce and tartare sauce from home, only to be told that they were not cooking meals that day and I could only have sandwiches. I took my sauce to a nearby store café, where of course I didn't need my own sauce anyway.

Then we had what seemed for a few minutes like a disaster. Roger's optician told him he had cataracts and must give up driving. It seemed like we would not be able to get Jessica to choir without regular taxis which we could not afford. This bombshell burst on a Wednesday, and we had to think about what to do next day. With some trepidation I sent an email to Mr Johnson, Jessica's head teacher at Chantry School, asking him if she could leave school forty minutes early on Mondays and Thursdays to catch a bus. He was very kind and readily agreed. I think he considered it a feather in the school's cap to have a Cathedral chorister!

Our new system was that she left Chantry at 2.45 and came directly to the bus station where we met her and caught a bus at 3.08. The later bus, at 23 past the hour, would also have done, but it would have involved a bit of a rush in Newcastle. When we got to Newcastle we cut through Marks and Spencer and the Eldon Square shopping mall to Nun Street and then walked down Bigg Market to the Cathedral. If Jessica was hungry, which she rarely was, there were several handy shops where she could buy a snack to eat on the hoof. Then afterwards we went home on the bus which generally fitted in well. The choir had to stay on after Evensong to rehearse till 6.30, then we hurried to town via Grey Street to Fenwick's where we got back into the dry and smoke-free atmosphere of the mall, and were then under cover till we got to Morpeth. As we passed through M&S we often bought sandwiches or other snacks to eat on the bus. They close at 7pm on Mondays, but we usually managed to get served in time, and on Thursday they were open till 8 so we had plenty of leisure. If it was cold we stayed in the shop on some nice courtesy chairs till our bus was due at 7.13. Failing that the bus station was enclosed and not especially cold, though the metal seats were often like ice. If we wanted a hot drink we could get one, on weekdays, for £1 from a machine in a little bus station newsagent. I did not have to pay for bus fares now I was a senior citizen, but Jessica had to pay £3.60 return. Eventually we got her an Arriva Teen Card which was not a lot of use on weekdays before 6, but saved us 10p. It cost her £2.50 single on the outward journey, and £1 coming back, so we only saved 10p, but at weekends it was a great help. Roger came with us on Mondays, but not Thursdays because he was glad of the rest after a busy morning running the Toddler group at our own church. He very kindly came to the bus station each time to collect Jessica's heavy school bag and take it home, then if he was coming he'd come on a later bus and join me at the Cathedral. We were generally home by 8, but as she was supposed to be in bed by 8.15 this necessitated late bedtimes.

On Sundays there was not an early enough bus to get us to the Cathedral for 9am when rehearsal began, so we had to take a taxi. This was not as bad as we might have thought because giving up the car saved us a huge amount of money. Car maintenance, petrol, parking, road tax, insurance and AA membership add up to far more than we ever realised! After morning service we had a choice. We could go home for about an hour, or we could have lunch in the city. The first was a bit of a rush, and the second was a bit of a drag. Finding somewhere we all liked for lunch was not easy, and after we had eaten we had to find somewhere to spend the rest of the time. The Central Library was open till at least 4, and Roger usually chose to go there, but Jessica preferred to mooch round shops. I can only take a certain amount of walking round and round brightly lit, smooth-floored shops and I always wanted to spend some of the time having a cup of coffee or similar, which Jessica found irritating. Often we went back to the Cathedral much earlier than we needed to for the 4.30pm rehearsal. In 2015 Michael, finding few people wanted to devote their whole day to the choir, changed the system so that the boys and/or girls only sang once on a Sunday, and the lay clerks filled in the other service. This worked well because we no longer had to stay over the lunch hours, and needed morning taxis a little less often.

Choristers at Newcastle are paid pocket money. Initiates get £24 a month, senior choristers £32, and Heads and Deputies more proportionately. This has been upgraded, and when Jessica started she got £9.80 a month. At many Cathedrals, where there is a choir school, the payment to choristers consists of a reduction in school fees which is no benefit at all to the chorister, but as we have no school the Dean and Chapter in their wisdom have decreed that pocket money shall be paid. Jessica likes this very much.

On all choir occasions uniform has to be worn, and this consists of black trousers, white shirts and choir ties for boys, black skirts with black tights or black trousers with black socks and white shirts but no ties for girls, and for both boys and girls a black blazer with the St Nicholas badge, supplied free against a £10 deposit. This was not very expensive for most people because it was often simply a doubling up of school uniform. Jessica's school uniform was grey trousers at first, but no one seemed to notice she was wearing them for choir. Cassocks cover a multitude of sins. At evening rehearsals school uniform may be worn, whatever it is, but if there has been a school non-uniform day the children must find time somehow to change into their school uniform. This probably dates from some child in the past turning up to rehearsal in something over-frivolous! Cassocks, surplices and tabards are provided free, which is a great relief. Unfortunately Jessica's first blazer, and her second when she grew out of the first, was supplied with a separate badge, and I had to get it attached. This taxed my sewing skills beyond their limit, and I had to pay £12 each time to have a local sewing repairs shop do it for me.

At first no one said anything about a blazer for Jessica, and maybe she was supposed to wait till she had been properly installed, but she was very anxious to have one. One night she asked the big girls when she would get one, and they promptly found her one in a cupboard. She was thrilled to bits. It transpired that she should have waited, and that I would have been charged £10 deposit, but no one seemed to object to her having it. I sent Michael the deposit, and also the £10 note I found in a pocket belonging to the previous wearer, and Michael told Jessica she looked very smart so everything seemed to be OK.

Another perk of being installed was to be given a tabard or surplice. Meanwhile the novice just wore the white cassock. If you took part in a public outside performance you were lent a tabard for that occasion only, to preserve the uniform appearance of the choir, but Jessica did not know this when, just before Christmas in 2012, the choir sang carols in the foyer of The Sage and she was the only one without a tabard.

As we attended services we were generally still indoors in the warm at meeting-out time, but most parents arrived at the Song School door and waited outside till some kind person let them in from inside. Roger, from his favourite position leaning against the hall radiator, would rush to open the door if he heard anyone knocking, though I (settled on the stairs with my Kindle) hesitated to do this because I didn't know whether the people outside had right of entry or were merely yobs looking for shelter. I had another reason for my reluctance too: many of the parents who came in did not bother to shut the door behind them, and I and my staircase were subjected to an icy blast straight off the River Tyne. At some point some bright spark suggested that parents should meet up in the bar of the Vermont during choir, but then no one needed that organised as they could do it anyway. And as only the most insensitive people would think of sitting in a hotel bar without buying drinks this was merely an added expense to those who otherwise might find it a good idea. Some parents were to be heard expressing dissatisfaction with the choir times, especially one lady who was a priest herself and should have known that the times of services were cast in ancient bronze and were more important than the family arrangements of the individual choristers. Being a chorister parent was no picnic.

A short respite from the hard staircase came when Michael offered me a temporary voluntary function as sitter-in. The Dean and Chapter had been discussing safeguarding and had realised that Michael, or James, or even both of them together, were having the charge of young girls with no lady present to protect them, or (maybe worse) there was no lady present to protect Michael and James from possible false allegations of abuse. I was asked to sit in the Song School (quite exciting because I had never been up there since Jessica's audition, and hardly then) where, if I cleared the junk off one, I could sit on a chair at some tiny unoccupied corner of a cluttered table. The Song School was full of all manner of stuff, mostly paper waiting in piles to be sorted or redistributed. I always felt I must be in the way. I had to sit there for the rehearsal before Evensong and the later rehearsal after it. In short, wherever the choir were, there I was supposed to be. On Sundays I wasn't needed because there would be lay clerks of both sexes to see fair play. Meanwhile a Music Assistant, who would be paid to do this job among others, was being advertised for. In my role as semi-trusted adult I was once asked by Father Kevin if I would go and sit in the Thomlinson Room with a senior chorister who was crying, and another time young Hugh Beney was brought to sit with me in the Sunday Eucharist because he felt ill. He did not require any help beyond a drink of water and kindly companionship while he recovered from whatever had upset him. I say semi-trusted because once a girl who was upset and crying was brought to sit with me in the Song School. Michael thought she should be taken home by car rather than sent home by herself, and seemed pleased when I said we would take her, but then he remembered that I had not (at that time) got a Cathedral CRB and therefore he could not take the risk of entrusting the girl to the back of our car. He fixed with a mum with a bigger car to take the girl and himself as well. I felt slightly hurt, especially as the girl in question was over 16.

During my short time in that role I overheard a couple of gems. Once a lay-clerk came up and said, "Michael …" to which he received a stony glare. "Sorry, Mr Stoddart," he quavered. Michael was very firm about how choristers, of whatever age, addressed him in choir time. Indeed his daughter Emily, when a chorister complained about this, said "Well, I have to call him Mr Stoddart, and he's my dad!" Another time James was complaining that Evensong had gone on for rather longer than usual. The prayers had been long, the readings had been long and the psalm had been long, he said. "Hmm. Anyone would think it was a church!" responded Michael acidly.

Waiting, whether at bus stops, in supermarket queues, or in cathedrals, has one advantage: it gives you a chance to count your blessings. I often had cause to be thankful that Jessica had taken to music and not sport. The idea of standing, or even sitting, by a freezing hockey pitch for as long as I sat in St Nicholas and other cathedrals, would have been dreadful to me. I had a lot of blessings to count.

We were not a musical family. Roger's mother recalled singing in the chorus of amateur operatics when she was a teenager, but that was about it. Other of his ancestors may have sung in the bath, but I wouldn't know. It was quite late in Roger's childhood that a wireless was acquired. When he was older and had a job he occasionally bought records which he played on a little Dansette record player. But having a record player did not mean you were musical. It meant you were "with it". Around the time he left school he bought a Spanish guitar and played it a lot, but sadly it was not always a pleasure for other people to listen to.

As a member of a chapel family I was accustomed to singing hymns, and we often had *Music While You Work* on the radio to lighten the morning housework. My grandfather had been a boy soprano and taken part in competitions, but as an adult his singing voice was never heard outside chapel. Once in a blue moon I was taken to our local YMCA to hear their operatic society's annual musical. I remember *Maritza* and *Gypsy Love*, both of which I found very moving. My mother once took me to a production of *White Horse Inn*, some of the lyrics of which stayed with me for years. She played the piano from time to time and was particularly fond of Ivor Novello. She was occasionally roped in to play for hymn singing at chapel, but not often because in those days there was no shortage of pianists.

When I was about six years old my grandmother had a cerebral haemorrhage and was in hospital for a few weeks. Her survival was not at all certain, and when my grandfather went in to see her every evening my mother and I sat waiting outside in a dark car. We did not have car radios in those days, and we passed the time singing hymns. One we sang very often was *In heavenly love abiding,* the words of which have stayed with me for life. If music has power to soothe the savage breast, it is also a comfort to the troubled soul. One of the differences I found between my non-conformist background and the Anglican Church was that the Anglicans don't know many really good hymns, and when they do they often sing them to the wrong tunes!

From her Nepalese mother's side Jessica might well have inherited musical leanings if they had been allowed to have free rein. Her mother told me that Nepalese ladies were not allowed to sing. It wasn't respectable. Servants sang, not ladies. It reminded me of how English girls of my generation were often forbidden to whistle. It was all right for errand boys, we were told, but not for young ladies. *A whistling woman and a crowing hen are neither good for God nor men,* went the old saying.

After our sons grew up and we were able to go out at night, we became subscribers to the Northern Sinfonia and attended all their concerts when they performed at the Newcastle City Hall. We also loved going to ballets and G&S operettas when we had the chance. Music gradually became embedded in our lives. Presumably the love of music had lain dormant within us in spite of our musically barren youth. But we were consumers, not performers.

When Roger and I took over Jessica's upbringing we sang to her every bedtime. I had a large repertoire of hymns, and of Roger's more eclectic offering she seemed to prefer hymns. One night, when she was about three, I had been singing to her *Blessed assurance.* After I tucked her up and went downstairs I heard the confident strains of the chorus: *This is my story, this is my song, praising my saviour all the day long!* I didn't know then, and I still don't know, how far Jessica's voice might take her, but I knew she had music in her soul!

Both Roger and I delighted in Cathedrals. They were certainly not a part of our childhood experience, with rare exceptions. Roger's grandmother took him to Canterbury Cathedral on a holiday, and I was taken to St Paul's by my own grandmother on a London trip. As a Boy Scout Roger was taken to a parade at Leicester Cathedral, but that was only an upgraded parish church and not terribly impressive in those days. When Roger and I were on holiday anywhere we always visited the local cathedral if there was one – Carlisle, St David's, Chichester, Ripon, and Canterbury again (a first for me). For some years, when we lived in Norfolk, we worshipped every Christmas Day in Norwich Cathedral.

Most Cathedrals were welcoming, but some were not. In the late 1960s we visited Durham Cathedral on a holiday.

As we opened the great north door we were confronted by a sour-looking cleric. "You can't come in," he said. "There's a service on." But that was a long time ago. Durham Cathedral now has a system of welcomers, who never turn us away. They largely ignore us.

Our visits to Southwell Minster, Nottingham's beautiful little cathedral, illustrated the importance of the initial welcome to a church. Our first visit was at 8 o'clock one summer morning, on a long journey which we decided to break at Southwell. We had not gone far into the church when an elderly lady came hurrying up to us smiling. It was so nice to see us, she said. If we wanted to explore the north aisle would we mind doing so first, perhaps, because a service would be taking place in a few minutes. Yes, we said, we knew, and we would like to join it. She was over the moon. "Mr Bloggs! Mr Bloggs!" she said to a colleague. "These lovely people are going to join in our service! Isn't that nice?" They escorted us to seats and found us prayer books, and made us feel thoroughly welcome and even rather special.

It was quite a few years before we went there again. Southwell isn't on the main route to anywhere special, but we made the necessary detour with some nostalgia. This time we arrived in time to take part in the main Sunday Eucharist service. The church was fairly full and there were lots of stewards, but no welcomers because it was Sunday (so not a tourist day). Not only did no one welcome us, but no one spoke to us at all. At the end we joined in the coffee mingle by helping ourselves to coffee. I looked for a contributions bowl but could not see one, so I asked a fellow worshipper where I might find it. He grunted that it was "over there". On our way out we decided to buy a CD of their music which we saw in a glass display case. This required a minimal amount of social contact because someone had to be found who had the key to the display case. Again, as it was not a tourist day, they were not geared up to selling their merchandise. But we were civilly dealt with. Happily our abiding memory of Southwell Minster will be the kindly old lady's welcome. She is probably with the Church Triumphant now, welcoming people into Heaven.

Roger was lucky enough to be able to take early retirement in his mid-fifties. We wondered how we might spend all the extra time we would have. One of the ideas that occurred to us was to visit all the Cathedrals of England, and maybe of Britain. That appealed to both of us. To Roger, a lapsed Christian who by then liked to think of himself as an atheist, the charm of cathedrals was their great age and the evidence they gave of cultural life throughout a millennium. We have very little that is older than our cathedrals, and their survival as living entities rather than ruins or museums is inspiring to even an atheist. I was less interested in the architecture than the atmosphere, and I love the sense of peace a cathedral gives. For the next few years we took all the opportunities we could to visit cathedrals.

Each of them had some memorable feature, though we did not necessarily appreciate the same things. Truro, for instance, has dozens of beautiful cross-stitch embroidered cushions on the stone benches in its niches, adding both comfort and colour. Wells has its swans, trained to ring a bell when they want a snack. Wells also has its scissor arch, and Exeter its cat door. Carlisle has stars painted inside its roof. Hereford has a memorial to Elinor Brent-Dyer, the author of the Chalet School books. We remember Chichester because as we passed their Treasury an alarm went off, and seven or eight men immediately rushed from all directions to save their treasures. We wondered if it was something we had done, but we were assured it wasn't. It seemed to have been a false alarm. We remember Gloucester for the young man who, clearing the sanctuary for an evening concert, asked us to leave and escorted us out. Perhaps he was a welcomer. At Bath Abbey our friend, wearing a woollen beanie to keep his bald head warm, was asked by a welcomer to remove his hat. We decided it was just as well they weren't a cathedral. They didn't deserve to be.

Most cathedrals had bookstalls or gift shops, and around the time we began visiting them a lot of them were setting up cafes. Mindful of Jesus's injunction "Make not my Father's house a house of merchandise" many people were unhappy about these ventures, but one of the justifications put forward for cafes was that they were an important part of the ministry of welcome. All I can say is that some cafés were more welcoming than others, but it was certainly an innovation we appreciated, especially on cold days.

Cathedrals were sometime surprisingly hard to find. It often happened, in a cathedral city, that the people we asked for directions were themselves visitors, though they often had maps and guide books which were quite helpful. It was an American who directed us to Bath Abbey! Looking for Bristol Cathedral, quite early one morning when there were few people about, we approached a couple of council workmen who we felt would be sure to know. Could they please tell us the way to the cathedral? *"Bristol* Cathedral?" repeated one of them incredulously. Yes, they knew the way to it alright, but seemed surprised that anybody should want to go there! A friend who owned a café in the small Norfolk village of Wells-next-the-Sea was asked by a visitor where the cathedral was. The Cathedral? Yes, Wells cathedral. This is Wells, isn't it? Our friend was mortified at having to tell the visitor that he was several hundred miles from where he wanted to be!

After we came to live in the north we visited Newcastle Cathedral occasionally, usually for special services. It is not generally a tourist attraction, but is frequented by the homeless and drop-outs who need a warm place to shelter without cost. In our early association with the

Cathedral it had a gift shop, situated in the then unused south doorway, but it was not much patronised and I think few people wanted to work in it because they did not feel safe. The shop presented too many challenges and it was closed. For a while stock from the shop was sold from display cases in the Lantern Café, but that fizzled out. It was possible to get good refreshments in the Lantern café on Mondays to Fridays, but it closed rather early. When I arrived on my choir sitting nights at 4.10pm it was always very, very closed.

Back to the present (as it was).

On her first choir Sunday Jess was very excited. She wore her favourite lime-green floral hairclips. Alas, Michael told her, kindly but firmly, such adornments were not allowed. Long hair must be tied back with a black band only. Choir was serious stuff! As the service progressed I suffered agonies of remorse. I had left undone those things which I ought to have done: I had not given her any collection. I was greatly relieved to learn that the collection plate was not passed to the choristers. Goodness, they make a big enough contribution, and this was obviously recognised. During the space between the *Kyrie* and the *Sanctus* the choir were not required, and the younger ones, under 11, were taken out to Sunday School. Jess enjoyed this. David and Gill Lawrence were the teachers then, and a pleasant twenty-five minutes or so were spent listening to a Bible story, drawing, chatting and having squash and biscuits. Apart from anything else, it solved the perennial problem of how to keep fidgety little choristers quiet. When the prayers of intercession began, someone would go up to Sunday School to warn the choristers that they were required back in church, and they would troop quietly back to their places in time for the offertory hymn. After the service there was a coffee mingle at the back, when different volunteers served coffee, tea and biscuits. The choristers, if they wanted to, joined the congregation for a few minutes (and a few biscuits if they could snaffle them without being noticed) before going back upstairs for a short rehearsal period.

Now we had to hang about till the afternoon rehearsal began at 4pm. We could have gone home, and at first we sometimes did, but eventually we began driving to the Little Chef at North Seaton where we had a good lunch with someone else to do the washing up. That suited us all. We knew that many cathedrals had their Sunday Evensong earlier than Newcastle, often as early as 3 o'clock, but Newcastle stuck with the traditional 5.30. Another ninety minutes to sit and wait, but it was all in a good cause and we didn't mind.

Evensong was held in the Quire. The congregation was always very small, and it was not unknown for us to be 100% of it. A nonconformist church might well have decided it wasn't worth having such a service, on the grounds that "nobody comes", but the Anglicans know that the service is for God, not the congregation. I was sorry to see that hardly any choir parents beside ourselves came to the service.

Since the Soham murders in 2002, when two young girls were murdered by their school caretaker, the issue of safeguarding was very much in the public awareness. People who took responsibility for children under 18 had to prove, by means of a Criminal Record Bureau check, that they had no criminal record of molesting children. A CRB did not, of course, testify to a person's good character, only that they had never been caught. It wasn't much, but it was something, and it was greatly revered. Churches made sure their clergy and staff were checked. No doubt Michael, and his assistant James, had CRBs. I did worry a bit that when we dropped Jess off at the Thomlinson Room on a Sunday morning shortly before 9 o'clock there was often nobody there. I insisted on waiting with her till someone reliable came, and usually it was the Stoddart family so I could leave her with a light heart. This naturally annoyed Jess. Whoever arrived first, she insisted, they would be very nice, and I was wrong to be so suspicious of people I didn't even know!

One person we met in early days was Pam Walker. She said she was sure she knew us from somewhere, and we eventually decided between us that we had met at a Messy Church event at Whalton. She told us that she had put the choir poster in Smail's window. I was glad to know that. Retrospectively, we owe Pam a lot.

Gordon once told us that, after many years at the Cathedral, he was still constantly finding new things of interest. He was a mine of information, and loved to take visitors round. However, I found the Gothic mouse-holes for myself. They are in the south Quire aisle. Less romantic people might suspect they are something to do with the heating or ventilation, but I know. I think John Betjeman would have liked them too. Many people must rush past them every day without seeing them, but it takes an observant chorister chaperone to notice and fully appreciate them.

In November Michael told us that there would be no more Evensong services for a few weeks so that the electricians could "crack on" with the lighting. This meant unrelieved two-hour rehearsals for the choir, often standing up all the time. For us, it sounded like two hours of sitting on the cold back stairs. Alan the verger, however, told us he was going to read Evening Prayer in the Eastern Chapels, and seemed surprised when we asked if we could join him. With one other person we were a congregation of three. Prayers have to be read, and presumably this is one of a verger's duties, on the odd occasions when the clergy think they have more important things to do. Alan did well. They're funny in the Church of England. Their priests spend years at university and theological colleges, and they have to convince a committee that they have been called to the

Ministry by God, but when necessary the services can be read by the verger who probably claims no divine calling and may have had limited education.

Nonconformists are often used to services starting five minutes late, but this never happened at the Cathedral. Eyes had to be kept on watches for preparation, of course, but the actual service began on the dot the Cathedral clock chimed. It was a very good clock with pleasant chimes.

As the electricians extended their work into the early evening we had to retreat to the Icon Room for Evening Prayer, but that was much nicer in all respects. It had comfier chairs for one thing. A feature of Evensong or Evening Prayer was that the officiant read out the prayer requests visitors had left. Once I heard Father Kevin read a prayer request for one John Goadby who was in Leicester Royal Infirmary. There was no more information than that. I am a Leicester girl, and the only Goadby I have ever heard of was a distant relative who I never met. I wondered if John Goadby was a relative, and I wrote to him at the Infirmary, telling him that we had prayed for him and wishing him well. Several years later I heard from one of his relatives (and mine as it turned out) that he had received the letter, and he had recovered. Chance or divine intervention we can't say, but it was probably encouraging to a sick man to know that a travelling friend had made a prayer request for him, and that strangers two hundred miles away had prayed for him.

I think Jessica's first outside engagement with the choir was a Sunday afternoon trip to St Andrew's Church in October. They were having a special service to round off a flower festival, and invited our choir to sing. It was a pleasant occasion. St Andrew's is the oldest church in Newcastle, and we had not been before. It's beautiful and well worth a visit. Sadly the choir were not offered refreshments to strengthen them for their walk back to the Cathedra, unless shortage of time forced them to decline.

Eventually pocket money was paid out. It was paid to a nominated bank on the 15th of every month. At that point Jessica trusted a building society to look after such of her finances as wouldn't fit into her piggy bank, and we duly filled in their details on the form we were given. Payday after payday went by. We enquired monthly if the Cathedral had paid? Yes. If the building society had received the payment? No. It was very frustrating. In the end the finance officer decided to send Jessica a cheque for the amount owing, and we decided Jessica should have her own proper bank account. After that everything was hunky-dory. The monthly sum was not large – £9.80 a month at first – but it was nice for a little girl to have. I remember my disgust, some months later, at hearing a choirboy's father say "Of course, we bank it for him. He doesn't have it to spend." The choristers worked very hard for their pittance, and if they had rushed into the nearest sweetshop and splurged the lot it would hardly have spoiled their tea.

The next exciting event was the Three Choirs Festival. This was an amalgamation of three Cathedral choirs – Newcastle, Carlisle and Edinburgh, who met to sing together once a year. This year it was held at Newcastle. It was an afternoon event. Roger and I, who are always early for these things, rewarded ourselves with seats near the front. Jessica was behind a bigger person, so we rarely saw her and she rarely saw us. Generally the choirs made a good sound, but it was not coming from all of them. Several children at the front seemed to be having to share music, and consequently one was hogging it and the other couldn't see it. I hasten to say that they were not Newcastle choristers. Michael had made proper provision. At a certain point it was teatime, and the choirs were to be entertained to tea in the Refectory. I imagine they were all looking forward to it. Edinburgh and Newcastle trotted off eagerly, but Carlisle were kept behind by their director to do a bit more rehearsing – oh, five minutes at least. In the Refectory Michael told his choristers to be polite little hosts and wait till everybody had eaten, or at least was eating, so they had nothing then. Edinburgh, who were under no such strictures, ate heartily. Finally, when Newcastle could hardly bear it any longer, Carlisle came in and cleared up what was left. If my sources are to be believed, Newcastle got nothing at all. It was a bad blow and caused much resentment. We had to make a very early stop at a chippy on the way home. Happy days!

Jessica liked Mr Stoddart and had great respect for him and for James. Between them they were teaching her a lot, and she valued what she was learning. Once she went so far as to quote Mr Stoddart to her piano teacher to settle a dispute. Mrs Hills retorted that she had been teaching for thirty-five years and she bet Mr Stoddart hadn't!

One night, just before the service, some yobs came in and started messing with the pulpit Bible. Gordon dealt with them firmly but courteously, and didn't throw them out. Maybe he hoped they might be inspired by what they heard. Later, on their way out, they yelled that it was a rotten choir. It was difficult for the choir and congregation to remain dignified, but we did.

Harvest was celebrated by a special Evensong with two harvest hymns. I was accustomed, and I believe many Anglican churches are, to seeing a festive array of harvest produce to remind us what we had to thank God for, but at the Cathedral there wasn't so must as a carrot. To be fair, we had a very small congregation to supply such a display, and as probably none of us were rural we would only have bought things from the supermarket. After this service we had a harvest supper, which I believe they do not always have and have not had since. We had a nice meal arranged by some of the Cathedral ladies, then the

Stoddart and Dalliston ladies gave us a lovely little concert.

Now, in the last few days of the lighting installation, the back hall to which we were generally banished when the Cathedral closed was painted. This was not before time, but it was rather inconvenient to me because the stairs where I usually sat were blocked by a huge stepladder. I had to sit on the stairs going down to the toilets, and they were very dirty. We understood that there was to be a cleaning-up day after the electricians had left, to be smart for the Bishop coming to bless the new lighting. We did not volunteer to help with that. The new lighting was paid for by the Heritage Lottery Fund.

The great day came and a large congregation assembled to see the new lighting and have it blessed. The order of service told us that we would begin the service in darkness and then as it progressed the lighting would be gradually increased to its full glory. I'm sure I was not the only person to feel thoroughly disillusioned. The lighting was functional in that wherever anyone was supposed to sit they could read their hymn sheet easily, but as for glory there was very little. The LED lamps, being short black tubes full of lots of tiny bulbs, were no adornment to the building, and the maximum light they put out was dismal. Even receiving Bishop Martin's blessing did nothing for it. Its great merit, of course, was that it would be cheaper to run. We can no longer afford to worship the Lord in the beauty of holiness. It has to be the economy of holiness. A day or two later I heard the Dean say the lighting still needed "a bit of tweaking." It certainly did.

Shortly afterwards, on a particularly cold evening, we were making our way to the loo and found the Refectory was open and apparently serving coffee. Desperate for inner warmth we asked if we could have a cup. "We're closed," snapped the Representative of the Ministry of Welcome. I could name her, but I won't. Yes, we knew, but we were chorister parents and we were having to wait in the Cathedral, and would love to buy some coffee if they were serving it because we were cold. She consulted with a colleague who glared at us, and reluctantly and ungraciously poured us some coffee. There were biscuits, but I didn't dare to ask for one. How much was the coffee? There wasn't a charge. Oh – was there a donations bowl? No. Back in the nave, slightly warmer, we saw Georgie Dalliston who was welcoming visitors as they arrived. Apparently we were unwittingly attending an All Faiths service. She gave us a friendly greeting. The Bishop passed through, and he brought us an order of service. What a nice man! It occurred to us later that, as we were eventually bona fide participants in the service, we would have been entitled to coffee anyway (and a biscuit), but we didn't know that then. There was only a small congregation, but the service was very interesting. Newcastle has many faiths among its citizens, and it is good that they should understand each other as much as possible, and be friends.

Meanwhile the Song School hall, where we usually ended up, had a good (old fashioned) light, a refreshing smell of paint and a warm radiator. For a while it was also very clean. Once my blow-up cushion was in place I felt quite comfy sitting on the stairs with my Kindle, provided no one left the outside door open. Once Father Kevin, as he passed, said the trouble with Kindles is that you can't tell what people are reading. In fact the reader herself cannot always remember the title.

Christmas was fast approaching, a very busy time for the Cathedral and especially the choir who had so much to learn, and apart from carols it was all new to Jessica. One incidental feature of Newcastle Advent was the Patronal Festival which was always held on a Saturday. For patronal festivals the choirs of Newcastle and Durham always joined forces, which was so nice. We generally had quite a decent congregation too. After the service buffet lunches were served, in the Eastern Chapels for adults and in the Refectory for the choirs, where they were able to mingle and get to know each other. As far as we were concerned the hot coffee was very welcome!

At the beginning of December the choir were invited to sing carols in the concourse of The Sage. A little platform was set up for them, and they sang against a dark background of the sky and the Tyne below. At a table to one side Elisabeth and Charlotte Stoddart were selling copies of a CD the choir had made the previous year. I looked forward to another one being made soon with Jessica on it, and I was assured it was on the cards, but eight years later it has not happened. The choir sang well (of course) and a lot of people sitting in the café enjoyed it and clapped. One bit of drama came when Michael, who was conducting, suddenly rushed forward and grabbed Rachel Dodd (the Head Chorister). She had fainted and was falling forwards towards him. Chairs and bottles of water were fetched, and a concerned crowd gathered round the casualty, but she was very plucky and insisted on continuing once she had been revived. She got tremendous applause for her courage, and it was well deserved. As time went by I noticed that a number of the older girls were given to fainting, and not surprisingly because they had to work very hard on top of a school day, and were probably at that awkward age when they preferred to skip breakfast and didn't leave enough time for lunch. It wasn't officially a concert, rather backfill for the Sage's other chargeable events, but it was wonderful, with entirely Christian content – not a single santa, snowman or reindeer. We were getting quite enough of those in the shops.

The weather continued cold. One night Alan the verger offered us a cup of tea! Tracy McKeever, the new assistant verger, often came over to chat to us as we sat and waited. She told us she had ordered a supply of cotton buds (normally used for cleaning babies' ears and noses) to poke around in the deeper recesses of the very dusty Hedley carvings. Tracy had formerly worked at Sunderland Minster, to whom we had recently lost a canon, Sheila Bamber. This was slightly before our time so we are not in a position to say whether it was a good swap, but I think it must have been. Tracy was good at her job. Among other things she was kind and welcoming to the homeless, but very firm with any breaches of order. She once told me how she had told a homeless man, who came in with his bottle of gin, that alcohol was not allowed in the Cathedral! I did not comment, but many images of the Dean and Chapter, and sometimes the Bishop, happily imbibing plonk in the transept, floated before my eyes. One day a Muslim girl came in. She was lonely and told Tracy she had no friends. "Yes you have," Tracy replied, "you've got me. Here's my phone number. Ring me up any time!"

The boys' choir had not been doing well. Michael was finding it hard to recruit new boys. About this time he asked the girls if any of them would be willing to come along and support the boys (voluntarily of course). Jessica was keen to help, and so were one or two others. It certainly boosted the sound! It meant more sitting around waiting, but we were now inured to that. This continued for many months, if not years.

A posh annual event was the Lord Mayor's Carol Service, which was naturally attended by the Lord Mayor and as many of his Corporation as were willing to turn out on a cold night. Before the service coffee and warm mince pies were served in the Refectory, and anyone attending the service was welcome to partake. There was a donations bowl which we were glad to contribute to. For this occasion the front few rows were roped off and reserved, and the *hoi poloi* like ourselves directed to the back. At a certain moment a loud voice instructed us all to stand while the civic party made their way up the aisle. There was a special carved headrest for the Mayor in the front row. It was not much used, and did not look at all comfy. The Lord Mayor was in his ceremonial robes, as were some of his staff, but many of the wives and other ladies were obviously total strangers to churches and did not know that hats are rarely worn nowadays. Some of them seemed to think they were there for a wedding, and most of them looked at least slightly stupid. The choir did their stuff well as always, and afterwards praise was duly transmitted to them from the Lord Mayor. Tonight the choir had new glass candleholders on their reading shelves, and they looked good, but Tracy told us they were very hard to clean and of course she was the one who had to do it. The congregation also got candles to hold, but they had a nasty tendency to drip wax on people's clothes. I wonder if the Lord Mayor and Corporation got any wax on their robes?

When new choristers join they are supposed to be given a handbook, telling them about all their responsibilities. We never had one, and it was some months before I knew one existed and asked for a copy. Consequently I did not know what I ought to have guessed, that choristers were expected to be on almost 24-hour duty over the whole of Christmas. In our first year we had planned, as was our custom, to go to Peebles Hydro for Christmas. As a cadet Jessica would still not have been expected to go to Midnight Mass, but she would have been required to attend the other services on December 24th and 25th. Our booking had been made back in the summer, and it did not occur to us to cancel it. Sadly it was our last such Scottish Christmas. When our choir would have been rehearsing for Midnight Mass we were singing carols in the hotel, and on Christmas morning when we should have been at the Cathedral we shared Eucharist with the lovely people at Peebles Scottish Episcopal church. We still hadn't got a handbook, but by now we realised we were not where we should be. Jessica was still only a cadet, but that would have made no difference. From now on, as the handbook made clear when we finally got it, choir must take precedence over just about everything.

January brought snow, as of course January should. We went to the Cathedral armed with blankets, though we never needed them because Gordon kept the Cathedral beautifully warm. We took extra flasks of hot cocoa too, and I had started carrying cereal bars and chocolate with me in case there was any homeless person there who might be glad of a bite to eat.

Choristers work hard all year, and they deserve a treat. There was no scope for one before Christmas, but now Michael proposed to take them to the cinema. Where should they go? Having fixed the date, he enquired what films were being shown in different places, and offered the choir a vote on which they would prefer of three: *Parental Guidance, Life of Pi,* and *Monsters Inc.* It wasn't a total treat as the choristers had to pay £5 for a ticket and take their own food. Jessica set off walking with Emily Stoddart, but in the film she sat between Georgie and Bella Dalliston. This was a matter of pride when related later, as she loved all the big girls and they were very kind to her. The chosen film, by a good margin, was *Life of Pi.* While we waited Roger and David Lawrence shovelled snow in the carpark. We went into town for a snack, and when we got back the Cathedral was locked. Few things look more rejecting than a locked Cathedral. In the end we managed to make ourselves heard by banging on the back door of the refectory, and someone heard us and kindly invited us in. The children were finishing up their tea and had had a very good time.

The snow continued. One day Michael emailed us all to say that choir would take place as usual but he would make allowances for children who lived in outlying areas. Well, we were in the most outlying area of all, and Jessica was there on time. Only five choristers turned up, and two of them were Emily and Celia Stoddart. One can only suspect some people, or their parents, were lacking in enthusiasm!

One evening at the beginning of February we celebrated Candlemas. This was important enough to invite the civic dignitaries. We all had candles, and the new lighting system was put through its limited paces. We had lots of hymns and readings, but there was still space in the programme for plenty of choir singing. At the end there was a finger buffet arranged down the south aisle. We were not planning to stay as we had promised ourselves supper out, but Jessica was very thirsty. We fought our way through the mob for a small glass of juice. A big one would have been better, but Cathedral juice glasses are always small. Buffets seem to bring out the worst manners in so many people. When people have got their drinks and nibbles they don't move away to allow others to have access, but stay where they are so they can reach of the next nibble. To get my poor thirsty chorister a drink I had to push past the Lord Mayor and Lord Lieutenant. Lord Mayors have such enormous Corporations. The carpark had been empty when we arrived, but it was now full. Our car was blocked in by another whose owner had parked very thoughtlessly. I went back in and asked Alan if he would ask whoever owned the car to move it. He kindly shouted out the offending registration number. Oh dear – it was the Bishop. He came out and moved his car with at least as much grace as one might expect in the circumstances, then went back to the gathering. I hoped he would drive home safely. Anglicans are very pious and always mindful of Paul's advice to Timothy in 1 Tim 5:23. A day or two later I heard the Dean say the lighting still needed tweaking.

During half term Jessica and I spent a day in Newcastle and had lunch in the Cathedral Refectory. Tracy was having lunch in there, as Cathedral staff generally did. "Does our relationship merit a hug or a handshake?" she asked. A hug, of course. After lunch we had planned to do the Cathedral's holiday Angel Trail. This involved walking all around the nave and quire looking for tiny plastic angels. It was fun. When we had located them all we took our entry form back to the Refectory where one of the staff gave Jessica a prize. It was the choice of a number of items left over from the former gift shop. Jessica chose a fat notepad with the Cathedral embossed on the front, which was a nice souvenir of a happy visit.

In early March Jessica was thrilled when Michael told her she would get her tabard on the following Sunday. When he announced it a lot of people clapped, so she felt very chuffed. She was told that some people had to wait a year. When the occasion came she was extra lucky to have the ceremony all to herself, where it is normal for several choristers to be processed together. This made it all the more special for her, and made it easier for the congregation to remember her name. She was presented to the Dean by Michael, and he asked her some questions which she answered clearly and sincerely. Rachel popped her tabard on, and the Dean said a prayer. He asked the congregation to pray for Jessica and her family, then he asked for a round of applause which was heartily given. She was very proud to be a full chorister at last.

Around this time I asked the Dean if the St Margaret Chapel could be converted into a Children's Corner with a carpet. He did not seem to like the idea. We already had a children's corner (a pop-up one for Sunday mornings only) and he had great plans for the eventual restoration of the St Margaret Chapel as a chapel. I wondered why as the Cathedral had many chapels, but I did not press the matter as I could see he was negative to it. He also said something rude about the south facing stained glass window in there, which he wants to have removed. This little chapel, off the south aisle, houses the Cathedral's only example of mediaeval glass – a little roundel high up on the east wall, showing Mary and baby Jesus. Visitors come to see it. Clearly too good for a children's corner. I thought that must be the end of it. The Dean's grandiose plans related to work that he hoped to have done with another Heritage Lottery Fund. We'd just had one for the lighting: now it seemed we wanted another. I already knew that plans were in an early stage for a hoped-for re-vamp of the Cathedral which would involve practically gutting it. I rather hoped it would not happen.

Michael sent a letter out to choir parents asking if any of them wanted to be on the Electoral Roll. It seemed you could be on it almost for asking, provided you had been baptised at some point in your life, and I thought I would apply. This gives the entitlement to vote at Parish Meetings, and could be useful.

We were near enough to Easter to be making plans for it. Confirmations are normally held at Easter, and Tracy told me she was to be confirmed then. She had been a Pentecostal when she was baptised by immersion, but it was a condition of her job that she should be confirmed (properly). The Pentecostals are not in communion with the Church of England. Tracy accepted this as necessary, but it irked her to have her baptism undervalued – in fact discounted. Another peculiarity of the Church of England seems to be that although any priest can baptise a baby, confirmation has to be performed by a Bishop. Does that mean confirmation is more important than baptism? Not that it worries me. I don't approve of infant baptism anyway.

On April 23 it was Durham's patronal festival, and our choir went to join theirs. In spite of widespread snow we went in the car, and when we reached Durham we took the wrong turn, as is so easily done there, and could not find the multi-story carpark. Roger dropped us off and carried on searching. Jessica had a suitcase with her gear, and we asked a lady welcomer where we could put it.

After debating with her colleagues she showed us to the Chapter Room which is normally out of bounds to the likes of us. It was very interesting, and accessed through a disguised door that looked like the wall it was set in. While we waited for Roger to join us we visited the shop and the refectory in the undercroft. We set up camp in the refectory and went off to choose some lunch. It's very good catering, but it ought to be because it is not at all cheap. Roger joined us having had great difficulty finding out how to pay for carparking, and a kind lady had rescued him. You get a plastic disc and have it time-recorded, then you hang onto it all day and if you lose it you pay £15. He was glad to have got to the Cathedral. I think he was already feeling like a nap, and probably wished he could curl up on a pew for forty winks. He could have done that at Newcastle, but at Durham he would have risked being thrown out by a welcomer.

At 2.30 I took Jessica back to the Chapter House where she needed to change into her choir uniform. The people whose permission I asked wore purple gowns and looked very official. They debated with themselves, and let us in, but one of them said if we had any questions out of the ordinary we should ask the vergers who wore black. They (who wore purple) were only volunteers and had no authority. They certainly looked as if they did. A lady was sitting on the floor surrounded by coloured carpet squares. She looked embarrassed. She told us that she was there to tell stories to any children who would like to listen, but none had come. Jessica very kindly drew up a carpet square and said she would like a story. So would I, but I begged to be allowed to sit on a chair as I am not very good at getting down onto carpet squares, and worse at getting up again. I have to say it was not a story I would have chosen for a Cathedral patronal festival. It was rather secular.

When I was at college about 1962 I remember hearing that someone had committed suicide by cutting his throat on the Durham altar. I wondered if anyone could tell me about it, and I asked a guide. He said it vaguely brought back a memory of a story he had heard, and he would go and look for a friend who had been working in the Cathedral for 70 years. Later he caught me up and said yes, his friend remembered it well and had been on duty that day. He had been headmaster of the choir school, and he remembered having to tell the children why the services were cancelled, and soothe their subsequent alarm. The self-selected sacrificial victim did not die on the altar but later in hospital. There had been blood everywhere so the vergers had to clean it up, and the Bishop came in to re-consecrate the defiled church early next morning. It had been very important to keep the Press out, he said. He thanked me for my question and for enabling them to keep history alive. I remember that week at college we had been studying the doctrine of sanctuary in our church history class. We feather-brained students found the Durham incident quite amusing.

Newcastle choir were late, and when they arrived the Durham choir had already settled themselves in the crossing for rehearsal. We sat in the nave to listen. At the beginning of the rehearsal there seemed to be a lot of people sitting in the pews, but by the end of it they had mostly disappeared. Was it something we said? Realising that the Refectory had now closed we rushed to The Café on the Green which was still open, and had a nice tea of soup and cake. Being a chorister chaperone is an expensive business, especially if you have a keen appetite as we both do. We hoped the children would be getting something to eat.

Back in the Cathedral we found the nave festooned with red rope to keep visitors out, unless they were there for bona fide purposes. It reminded me of a family visit we made to the Cathedral on a Christmas Day many years ago. As we turned from the west end to walk up the aisle we were faced with these red ropes, draped to prevent access except through a small, guarded gap. A fat man in a frock who looked canonical to my untutored nonconformist eye, glared at us. "Are you attending the service?" he asked. "Yes. Are you?" I replied. He gave a sarcastic bow and let us pass. But that was a long time ago. Now the Cathedral has its purple-clad welcomers to man the red ropes. But perhaps I am unjust. Durham Cathedral is such a treasured heritage, and such care has to be taken of it. Many people must be involved in its protection, and they haven't all got the gifts of sharing and welcoming.

The patronal Eucharist that followed was presided over by the Bishop of Jarrow, and Canon Rosalind Brown was the preacher. The joint choir sang beautifully, and we had a good view of Jessica who was singing lustily. Canon Rosalind talked about how the Press had dealt with the recent appointment of Justin Welby as Archbishop of Canterbury, and ended by asking what we thought the Press might say about us. Amen. The service concluded with everyone trooping up to the East End ("Had we better take our handbags?") to pay our respects to St Cuthbert, and then we were funnelled out past stewards with collecting buckets. There was no escape. They'd got us cornered. A lady clergyman said "Happy Petertide!" as I passed her. Pardon? She repeated it with some hint of embarrassment. I had forgotten, with all the fuss about Cuthbert, that Peter is Durham's patron saint, not Cuthbert.

As we emerged at the top of the south aisle Michael met us. He looked a bit harassed. The choir were to gather at the north door ready to leave immediately to catch their train. However he knew Jessica was with us, and he kindly took ninety seconds or so to show us where we could find her in the Chapter House, not realising that we knew. It must have been a stressful day for Michael, getting a party of children to Durham by train (which was running late due to widespread bad weather), and then having to get them to the station for a return train which would be sure to be on time. He did well.

In the Chapter House one of the Durham girl choristers was sobbing, and her friends were gathered round her trying to comfort her. It seems that the conductor, who shall be nameless, had kept glaring at her all the way through the service. The Durham choristers, of course, all attended the Cathedral School. If they got fed up of choir, or didn't like the way they were treated, they couldn't leave. It was boarding school, and everyone, even Enid Blyton, knows boarding school can be hell. I reminded Jessica how lucky she was to be in a choir where you not only went home at night but also got pocket money. These poor children did not get pocket money, they just got a reduction off their fees, which only benefited their parents.

We walked down to the multi-story carpark where Roger found his parking disc in his pocket and sussed out how to finalise the transaction. He had to put £11 in the slot before it let us go. It comforted him to know that he had saved £4 by not losing his disc. I think he was relieved to go home. Supper at a pitstop rounded off what had been a pretty good day. Chaperoning was obviously going to provide a lot of interest.

On Maundy Thursday there was foot-washing service. It was fascinating. Tracy was going to have her feet washed in readiness for her confirmation on Easter Sunday. Maybe she would wash them again before Sunday, but it might not be the same. An arc of twelve chairs were arranged on the crossing dais, and seated upon them were previously chosen victims. Maybe they were people who were known to have clean feet already. Each person had water poured over one foot, then it was dried with a fluffy white towel, they replaced their sock and they were done. I couldn't help wondering what would have happened if the person wore tights, but presumably they had been warned not to. And what about the other foot? The Gospel clearly says "feet". Was it to save time? Were we in a hurry? I think each person got a fluffy white towel, and I supposed Tracy would have to wash them ready for next Maundy Thursday. We in the congregation, of course, just watched and stayed dirty.

Another odd custom to me was that all crosses in the Cathedral were covered with little purple bags. Nobody could tell me why. They were removed on Easter Sunday morning. Even on Good Friday the little bags stayed in place, as though the crosses were somehow improper. It *was* improper, and indeed outrageous, to crucify the Son of God, but why, at this very time when we remembered his crucifixion, did these symbols have to be outlawed as though we didn't want to think about it? There was one cross allowed on Good Friday, and that was a large wooden one that was ceremonially carried into church from the outside in a solemn procession, and set up in a socket on the crossing dais, and a stream of people went out and touched it or, if they wanted to look specially pious, kissed it. It seemed to me that for the weeks of Lent the Cathedral tried to pretend that God was dead, so they could tell us on Easter morning that he was risen. It is good to remember Christ's passion and death, but his resurrection was once and for all, not an annual event.

One night in the snow, as we drove up the little hill from the carpark, we saw an old man lying at the side of the road in the warmth from a kitchen ventilator. We wished we could do something for him, but could only think of our emergency chocolate in the glove box. He seemed pleased with that. Later we often noticed him in the Cathedral, sitting usually next to the Lord Mayor's stall. The vergers sometimes gave him a hot drink. He told me his name was Eddie. He was homeless, but had from time to time been provided with housing which he invariably lost because he drank his rent money. He was a nice chap and probably only in his fifties, and I wished I knew his story. He seemed intelligent. He did not come to church services, but often dropped in to get warm when he knew the service was over. He came in that Easter Sunday. The Dean was standing at the back with a huge bowl of mini-eggs for anyone to help themselves to as they passed him. Nobody offered poor Eddie an egg, but happily I had some of our own so I was able to give him some. He was pleased. Over the years Eddie would come for weeks on end, then we wouldn't see him for months. He'd get a flat, then he'd lose it again. It is several years now since I have seen him, and I fear he may be dead. Many such people come and go in the Cathedral, but I shall never forget Eddie.

In April, when the fruit trees were coming into blossom, Michael was invited by the Duchess of Northumberland to take the choir to sing in the cherry orchard at the Alnwick Garden. I took Jessica to the Cathedral where we joined the coach party to Alnwick. Roger was to join us later in Alnwick, as we thought parking in Newcastle, and then having to drive back from Newcastle at night, might be avoided. The Duchess had invited bereaved people to sponsor a cherry tree in memory of a loved one, and every year she hosted a little gathering where they could be entertained and could walk among the cherry trees. I think they had to pay a one-off £100 for the privilege. This year the Bishop was invited to lead a short service of remembrance, and the choir sang. Later in the atrium coffee and cakes were served and the choir sang some more. Cherry blossom being a very Japanese thing, the Japanese Ambassador was also invited and was very flattering about the choir and chatted to all of them. Michael invited me to go in as well, and I was lucky enough to get some refreshments which were large cup-cakes beautifully iced with cherry blossoms by the Duchess's chef. I kept my cupcake for Jessica. Later, when it was over, we learnt that the choir had not been given any refreshments, but had been given some tea when they arrived. They had also been given complimentary tickets to go round the garden and castle as time allowed. As they left they were each given a paper carrier with a bottle of water, an oat cookie and a Golden Delicious apple. By now Roger had been able to join us and we had the car to go home in. The weather had been kind and everyone had had a really enjoyable afternoon and evening.

In years gone by the Cathedral choirs had been supported by an organisation called the Cathedral Choirs Association. They raised money for the choirs and did other helpful things. They had become moribund, and Michael wanted to revive them. He admitted at this point that the boys' choir was failing, and he wanted to start again from scratch. He would be requiring the girls to do more, especially on Sundays. I asked him if he planned to amalgamate the two choirs, but no, he didn't. I suppose there are musical technicalities I wouldn't understand. On a Sunday at the end of April we duly attended a meeting in the Thomlinson Room after morning service. Most of us didn't know each other. One or two choristers came, including Jessica, while others preferred to stay outside and play.

We sat in a semicircle, and Michael kicked off. His wife, Elisabeth, sat by him and took minutes on her laptop. Two people rapidly offered themselves to be Treasurer and Secretary. Maybe someone would similarly have volunteered to be Chairman but Michael said it was in the constitution that he should be Chairman. (Phew, thank goodness.) It became clear that everyone thought the main purpose of the association would be to raise money, and maybe it was. Someone suggested that we could raise money by charging for concerts. Another mum whinged that her son couldn't manage Tuesdays and it was a shame to penalise a child because he couldn't manage Tuesdays, etc. James replied that there was a lot of hard work and practice necessary, and the rest of them couldn't be held back by a few people who couldn't come on Tuesdays. It wasn't fair to everyone else, he said. He was uncompromising, and I think braver than Michael would have been. A lot of people seemed to resent the required commitment and wanted more flexibility. One mum said "We want to see more of our children," and I replied, "Why not come to the services, then you can feast your eyes upon them for an hour." This did not go down well. The meeting ended so that people could get home (and see more of their children and doubtless their dinner). We had now established a committee, and they would take it from there.

About this time a new canon was installed – Father Steven Harvey. He was to replace Sheila Bamber, and he was to be Canon for Education. One of his first projects was to ask the congregation, in an open letter, if we had any visions for the Cathedral. There was a small space to fill in and return, if we had. I took full advantage of this to press my idea of a Children's Corner in the St Margaret Chapel. The little space for reply was not nearly big enough so on a separate sheet of paper I described what I would like to see. I would like to see the St Margaret Chapel fitted out as a permanent Children's Corner, with a carpet (for both comfort and quiet), some bean bags to sit on, a bookcase full of nice Bible story books, a table for colouring and some soft toys. The essence of it should be that the children could play quietly without disturbing worship. I hoped that visiting families, during the week, might play there with their children, and feel that their children were welcome. I hoped, I said, that in years to come people might look back and say, "I used to love going to play at the Cathedral!" I sent it in, and forgot about it. Nothing was said about it. Maybe the Dean had had apoplexy.

Several months later I got a lovely surprise when I went into the Cathedral. The St Margaret Chapel had been turned into my dream! A cream carpet, not in pristine condition but cosier-looking than most Cathedral furnishings, was surrounded by a smart bookcase with Bible stories, a small rattan chest of drawers with soft toys in, several cushions, a table with crayons and paper on, and two beautiful soft toys that were an inspiration: a cloth Noah's Ark with animals and a cloth church with little people. I suspect Helen Robertson had helped him. It was a paradise for children who could play happily with hardly any noise at all. I felt sure St Margaret would approve. I was telling Tracy how thrilled I was. "Yes," she said, "Father Steven listens!"

It wasn't long before we had a chance to visit Durham again, this time for a Cathedrals Sports Day. I gathered that choristers from the Northern Region (Peterborough northwards) came together for sports and singing in different locations every year. It sounded fun. They had sports in the morning, then a rehearsal, then Evensong. For choir schools this was written into their annual timetable, but children from other schools would have to get permission. The only problem with this was that it took place during SATS fortnight when nobody was allowed to go on holiday or be off school. I decided to risk applying for leave, as the day in question did not affect exams for Jessica's year. To my surprise and joy the Headmaster not only consented but seemed pleased. He said he would make a point of wishing Jessica well the day before. Mr Johnson was a very nice man.

One day in late May we assembled at Central Station to go by train to Durham. Michael was in charge of the party, and James was with him. I had decided to go along too, but to keep at a polite distance as I knew I was not required. I travelled in another carriage on the same train, but told Michael that although I might be around from time to time Jessica was in his care and he was to ignore me. I hung back at Durham so she did not see me, then I had a lovely morning browsing in the city – a very good place to browse. I had a cup of coffee in St

Nicholas's Church in the Market Place, then looked in some charity shops, a favourite hobby. They have very good charity shops in Durham. Toward the end of the morning I went up to the Cathedral. I was dismayed to see that the Café on the Green, where Roger and I had snacked recently, closed at 3 o'clock today. Oh dear! I had an excellent lunch in the Undercroft refectory and I had planned to sit there and do crosswords and read, but it was crowded and my conscience drove me out after I had finished my pud. I sat in the nave to listen to the rehearsal, but not in the greatest comfort. The front few rows of the nave were reserved for the choirs and the seats further back had no cushioning. Evensong was delightful with so many visiting choirs, and afterwards there was a short presentation ceremony of little awards for the sports. I found myself sitting next to Grace McCombie, who I had never met. Her husband had taught Jessica's father. They had given Jessica a little suit when she was born, but had never seen her. Now the Babygro had been replaced by a cassock. Small world. Jessica had had a very good day, and it was yet another unexpected perk of being a chorister. I phoned for a taxi and got myself to the station about the same time as the choir who had to walk. Surely they must have run? Yes, they had! Rather them than me – it's uphill! Again I made for the opposite end of the train. Passing through the buffet I came upon Michael and James. I will not record what they were buying, or what I thought about it. They'd had a busy day and they are, after all, only human.

On another occasion in May the girls' choir had to sing in a concert with Newcastle University Choir. We spent the time we were not required having tea in Marc Toney's in Grainger Street. They did a decent egg and chips, and their chairs were a bit more comfortable than hard pews. The choristers had to take packed teas. We had thought, till a few days ago, that "sandwiches in the Thomlinson Room" meant that the Dean and Chapter were treating the choir to a feed, and very properly too, but it was not so. They had to take their own sandwiches, which in most cases would have had to be prepared before school in the morning. I gave Jessica extra cakes to share, and they all got eaten. Our choir was not singing till the second half, when they sang three pieces on their own and then joined the University choir for a Dvorak mass. They did very well. It went on till 10 o'clock which is late for little girls to give of their best, but they did.

May was a busy month. One evening we had a big performance of Britten's *Saint Nicholas* with lots of different school choirs and orchestras. Michael wanted our choir to be there by 4 o'clock so we had to ask permission for Jessica to leave school early. It was another packed tea occasion, and we took packed teas ourselves and ate them discreetly in our pew. It was a very good performance. Many of the visiting children looked tired, but the conductor was nice and kept things going. Britten is not our favourite composer, but we endured him in a good cause and were pleasantly surprised. I learnt, to my horror, the origin of the three boys in a tub on a small St Nicholas statue near the organ. If you don't know it, Google it, then come and see it.

At the beginning of June the newly formed Choirs Association had a meeting after Sunday Eucharist. It was held in the Education Suite. Two of the committee, who shall be nameless, took over the proceedings. Michael was there in his capacity as Chairman, but he said very little. One executive member started by saying that they wanted the children to go into the next room to do something special. Would they please take a brownie and a cookie and go. They did. We had already had coffee after the service, but some kind person had brought brownies and cookies for the meeting. Those of us who were not being dismissed could also have a brownie and a cookie if we wished. For the next hour and a half we had to discuss ways of raising money. Roger and I both spoke occasionally but really we have no interest in fundraising. We would prefer to skip the gimmicks and just make a donation if we have to. It would be cheaper and less stressful. The trouble is we know Jessica will want to be involved in some of the activities so we can't boycott them. One popular suggestion was bag-packing in a big supermarket before Christmas. We knew Jessica would be very keen to do that, and we should have to wait for her all day and waste money on store refreshments. My own feeling is that the choir earns its existence by singing, and the parents do their bit by getting them to the right place at the right time, and if the congregation want a choir they should pay for it themselves. It seemed to me that the children already did quite enough without having to raise money. I also got a sneaky feeling that some of the committee were trying to create a social life for themselves on their children's backs. OK, I am an arch misery, but in my defence I should say that I have Asperger's Syndrome.

Then we had to discuss recruitment, and how to get children to join the choir. Well, Jessica joined because she genuinely wanted to sing in the services, but many of them don't. They join, or their parents join them, and then they make all sorts of lame excuses for not turning up. It sounds good to say your child is in the Cathedral Choir, but the commitment is too great for some families. And of course many children join for the novelty and lose interest when they find how hard they have to work. It was rather like a PTA meeting – we nattered on and got nowhere. Probably rumbling tummies brought the meeting to an end at 1pm. We had sort of decided on bag-packing, a ceilidh, a Sunday lunch, a concert or two and maybe a Fifty Club. What larks.

I didn't know what special things the children were doing in the next room, but there was a fair amount of noise.

Suddenly a female voice shouted "Be quiet, you two!" I wondered which CCA lady was having to tell them off, but I later learned that there was no adult in charge of them, and it was actually Jessica shouting at two younger boys who were stunned into silence for several minutes. The "special" task was to discuss and list ideas for a new choir handbook. I'm not sure if, at that point, we had even received a copy of the old handbook. They had been given nothing to wash their brownies down, and they were probably dying of thirst as well as hunger. Thus the new CCA was established, and flourished. I found I was allergic to Choirs Associations, and I continued to be.

On an early June Saturday Michael held another *Be a Chorister for a Day*. This time it was in the morning, from 9.30 till 1 with a service at 12.30. There were more parents there today, maybe 20, and the available seats in the Quire were almost filled. One granny was bent on videoing it all, but I leant across and whispered "Please don't!" and as far as I know she stopped. Some people do not understand the difference between an act of worship and an entertainment. Afterwards we had been asked to go up to the Thomlinson Room to mingle, but there wasn't much mingling and I think most children were ready to go home.

Around this time I heard *Locus Iste* for the first time. I loved it, and have always delighted in hearing it since. The choir seemed to like it too. It occurred to me that it would be an advantage to Jessica to learn Latin if she got the chance, so that she would more readily understand what she was singing. It is not the most exciting prospect to a child, so I decided I would offer a substantial bribe. But she was still in middle school, and such treats seemed far in the future.

Next day our choir joined with a visiting children's choir in connection with RSCM. I reminded Jessica to be friendly and say "Hello, I'm Jessica." She did, but one of the visitors she said it to didn't answer but moved away and said to her friend "Weird kid!" Someone had provided some cake, but otherwise it was a social flop. It was not the first. Most children, if they have their own familiar social group around them, are not interested in extending it to strangers, especially if they are off their home ground and feeling insecure.

We had a special Choral Evensong to celebrate a hundred years since the death of Ralph Hedley who, with his son and apprentices, had undertaken much of the decorative carving in the Cathedral including the choir stalls, font cover and rood screen. Gordon, Alan and Tracy, possibly with volunteer help, had dusted and polished all the woodwork they could safely reach. It certainly smelled good. After the service was the inevitable drinks reception with some local songs sung and played by Kim Bibby-Wilson. A Mrs Brown, one of Hedley's grand-daughters, made a nice little speech of thanks. She paid tribute to the vergers for polishing the carvings so nicely. "They're a bugger to dust!" she said. The Dean studied the floor to hide his embarrassment. The carvings, while beautiful in themselves, are rather wasted in their setting. In many cathedrals such carvings are arranged in front of a plain stone wall, so their detail can be readily appreciated, but at Newcastle they have no background and their detail is hard to see. Wherever you are, you are looking through them at something else. It's rather like a doily on a cake plate. If the plate is a plain, solid colour the doily is seen in contrast, but if the plate is patterned the contrast of the doily design is lost and just looks a mess. In the case of a cake plate the problem can be solved by putting a cake on it, but there was rarely any cake on the Hedley carvings.

Once, when the Dean had been publicly worrying about how the Cathedral was going to pay its bills, I wrote to him and suggested he should sell the Hedley carvings to the Americans, so that a different congregation could enjoy what had perhaps delighted us long enough. Not surprisingly he did not reply.

One good thing the new CCA did was to arrange with a local laundry to wash our choir cassocks in return for advertising. Cassocks got very dirty, especially at the bottom, from walking up and down dusty staircases. In fact I suspect most of the sweeping of the Song School stairs was done by cassocks. Previously parents had been asked to take cassocks home and wash them in the holidays, which was reasonable enough and not difficult as they were polyester and dried easily without needing to be ironed. I don't know if there was any charge, but part of the deal was that whenever we printed any reports or newsletters we should include a small advert. It seemed harmless, but didn't last long. I suppose after a year or two the laundry would realise that their target audience was saturated. I won't mention the name of the laundry. I have no such deal with them.

One Sunday in June we had a more local trip out. The choir had been invited to sing Evensong at St. Columba's, Wideopen, to help celebrate 50 years of existence of that building. It was a beautiful, modern church that had for a time been used jointly by Anglicans and Methodists, but recently the Methodists had departed. There's a story there, but it's not within my remit. The choir sang beautifully, but poor Alison Russo, a senior chorister, had to be taken out by Elisabeth because she felt faint. Unlike Rachel she did not feel able to carry on. Jessica said later that, at the beginning, Alison had said she was thirsty but hadn't had time to get a drink. The choir really needed a kindly matron to remind them all: "Have you been to the loo? Have you had a drink? Go now!" Alison was one of the strongest singers, so she would be missed. Evensong was followed by two hymns (nice enough) and a sermon (quite unnecessary). The sermon began with a reminder that there were refreshments afterwards with Pimms, but that sadly the young ladies of the choir would not be able to have Pimms! Well, if Pimms isn't suitable for young ladies, is it suitable for anyone? Most of them were driving! In fact it was a very good and generous finger buffet with plenty of innocent drinks. The choir enjoyed themselves, and I hope thought it was worth tolerating a sermon for. Later, as we waited for Jessica, I got into conversation with Robert and Joan Malcolm who I had not met before. They were Wideopen people, but now attended the Cathedral. They both had severe health problems, but were extremely cheerful.

The following night, during choir rehearsal, a drunk came in and shouted something about money, but he did not seem aggressive. After a while he sat down in front of us and turned round and greeted us pleasantly. I told him my name, and asked him his which was Andrew. Then Gordon came and saw him off. He just said "Come on, Andrew!" and led him kindly by his arm. I supposed he was a regular. I gave him a chocolate frog. He looked 50 but we guessed he might only be in his twenties. Gordon would only be turning him out because Evensong was about to begin, and poor Andrew was probably known to be a disturbance. Whatever Gordon did, he did with courtesy. I wondered if Andrew had ever had a chance in life. Had anybody ever loved him? Michael and James always seemed unruffled by such disturbances. I suppose they were used to them.

One night as I was coming away from the Song School I found a large bee struggling on the path. He looked OK, but he obviously couldn't fly. We scooped him up twice, once to a safe gutter and once to some tired-looking grass so he did not get trodden on. I knew the flower ladies were doing the weekend flowers, so I went in and asked them if they had perhaps got a broken flower to spare for a bee in distress. They clearly thought I was as mad as a hatter. No, they hadn't got a broken flower. If positions had been reversed I would have found a small spare flower, broken or not. I have never felt much affection for the flower ladies since. I hope our poor bee survived, but it was a hostile environment. The Dean, who was watching us, told us St John's Church (at the bottom of Grainger Street) had a beehive on their roof in an effort to save urban bees. Maybe it was one of theirs.

Among people who always gave us a friendly word were Ron and Margaret Smithers. Margaret told us that the following week there were to be ordinations. The candidates were given numbered seats for their families and friends, and there would be very little room left for the normal congregation who would have to sit at the back of the north aisle – a sort of naughty corner. She said lots of people would be there before 9! We were glad of the warning. It was clearly a very important date in the church calendar. At the end of choir rehearsal James told the choristers that they must sing their very best. There would be 900 people from the diocese, and they *must* make a good impression. As we left I told him that they should be singing to the glory of God, not to impress the diocese. He replied, "Yes, I know, but ... "

After the Bishop had ordained the new batch of priests the choirs got down to the serious business of the day – a lunch party at 50 Moorside South, the home of the Stoddart family. It was a lovely warm sunny day and the choristers were mostly still wearing their choir uniform. Celia, taking pity on them, took them all to her bedroom and invited them to help themselves to any of her clothes that might be cooler and less formal. She was a lovely girl. The parents stood around in the garden, as people do, chatting. There was nothing to sit on but two garden chairs. No one sat on them, and after about half an hour we decided to avail ourselves of them, as we were the eldest of the assembled company by at least twenty years. It enabled me to do the knitting I had brought with me. When it was time to eat there was a very good spread of the different goodies we had all taken. We are not party people, but we have to endure them once in a while for Jessica's sake. Today she was having a whale of a time. The party broke up when it was time to go back for Evensong rehearsal.

The end of the choir year was rapidly approaching. One excitement still in store was an ecumenical pilgrimage to Holy Island where the various choirs were to sing. It was very hot weather and I was quite worried about whether the children would suffer from heat exposure. There is hardly any shade on the island. 94°F was forecast. I asked Michael but he admitted he had not thought about it. I emailed the pilgrimage office about it, but as far as I recall I got no response. They were probably much too busy to bother with old grannies making a fuss.

It took place on Saturday, July 13th. The choir were going by coach, but as we were already 13 miles on the way to Holy Island we decided to drive there. The weather was everything the Met Office had promised – sunny and nice but very hot. We parked in the big car park and walked on to the village, passing several stalls islanders had set up in front of their homes – strawberries, potatoes, eggs, honey, paintings and books. We did not want to buy anything then, and doubted if there would be any strawberries left on our return. We were still early and we stopped off at the Oasis Café, which was very nice and clean and had a most appetising array of food, but we were not hungry yet. My main aim in going there was to keep us in the shade for as long as possible. It was a mistake. Our drinks were unpalatable. Roger's tea was poor, but he drank it, Jessica's hot chocolate was weak and tasteless but she drank it, and my coffee might have been good without UHT milk. I couldn't go back to the counter to ask for fresh milk because it would have meant jumping the rapidly growing queue. Knowing that toilet accommodation on the island might be oversubscribed I availed myself of the one at the café. This consisted of one ladies and one gents with a common concourse, so ladies queuing had to wait ages while the gents was available. I decided to skip the queue and go to the gents, despite the horrified gasp. It was in all respects the same as the ladies and very satisfactory, but when I came out there were two men waiting. I smiled apologetically, and fled.

By now Cathedral people were coming to join the café queue. The Cathedral coach (not for the choir) must have arrived about the same time as we did. The Dean and Canon Kevin were among those queuing when we left the café. We had arranged with Michael that we should go straight to St Mary's Church and wait there till he and the choir joined us. We stood around for ages but saw no sign of them. We figured they should be there about 11.15 which was not yet. Meanwhile in the time we had available we visited St Cuthbert's URC and the Lindisfarne Mead Shop which is a tourist's paradise. There were very few places to sit, and as far as we ever knew no extra seating at all was provided for the event, and the public benches in the old market square were always full. Perhaps pilgrimages are not about comfort. It was quite tiring and frustrating because we knew the choir were somewhere, but where? They were supposed to perform in the Priory at 12.45, fifteen minutes before the main service began. We tried to find shady spots to stand in, and we found a good place near a very old gravestone in the shadow of the Priory walls, but a bossy usherette (sorry, English Heritage assistant custodian) told us sharply to get off the graves. I was offended, but we *were* the wrong side of a polite rope barrier they had put up to prevent us from enjoying ourselves. At 12.30 a lady in the church told us the choir had been delayed by a breakdown. They were hoping to be here soon. We decided it was a good moment to eat our packed lunches, so we sat on some nice comfy grass and tucked in.

Just before 1 o'clock the choir arrived and Jessica ran off to join them. We went to the Priory. There had been a very long queue, but in the end it paid not to have queued because we were able to just walk in at the back. Admission was by wristbands, so that pilgrims did not have to pay the full English Heritage price. There was no seating in the Priory, and we were not allowed to sit on the walls. If you don't know Lindisfarne Priory, dear Reader, it is fully open to the elements. As most of the pilgrims were in the second half of life I don't know how they managed. Roger and I found a spot right at the back where we could lean against a wall (nobody stopped us leaning) and just see the choir a long way off, but the order of service we had been given made no mention of the choir doing anything at all. After a couple of minutes I left, telling Roger I would see him in the church before 2.30 when the choir were to give a concert. I found a space on a seat in the square and finished my packed lunch, but after about ten minutes I couldn't stand the heat any longer. I paid a second visit to the Lindisfarne Mead Shop to keep out of the sun. I noticed that Lindisfarne mead contains sulphites. What would the monks think? At some point I chanced to meet up with Roger. He had also not stayed long for the same reason. In the excellent Island Shop I bought myself a banana for my daily potassium. I think the owners of the few island shops would have made enough money to retire by the end of the day. In addition to the Diocesan Pilgrims there were all the usual hungry and thirsty tourists. Holy Island is usually an oasis of peace, but not today! Just before 2.30 we found ourselves relatively comfy seats on the back row of the church. Only hard wooden pews, but infinitely better than standing in the Priory, and a roof to provide shade. The nave was encouragingly full. The choir sang eight pieces beautifully, and surprisingly, in spite of the heat, no one fainted today! There had been a slight sea breeze over the island all day, and it mitigated the heat.

After that Jessica came to tell us that Michael said they could all have half an hour to "go off". He probably needed half an hour's peace himself. I think they mostly queued up for ice creams. We asked Michael where we would find Jessica after the half hour, and he said at the coach. Good idea. On the way there I had an ice cream myself. That was nice. Chorister chaperones don't always find themselves near decent ice cream. To our surprise the strawberries on the little stalls were still there, and in very good condition. Maybe the islanders had been picking them all day. We bought a box to eat and share. They were the best strawberries I had ever eaten. Back at the carpark Cathedral people were assembling for their coach. The choir drifted along, and there was a long farewell session as Jessica watched them get on their coach and drive away. Then we drove off ourselves, and a lot of the time we could see the coach far in front of us.

It had been a good day, but I didn't feel it was a pilgrimage. It was organised, I eventually discovered by Holy Island Churches Acting Together, and therefore ecumenical but I think heavily C of E. George and Marjorie Brigham, from our church, believed themselves to be the only Methodists on their coach. The idea of a coach trip to such a beautiful place in friendly company for only about £15 would appeal to many people regardless of any spiritual element. If the supplementary cost is to pretend to be holy, so be it. I very much appreciated the day, but I regarded myself as a tourist, not a pilgrim.

The following day was sad for Jessica because she had to say goodbye to some choristers who were leaving, among them Emily Stoddart and Rachel Dodd who were off to the next stage of their lives. Michael would present the leavers to the Dean and ask him to bless them. Part of the ritual was to say that the chorister "had always given of her best." It was very often true. The Dean gave them each a copy of Handel's *Messiah* and prayed for them. It was emotional for the congregation as well, as we reflected the individual talent and devotion that made up our choir, and the cheerful little faces that we might not see again.

Now we had a long summer holiday.

2013-2014

As a new year began we continued to sit at the back of the Song School to protect Michael and James. Evensong does not begin till the second week of term, so the first week the choristers had to endure two-hour rehearsals, standing while Michael sat at the piano. If they were lucky he remembered to give them a ten minute break in the middle. We heard Jessica being congratulated for being the first person to return her registration forms. We heard Alison Russo being congratulated on becoming Head Chorister and Bella Dalliston on becoming Deputy Head Chorister. We all clapped, including ourselves hidden behind the stacks, and later Jessica told us off for clapping longer than anyone else (about half a second). I asked Michael if there would be another CD soon, and he said yes, he hoped so. I'm afraid he didn't hope hard enough. The next recording was some years away.

As we had to be so early on Sundays and time dragged for us I began taking my knitting. One Sunday I was sitting in the back pew knitting, and Geoff Miller the archdeacon, who was to preach, went into the pulpit to test the sound equipment. His voice boomed across the church, and I might have winced. He must have seen me because later he came across and apologised most humbly for disturbing me when I was praying. I assured him I had not been praying ("at that particular moment" I added). I suppose at a quick glance a knitter in a pew does look devout.

Our first outing of the year, on a beautiful late summer evening, was to Ford. The choir had been invited to sing at St Michael's Church at a special Evensong as part of their Flodden 500 celebrations and to mark their patronal festival. As the church was actually dedicated to St Michael and All Angels, they had quite a lot of celebrating to do.

We drove there, and were kindly welcomed by the churchwarden (one of the angels) who was looking out for the choir coach. It arrived in ten minutes, and Jessica trotted off with the choir who we understand were given drinks and biscuits in the vestry. We found a nice tearoom called the Old Dairy, and had tea and cakes while we waited for Evensong. About 3 o'clock we went across to the church to wait for the service. A nice lady (surely another angel) came and asked me if I would like a cup of coffee! That was very kind, but as I was full of coffee from the Old Dairy I declined with thanks. It was a lovely church and the service went well. The choir did themselves credit. Afterwards at the back there was a table with elegant tea and coffee in pretty china cups! More angels were serving it to their thirsty visitors. As I was drinking my coffee Michael appeared and said the choir were going to be taken to the Lady Waterford Hall for a meal, and we would be very welcome to join them! Roger had gone to the car for a nap, but I accepted. The hall was set out with a lovely buffet tea, which the choristers polished off with gusto. More angels stood around happily watching them tuck in. St Michael's, Ford, seemed very well off for angels. Jessica seemed happy enough to have me around, and I tried not to cramp her style. Ford is in such beautiful countryside. It was a pity to be able to spend so little time there, but we had lovely scenery all the way. It was a long day but very pleasant. The round trip was 147 miles.

Being keen to recruit choristers Michael had another *Be a Chorister for a Day.* Again it was a very short "day" of under three hours. Tracy took them all up the tower, having made a preliminary visit beforehand, and she was exhausted when she had finished. There were only two little new boys who didn't look hopeful. Boys can join the choir at 7 but they are too young, in my opinion, to make the necessary commitment. Jessica told us one little boy had just cried all the time and his parents had to be phoned to fetch him. Did he think he'd been abandoned?

In a village church where a child lived nearby it might be fine, but for all Newcastle choristers it involves travel and supervision after a long day at school. The day ended with a nice little service, but there were very few in the congregation – I think fewer than ten.

Perhaps the tearful little boy would have been happier if there was a nice motherly person there to look after him, and a few days later there would have been. One night at the end of September Roger and I were sitting at the back of the Song Room as usual. Michael brought a tall, slim young lady up with him and introduced her to the choir as "someone who is going to look after us." Her name was Hannah Davidson and she was a part-time Music Assistant. The Music Department certainly needed assistance, but her main job, I think, was to safeguard the girls and children. She was nice. Michael also told them that a new singing teacher had come and would be taking them for individual singing lessons. One girl could go down for a singing lesson now. Who should it be? "Who do you most want to get rid of, Mr Norrey?" he asked. Realising his tactlessness, he changed it to "Who can you most easily spare?" which was about as bad. Two girls were sent down in turn. James continued with the rehearsal. Once he asked them what special feast day we had been celebrating that weekend. Jessica said,

"St Michael."

"And ... ?" asked Mr Norrey.

"The dragon?" said Jessica.

It might have been better if we had not been present to witness such a gaffe, and indeed now Hannah had come we were no longer required. It was back to the radiator and the draughty staircase for us.

An annual event at the Cathedral is the Reading of the Letters Patent which I suppose are Royal licenses for the judges to dispense justice. It was held at the beginning of the legal year. As usual when the great and good were present, the front rows were reserved for them and the usual congregation, if they should attend, had to sit in the naughty corner. As I made for our favourite seats Gordon had to tell me (kindly) to buzz off. I remembered that Roger was having a nap in the carpark at the back, and I went to wake him and tell him that he would have to clear out to make room for the cars of dignitaries. I collected my cushion and went to sit on the back row by a radiator. A nice steward said he would have to ask me to move for – er – "For more important people," I said. He said well – not really more important, but – well ... I assured him I understood perfectly. On special occasions in the church year the regular faithful have to move out to accommodate people who never darken the door for the rest of the year (I didn't actually say that). Father Kevin came in and greeted me very warmly like an old friend. He has always given us civil nods, but this was quite a shock. He had just returned from a holiday in New York, and was perhaps still under the influence of their much greater friendliness.

Roger came back and said he had gone to Castle Garth and it was full, no doubt with the judicial dignitaries who were assembling for blessing. He had to drive all round the Wrekin (via Swan House roundabout) till he got back to Dean Street where he had to pay £1.80 for one hour. He came back to the Cathedral by the back way and noticed to his annoyance that there were now at least four empty spaces. He whispered to me that he would have to leave at 5.25 to go back for the car, but he would park in the Cathedral carpark if there was any space. And that is what he did. It was such a pity because he could have stayed where he was all the time, but we didn't want to be in the doghouse with the Verger. We wonder where the Lord Mayor's driver parks on such occasions. Maybe he goes home and the Lord Mayor phones him when he wants to leave.

Anyway, Roger left me at 5.25 and I sat quietly reading my *What Doctor's Don't Tell You* magazine which was gripping. I suddenly woke up to the fact that the congregation was standing and the procession of dignitaries had walked up the aisle. At the back a steward was glaring at me. I suppose I looked as if I was showing contempt, but of course I wasn't. As Roger said later, you'd expect an usher to call out "Be upstanding for the High Sherriff and justices!" or something. It was all very low key. I leapt to my feet and hid my mag under my cushion. Roger joined me just after the sermon (oh Roger, you missed the best bit!). There were many empty seats and we could have sat further forward at the sides. Rows of bewigged judges sat on the south side, with their legal subordinates and a few wives on our side. Two of the ladies were wearing large black fashion hats, but most were not. Hats don't seem much worn nowadays except at weddings and Ascot, I'm glad to say. St Paul liked woman to keep their heads covered in church, of course, but I think these particular hats would have had him rolling over in his grave. The actual Letters Patent, which must be very long and boring and perhaps barely comprehensible to the legal laity, were read elsewhere in advance, and a declaration had to be made in the service to that effect. In the words of the Immortal Bard, for this relief much thanks. There is no doubt, and I think most of the congregation would agree, that the high spots of the service were the choir singing. The High Sherriff would undoubtedly have sent his thanks to them, and would surely have been sincere. Back in the Song School hallway we happily did not have to wait long for the children to come down. Roger could not have leaned against the radiator as usual because there was a bike parked against it. It wasn't Roger's day. He was glad to go home.

In early October the choir were invited to give a little con-cert at St Gabriel's Church, Heaton, as part of their Harvest Supper. Parents might join the fun for £6.50, and it never occurred to us to do other than pay, attend and eat. Of the nine girls who went to sing, only four stayed for the supper. It was free for the children, so they really missed out. Jessica, Yashia, Bella and Jude stayed, but the other parents came back for them afterwards, so Roger and I were the only parents staying for supper. Those Hawkinses never miss a feed! It was elegant and appetising, and we ate lots. We think at least half of the food must have been wasted. We did not know that we had been asked to take drinks, but there was plenty of juice. Anne Ramsay and her husband welcomed us cordially and sat with the girls. There was no heating on and it was a bit chilly, but as I had taken no jumper that was entirely my fault. At the end Jessica said she would like to hang about till Jude's father came to fetch her so she wasn't on her own. It had been a very enjoyable evening, and the choir thoroughly deserved the very good supper that most of them sadly didn't stay for.

The system in the Music Department was that choristers got occasional individual singing lessons if there was currently a teacher. A new lady teacher, Rebecca Coulson, came about now. Jessica got a lesson with her, and she told Jessica that she was a very good singer. That night at Evensong there were only four in the congregation. The canticles were to a setting a priest would not know, so Bella sang the cantor's part because she knew it. She has a very pure, clear voice. About now Jess hurt her arm and had to wear a sling. Michael, Elisabeth and Celia were most kind and solicitous. Rachel Peutherer, who stood beside her in choir, turned the pages for her which was a great help. A new organ came at last. It is only temporary, but we suspect will be temporary for a very long time. We have to raise money for our next project first, then for a new organ. It could take many years.

On Saturday, October 19th, we had a trip to Carlisle for the Borders Festival. We had to leave home at 9.15. We stopped for hot drinks at the Little Chef at Bardon Mill, and the choir coach, which left the Cathedral at 10, probably passed us. It was a wet day, but not raining then. In Carlisle Roger dropped us off within sight of the Cathedral while he went off to look for parking. He had researched this on the internet the night before but was not very enlightened. Carlisle is a very one-way city and if you get it wrong you have to go all the way round again. In the Cathedral a welcomer told us she thought some of our people might be across the way (pointing to a café we knew) but she didn't know who was who. We thanked her and went across to the Prior's Kitchen, but we did not recognise any of the faces we saw and we went back into church. We browsed their gift shop which was very nice but happily had little to tempt us except some notebooks with jolly mice on. After a few minutes the kind welcomer told us she believed more people were assembling in the Fratry. We didn't know where that was, but she kindly showed us. She was a very welcoming welcomer, and an example to all of them. The Fratry was in the upper part of the building under which the Priors Kitchen nestles. We went up some stone stairs to a large hall where lots of people were mingling, and we saw Celia at one end. Jessica ran off to join her. Down the room were three rows of tables set simply for lunch with basic cutlery, and every couple of feet or so was a bowl of cut-up oranges which smelled divine. It looked as if the children were being lovingly catered for by the Carlisle ladies.

I went back to the Prior's Kitchen to get my special bargain. This was a free cup of tea or coffee if I bought a cake or scone. I claimed it with a voucher I had found by accident on the Cathedrals' website and downloaded. It was valid up to 12 and after 2 till they closed at 3.30. It was now about 11.45. I got my free coffee and a lovely slice of Paradise cake. As noon approached and Roger still had not appeared I got him his special offer tea and scone. He was pleased to find it when he came in ten minutes later. We had a schedule for the day and we knew there was to be a rehearsal from midday till 1 o'clock. I wanted to hear it, so I asked Roger to hold the camp while I went into the church to listen. He had his lunch while I was away. After that I went back and had my lunch. We were glad we had done that as the café was busy and we might not have got a table later. In the afternoon the choirs were to be joined by the lay clerks. There were eight of our girls, and about a dozen each from Hexham and Carlisle. Roger went off to find what he called the Toll House, though he realised later he had got the name wrong and he really wanted the Tullie House. I think he found something to his satisfaction. I ate my lunch and read a book till 2 o'clock when I went back into the church to hear the second rehearsal. Our girls were wearing their choir uniform, Carlisle were wearing uniform red sweatshirts and Hexham had no uniform. The singing was such as to make you think, "Well, let's hope it will be alright on the night!" I went for another cup of coffee, then carried on listening to the choir till 4 o'clock when they went off for their tea (which I later heard was tea and lots of biscuits). It was now my intention to bag the best seats I could and sit on them till the concert at 5, popping out when necessary to buy our tickets at £8 each. But that was not to be. A chap in a long black frock approached me from behind and asked if I would like to take part in Evening Prayer which was just starting. I had to say yes. I think if I hadn't he would have escorted me out! Two lady priests (or one and a hanger-on) sat at the very back in canonical stalls. I sat at right angles to them. I am pretty clued up now about Evening Prayer and I think I did all the right things. That took about twenty minutes, and after the robed ladies had recessed I ran to the seats I wanted and stuck my luggage on one of them. I went to the crossing to get tickets and found Roger. Our seats were at the middle end of the second row, and after a while, as no one sat in front of us, we moved to the front row, thereby getting the best possible view. By now there were about 80 children all together, plus lay clerks. I don't know where the extra children had come from. On the front row sat lots of little Hexham boys in red gowns and pie frills. Some of them looked much too young to be under so much stress and several were not singing at all apart from an occasional goldfish impression to impress the conductor. Hexham were now wearing purple cassocks, Carlisle green ones and Newcastle just their white cassocks and not their tabards. This would make them look more uniform as some of them do not yet have tabards. It was a very good concert, lasting about an hour. Yes, it was worth £8. Jessica was very pleased with it all and they had been given a good lunch.

Now it was time to go home, and it was raining. Roger said there was no point in him fetching the car because he would not have known how to get back to us. We should have to walk. It might take us ten or fifteen minutes. He could remember the way he had walked. The rain got heavier. We had no umbrellas, and I had deliberately left my cagoule in the car so as not to be lumbered with it all day. I just had a cardigan, and Jessica's coat had no hood – the only hoodless coat she possessed. We just put our heads down and ran out into the rain. It actually took us thirteen minutes to reach the car, but we were saturated after the first few seconds. Rapidly forming puddles sent up spray to meet what was coming down. By the time we reached the car we were soaked to the skin and past caring. I found some old towels in the boot to dry our hair a bit, then we just snuggled under rugs. The car heating soon warmed us up, and Roger (who had been wearing a coat) drove us to Bardon Mill Little Chef where we found the rain had substantially stopped. We had a good hot meal and soon felt a lot better. It had been a very good day, and getting wet was a small thing in the end.

It was in November that Roger had to give up driving. Our choir routine changed a good deal. I set myself up with a small backpack so I could have two hands free for the handrails when I went upstairs on the bus. It had useful side nets for our small flasks. However I no longer had carrying capacity for my latex cushion. For a while I managed with a small inflatable one, but then Jessica asked Hannah if I could leave my latex cushion in a cupboard in the Thomlinson Room, and Hannah very kindly said yes. We found there was no bus on Sunday that would get Jessica to the Cathedral in time for rehearsal, so we reluctantly decided to get taxis on choir Sundays. It seemed expensive at first, but as the weeks went by we realised how much we were saving by not running a car!

On Sunday November 24th Jessica was confirmed at our own church. I emailed the office to ask if the Cathedral would pray for her that day, and they did. Now when she went up to the communion rail she could hold out her hands to receive, rather than keeping them by her side to get a blessing. A few days later Father Kevin sent Jessica a lovely card "from the whole Cathedral" congratulating her.

Less agreeably, we had an email from the CCA asking for a sub of £12 each. We had believed parents were automatically members and did not need to pay, but apparently most people were stumping up. Crawlers! We considered this a rip-off, and determined we would not pay till it became embarrassing not to do so. They had a special little concert one night for a development launch for a choir fundraising scheme for scholarships, and lots of influential people were invited. There were only seven girls singing, but they did brilliantly and were much appreciated.

One night in Evensong Mr Norrey had all the girls singing little bits of solo, just a few words each, in the *Magnificat*. Most sang timidly like little mice, but Jessica was more confident. It was a nice little opportunity for them all, as most of the younger ones had never sung by themselves. Mr Norrey is very nice to the girls, and they respect him.

Advent was with us and Christmas was coming. On the 12th of December a Street Nativity was held, organised by several churches in the city. Our choir were detailed to sing carols from time to time. The event began at the Hub at the top of Northumberland Street, so I made my way there. I stopped at M&S and bought myself a chicken satay snack with a peanut dip. Well, chaperones have to keep their strength up! I sat on a seat to eat it. After a while I heard someone say "Here's a choir!" and when I looked our choir were just passing behind me. I followed them along to the Hub where church people were assembling. The vicar of a local church, who shall be nameless, was trying to jolly people up and hit Jessica on the head with a carol sheet which may not have been dangerous but was certainly not dignified. The small crowd, mostly supporters, thickened a bit, and it was soon impossible for me to see what was going on.

The performance started with a dance by professionals which I could not see. Then John Grundy (a local TV star, dear Reader) appeared as the Angel Gabriel to a young girl (Bella Dalliston) and exchanged a lot of Geordie jokes. Again I couldn't see (I never could) but I could hear, and I decided I didn't like it at all. I stayed around to support Jessica and the choir, and the action moved from one side of the pedestrianised street to the other for different scenes. Passers-by were attracted by the novelty, but I heard many people saying to their friends, "I don't know what's going on." The story, as it unwound, was that a young couple, Joseph and Mary, had been moved from Camden to Tyneside where they hoped he would get a job and they would be rehoused. The Angel Gabriel followed them round and spread the Geordie humour on thickly. It was supposed to tell the story of the Nativity with a new twist that the people of Tyneside would understand. There was a fair sprinkling of bad language too, which again was supposed to be what the Geordie audience would appreciate. I found it most offensive. The real Joseph had been neither unemployed nor homeless, far from it, and the comparison between the Roman Census and the pert, unhelpful Local Government clerk was inappropriate. Eventually the baby was born in Fenwick's doorway. If the contemporary theme had been continued to its logical conclusion a social worker would have appeared and made off with the baby, but no. A doll was put into a box of straw, and was visited by shepherds and wise men. During all this we stopped occasionally to sing a traditional carol, and they were the only good bits. Our choir was leading the singing and giving the whole performance the only bit of grace it had.

The farce ended with a variety of priests doing a very short prayer each, then we said the Lord's Prayer on the assumption that most people knew it (which they no longer do), and the Bishop gave a final blessing. I saw Father Kevin standing with a colleague in his good black mufti, and I got the feeling that although he was trying to be positive he really didn't like it very much. At least I hope he didn't.

I was glad to leave the scene and hurry back to the Cathedral. As I passed Fenwick's windows, where young families were queuing to see their famous fairy tale Christmas window display, I felt they had the better deal. It may not have been religious, but there was nothing crude or vulgar about it.

It's a fine thing to take the Gospel to the streets, but this was not the Gospel. It was confused exhibitionism. Everyone who took part did well, but the whole thing was rubbish. Souls are not won for the Kingdom of God with corny jokes and modern-day mythology. The Nativity is history, and should have been presented as history. It's a wonderful story on which no one could ever improve. I can say now, years later, with relief, that the Street Nativity was never repeated.

A few days later, in Evensong, Jessica and Harriet Watts-Williamson sang a short duet in the *Nunc Dimitis*. They sang different parts, and did very well. It was quite short, but by far the longest piece Jess had sung so far. It showed Michael had confidence in her. Harriet was a few years older, and a more experienced chorister. The same day was special because the Dean returned from a long sick leave. He was not ill, but he had had a foot operation and was not allowed to walk. Now he was hobbling round dramatically in protective footwear and with a stick. It was good to have him back.

On the 19th the choir were due to sing carols at Monument Metro Station as a money-raising venture. I stayed behind in the Thomlinson Room to make hot chocolate for their return. Knowing that the choristers would not be expected to wear coats, and it being December, I urged Jessica to wrap up warmly under her cassock, which she obligingly did. Later I heard that she had become overheated, and Hugh Beney's mum and Elisabeth had taken her into Fenwick's to cool her down and unwrap her in their loo. A passing manager invited them to take the choir to sing in the store, but they did not make so much money in there. Maybe the customers thought Fenwick's were paying them. When they arrived back with their buckets they seemed pleased with the result. I thanked Elisabeth for looking after Jessica and apologised for being the cause of the trouble, but Elisabeth kindly said she had given Celia exactly the same advice. It was quite a busy day and I offered supper out, but Jessica wanted to get home. It was not till later that we remembered we had forgotten our Golden Wedding.

On the 23rd we attended the Crib Service at which the younger girls were singing. At 3 o'clock we were all invited to go to the Font. There were only about 20 or fewer of us, and I think we were all from the usual congregation. The Dean, Father Kevin and Father Steven shared the leading of it. Father Steven seemed to be in charge, and I suppose it fell into his brief as Canon for Education. He asked a volunteer to be Mary, and the angel was already self-appointed. We sang several carols as we walked around. He gave Mary a blue wrap. It was a sort of walking *tableau vivant.* The first stop was the St Margaret Chapel where he had to introduce Joseph. No child was willing to be Joseph, so an adult had to be enlisted. Roger kindly took on the role and had a teatowel draped over his head, and was given a brown jerkin. On to the crossing where we took on the donkey. Most of these roles were played by very tiny girls who hardly realised they were volunteering. Back to the south side where the choir were given tinselled haloes and the angel appeared to the shepherds, on to the chancel which was Herod's palace and three ladies were decked out as kings, then finally to the Chapel of the Incarnation where it all came together and the angels sang from the choir. It was all very nice, infinitely better than the street nativity. But it was a pity so few people attended. It was also a pity that the angel's grandpa danced around flashing his camera all the time. At the end there was juice and biscuits which was nice. Roger told Steven he would like to be the donkey next year. I made friends with a tiny new black baby girl, the youngest of three, who was smiling in her pram, and asked her name. When they told me I feared I would never be able to remember it, and asked how to spell it. Jaachi, I hope you're reading this!

Christmas Eve called for special arrangements. Buses did not run after early teatime, and of course there were none at all on Christmas Day, and we didn't want to keep taking taxis when we, and the drivers, might be tired. We booked a family room at the nearby Vermont Hotel. Jessica and I went on the bus with our luggage and settled in, and Roger joined us by the last bus. About

4.20 I took Jessica to the rehearsal for Nine Lessons and Carols. It was dark as we followed the board walk between the railway arch and the Black Gate. I knew at one point there was a step down – or was it two steps? I took them very carefully in case there were two. Oh dear – there were three! I jolted my back, but fortunately not badly and it was soon better. Roger and I spent the time reading, doing crosswords and snacking. I read the fire precautions booklet, which ran to two pages of smallish print. I was left with the impression that a towering inferno was quite likely, and the chance of survival on the eleventh floor, where we were, was virtually nil. I decided to keep my coat by the bed. Through our window we could see the illuminated Castle in all its glory a few dozen cobbled feet away, and around and beyond it the railway, river and their lights. When it was quiet we could hear the Cathedral clock (chiming, not ticking).

About 5.30 we set off for the Cathedral to wait for the service of Nine Lessons and Carols. It was very well attended. We sat in our usual spot (two rows back on the south side) but Gordon had to flush us out because the Lord Mayor was coming and two rows had to be kept for her and her retinue. The Bishop gave a short sermon and the choir sang sweetly. We had candles to hold, and all tried not to get wax drips on our clothes. It wasn't easy.

Then back to the Vermont to stay awake till Midnight Mass. Now it was time to eat, and we had a very good fish and chips supper served in our room. There was only one chair and one dressing-table stool, but Roger very handsomely said he would sit on the floor. Jessica and I ate at the dressing table. The food was delicious, and we were ready for it. Afterwards she managed to keep awake, and at 10.10 we took her back for rehearsal, then went back to our room for an hour. We too were feeling tired, maybe more tired than we would have felt at the same time at home, and knowing we had to stay awake for another few hours was hard.

We went back to the Cathedral at 11.15. We sat in the Quire with another family but no one came to light our candles. I went off to seek a light, and the nice man who swings the incense gave me one. Of course it was mass, and a pretty special one, so there was no escaping the incense. There was a good turn-out of the choir, but it was augmented by Georgie, Emily and Rachel who were all on holiday from uni. The Dean preached for eleven minutes on the theme "The waiting is over!" I wasn't waiting for anything, but I got his drift. There weren't many children there, but if there had been their waiting would have had to go on for a few more hours. As well as forgetting to light our candles the stewards forgot to collect our offering, so we kept it. When midnight came, and everyone was whispering "Happy Christmas!" to each other, I whispered "Happy Birthday!" to Roger who was 73 on Christmas Day. Elisabeth asked how we were getting home. A few weeks ago she warmly invited us to go to their house to kill time between services on Sundays, but I told her we managed very well but would be grateful to keep the offer in mind for an emergency. She seemed pleased we were staying at the Vermont. Tracy, who lived in Sunderland, was getting a taxi home at the Cathedral's expense, she told me, but then that was her Christmas stint finished. Gordon, and maybe Alan, would be looking after us next day. Back to our room where we had a warm drink, set two alarm clocks for 7.30, and went to bed.

We had worried about how Jessica would take to such reduced hours of sleep, but she woke up easily and cheerfully. We were down for breakfast at 8. She had Frosties, cranberry juice and toast, and made a water lily with her serviette into which we put the waitress's tip. Then Roger took her to the Cathedral for the last time. Michael had been merciful and only required them to be there at 9.30 for the 10 o'clock service. Most of them would have been up for hours doing what kids do on Christmas morning, but Jessica had left her prezzies at home to open later. We finished our breakfast, then packed up and left.

I had felt very embarrassed at breakfast because poor Jessica was in her choir uniform, with blazer and black stockings. The other guests must have wondered why a child was being required to wear school uniform today of all days! Had those elderly grandparents no imagination? Had the poor child no other clothes? I wanted to shout out, "It's not school uniform! She's in the Cathedral choir!" but of course one doesn't do that sort of thing.

Today Gordon turned us out of our seats (not again!) because the Bishop's wife was coming. We weren't in her seat, but she came with an impressive retinue of children and grandchildren. Well, it says something for a Bishop if his children go to church (depending on whether they go the other 51 weeks of course). From the way they sang we guessed they often went. The Bishop preached a short sermon about Advent calendars and the excitement of wondering what was behind each little door, but knowing that door 24 would always be a crib scene. In life, he said, we are constantly facing surprises, but we knew that at the end Jesus would be waiting for us.

Afterwards it was mingling time. Joan Malcolm was going round with a basket containing, she said, "gold, frankincense and myrrh" and inviting people to dip in. It seemed to be chocolate coins. That was very nice of her. Michael gave the choir a big tin of sweets to tuck into. There was no coffee today because it was supposed that everyone would be anxious to rush off home and baste their turkey. Now at last we could go home. In our innocence we thought there would still be taxis waiting on the ranks. There weren't. We got as far as the Theatre Royal, and realised to our embarrassment we had not thought ahead. At that time we did not carry mobile phones. Eventually a nice Indian cab driver appeared and stopped to ask us if we were alright. He was not on duty, and he was taking his wife and children out, but he would be very pleased to ring a friend who was working. We were so grateful. The friend soon came for us, and it was so good to be on our way home. When we got to Morpeth we gave the driver £40 and Joan's gold coin. We would know better next time! I told Jessica that the first taxi driver had been what I call an angel – someone you don't know who just comes into your life unexpectedly at the right moment to help you. Now Jessica had three weeks of choir holiday to look forward to.

January came, as it does. On the first Sunday, four new choristers were installed, Alison Russo and Bella Dalliston were installed as Head Chorister and Deputy Head Chorister respectively, and two boys were leaving. It was a little bit of a shambles in a way because Michael and the Dean both had orders of service in one hand and had to do the robing with the other. Michael seemed particularly cack-handed and surplices and tabards were rather thrown on with one hand, and looked dreadful from behind. Today we had decided to try going home and coming back, to see if we had enough time. The service had been long with the installations, and we missed two of the likeliest buses. As we waited for the third we fed pigeons in the bus station. I bought them a soft roll from Gregg's. Some people call them rats with wings, but I find them charming, and so many of them have badly injured feet and legs which makes their lives hard and short. Some of them ate out of Jessica's hand. Over time I noticed that pigeons in other parts of the city rarely had such injuries, and I came to the conclusion that the bus station birds fell victim to a nasty trap. On two or three of the poles are signboards pointing to different places in the city, and on top of these box-shaped boards are a layer of sharp needles. They are almost invisible. Birds fly across them without seeing them and catch their feet, and there is no escape but to struggle off and leave their feet behind. Unlike most animals a bird cannot lie down and rest while it recovers. A pigeon must carry on balancing and walking on a bleeding stump, or it will starve to death. They show tremendous courage, and we named one of them Hardy because of his dauntless spirit. There are notices up telling us not to feed pigeons, but I fear I don't always see them.

Our experiment worked and we caught a bus back for Evensong with relative ease. Roger even managed a short nap during our time at home. It was Epiphany, and we had a candlelit carols service in the evening. There was a very good congregation, almost as good as at Christmas, whereas on most Sunday nights there is only a small handful. One item in the service was a commission that went along the lines of:

Will you dare to embrace each other and grow together in love?

And the congregation droned *We will.*

Will you dare to share your riches in common and to minister to each other in need?

We will.

Will you dare to pray for each other until your hearts beat with the longings of God?

We will.

In our defence let it be said that Roger and I made no response. We did not believe that the people standing around us really meant to embrace each other, pray for each other until it hurt, and share their riches in common – no way! People are unlikely to change their whole philosophy and way of life because a priest has made them say so in a service. As for "We will," it is an expression I don't like. I can make a promise for myself, but not for anyone else, and no one else can make a promise for me. I can only say "I will," and of course sometimes I know that I won't so it isn't right for me to say I will. The choir sang seven anthems, which represented lot of hard work, and they did very well.

Jessica told us Michael had asked her how she got the Cathedral now (still always in very good time). He was worried when he knew we took taxis. It's a funny thing about taxis. People who are otherwise polite and discreet feel quite free to criticise another person's expenditure on a taxi. They would never dream of saying "What a posh car! Did you really need something so expensive?" or "That's three new coats you've had this year – how extravagant!" but they feel quite free to say "A taxi? That must have cost you a lot!" as if it was their money you were splashing about. If Jessica was to continue in choir it was necessary for us to get taxis, but we were quite happy about this. The money we were saving by not having a car was quite enough to provide for more taxis than we ever needed. But Michael worried. He thought he had a solution to the problem. He said we really needed to get some more Morpeth choristers so that we could share lifts. I think he hoped we would recruit some from among Jessica's friends. We thought it was a rotten idea, and hoped it wouldn't happen. We had always bent over backwards to get Jessica to choir in time, and if other people became involved there would be inevitable delays as people kept each other waiting. Also we did not want to entrust Jessica's safety to a driver we did not know. We privately determined that if Michael did recruit anyone from Morpeth we should continue independently of anyone else. But he never did.

The Choirs Association were busy planning treats. One was to be a ceilidh at St Basil and St James at Fenham. It would take place on a Saturday evening between *Be a Chorister for a Day* and Sunday Eucharist. The cost was

£5 which included "free" tea and cake (and we must provide the cake ourselves). Ceilidh tickets were sent out unsolicited. We had to either send the money or send the tickets back. We sent the tickets back. We didn't go, but we know it was a success and it was continued annually. The following day after Eucharist the CCA raised even more money by selling the left-over cake. I took Eddie a piece because he had come in to keep warm. He is one of the marginalised people we sit and pretend we care about in sermons, but too often ignore when they are near us.

The next *Be a Chorister for a Day* was quite a success. Eight new people came, and each had a designated chorister looking after them. I saw Jessica being very kind to a little boy and helping him to follow the music, but another choirboy who shall be nameless was being very stingy and unhelpful to his little protégé who must have had great difficulty seeing what he was supposed to see. Afterwards Hannah had organised flask drinks and biscuits in the south aisle for parents, and decent quality fruit juice for the children. I congratulated her as this is the first time parents have had refreshments or any meaningful recognition. Hannah was a great asset to the Music Department.

One Monday night in early March I was the only congregation at Evensong. Father Kevin said, as usual, "The congregation may be seated." I gave him a smile as I sat, and later he apologised most profusely in case he had embarrassed me. Well, I'd have been embarrassed if he had said "Christine may be seated!"

On Ash Wednesday there was an evening choral Eucharist with ashing. I don't remember it happening last year. At an appropriate moment the celebrant (was it the Dean?) stood with a bowl of black powder and dabbed it on to the foreheads and wrists of the congregation as they filed past him. We did not go up, but Jessica did. As a chorister it would have been very conspicuous if she hadn't, but she was quite keen. I had never seen black ash before. It has always been grey in my experience. I am told these black ashes are made from the slow burning of last year's surplus palm crosses. Jessica did not want to wash it off at bedtime, so next morning we had to remind her to be sure to get it off or her teacher would think she had not washed. It was really mucky stuff.

At the next CCA meeting there were lots of references to "parent and associate members" and "fully paid-up members." No one beyond the Treasurer should have known which was which, but we began to feel we were considered second class. The meeting was boring, and we didn't really want to go on attending, but we felt we had to for Jessica's sake. We decided that if we did have to pay, only one of us would. It wasn't the money, it was the principle.

In March the choir went to Durham again to help celebrate their patronal festival. This time we went with the choir in the coach, paying a contribution towards the hire cost. Hannah had thoughtfully asked permission of the proprietors, Howard Snaith Coaches, for the children to eat their packed teas in the coach. The driver did not want to drive up to Palace Green so he dropped us all off in the town centre to walk up. Roger and I had 90 minutes to wait while the choirs rehearsed. Unfortunately I had forgotten my cushion, but this time the front pews were empty and they had nice thick seat-pads.

After the rehearsal some nice lady ushers saw us into seats in the choir. At first we were in little stalls with roofs over our heads. I didn't like that at all. Goodness knew what might be lurking in the little roof, and I was afraid I would bang my stupid head when we had to stand up. Worst of all the seats were very narrow, front to back, and I felt as if I was slipping off. I told Roger I wanted to move again and he was a bit peeved. He loved his little roof and the gargoyles and carved armrests. We moved to a slightly more modern and less intimidating bench, and happened to fetch up directly opposite Michael who seemed to have no function once he had delivered up his choir to his counterpart, James Lancelot. The service was rather boring, but I gathered it was supposed to be very joyful and, as a patronal privilege, we were allowed to sing Hallelujah with gusto. It seems that the Church of England does not normally sing or say Hallelujah in Lent. Why not? Roger says he believes we are supposed to be sad in Lent. Sad, for six weeks, when God's in his heaven and we are redeemed? What rot. There was no collection this year. Last year we remembered stewards with buckets who we could hardly avoid. I put my collection in one of the big donations boxes as we left.

We didn't want to interfere afterwards and we meant to keep well away from the choir, but I slipped into the Chapter House to use one of the two loos. As I came out Michael appeared and invited us to join them officially. We met up with Jessica, though she was still with the group that Hannah was organising very efficiently. We trotted off, more or less in a double crocodile, down to where we had left the coach. It was waiting for us, and it was good to get back into our comfy seats after three hours on pews. We all finished our snacks. Jessica was sitting somewhere at the back with Deimante, the daughter of Neringa the Cathedral Finance Manager, who joined the choir for a while. When we got back I reminded Hannah that she wanted some money from us, and she was pleased to be reminded because she had forgotten. It was £5 each which was very reasonable.

Today we had an email from Michael about a proposed summer club for the first week of the summer holidays. It consisted of five long days (08.00 to 18.00) at the Cathedral singing and "doing other activities" (what?). So far so good. Then it said they were thinking of charging up to £150. Good grief! We both said no, but worried about how Jessica would take it. It wasn't the £150, which we would gladly afford if it was worth it, but this seemed like blatant fund-raising. The staff would either be already salaried or volunteers, there would in all probability be no food included, the premises are already there and paid for, and at this time of year there would be no heating costs. The only cost I could think of would be extra insurance. We decided not to raise the matter with Jessica tonight in case she got unduly upset at bedtime. We wondered if she would have heard about it from other children on the coach. But they probably hadn't heard yet as most of them came directly from school. I sent Michal an email telling him what I thought, and he sent me a friendly reply. He did not like the summer club idea either, but he had been outvoted. It seems some of the ladies of the CCA were shameless about wanting cheaper childcare. Childminding is not one of the functions of a cathedral. Michael said he was very pleased to have our (albeit negative) response, and it would arm him in his struggle. I think he was already beginning to discover that CCAs, like PTAs, are a mixed blessing. At a subsequent meeting, when I raised the matter, one of the fathers said, "We have to pay for child care anyway, and we would rather the money went to the Cathedral." There's no answer to that. Later a new scheme was worked out whereby children (like Jessica perhaps) who did not have to be put in child care but just fancied a day with choir friends could come for a reduced number of hours at a reduced price. I knew Jessica would want to go, and I was happy to take her, but I felt we were all being ripped off. But that was later.

On March 30th came Mothering Sunday. The Cathedral was giving out little posies of daffodils, first to mums, then to everyone. First the posies were blessed, then the choristers and other children distributed them around the congregation. Jessica had been told nothing about this and did not know what to do, but having done it at our own church she guessed and coped. She brought one to me, and as she took them round to other people she gave one to Harriet's little sister Anastasia and said "I'm sure you'll be a mother some day!" On our way to the bus station afterwards I was still holding my posy and looking for someone I might give it to when I saw a biggish little Mongol boy in a buggy being pushed along by his father. I asked if I could give the posy to the little boy and his father was most overcome with gratitude and appreciation. As for the little boy, he looked delighted. It was nice to pass on the blessing.

The following night the new singing teacher, Mrs Rebecca Coulson, came. Jessica and a girl I will call Ermintrude had lessons. Ermintrude seemed not to have her heart in singing. At the end of Jessica's lesson Mrs Coulson said "Very nice, Jessica." At the end of Ermintrude's lesson she said "Very nice, Ermintrude. Try to get the notes right." Jessica felt it wasn't worth doing well if equal praise was given to rubbish. She said that Ermintrude, who up to now had not sung at all but only mimed, now sings but gets the notes wrong and puts Jessica off. Apparently when it was her turn to have a singing lesson tonight she acted bolshie and refused, and Hannah said "But Ermintrude, you're in the choir!" The refusal continued, and Hannah said Ermintrude had better get to her lesson sharpish or she would be very angry, and Ermintrude would see the other side of her! Presumably this terrified Ermintrude, who scuttled off to her lesson with Jessica.

By now I was slowly getting absorbed into some of the other Cathedral activities, and during Lent I attended a short series of daytime talks by the clergy about notable Anglicans who each of them had chosen. On the day Canon John Sinclair was talking about Dorothy L. Sayers I met Yvonne Hall. I had actually come across her before (she was a server), but today she made a point of introducing herself to me. She was the new Chairman of the Mother's Union, she said. I knew, because I had been at her recent installation into that role. "Yes, there are going to be some great changes in the Mothers' Union!" she said. I asked whether she meant changes in the movement or here, and she said "Here!" in a rather threatening voice. Oh, she had plans for *great* changes, she said. For one thing she wanted the meetings to change to Saturdays, so that husbands and children could come too! Oh yes, she said, she had *lots* of plans, and it was all the doing of the Holy Spirit! I received this information cautiously. I fear the Holy Spirit has been unfairly blamed for a lot of evil in our world. I decided that, if Jessica would like to go too, I would give it a try when it started, but if not, not. Mums should be available for their children on Saturdays. I was sceptical, however. I imagined a man going back to work on Monday morning, and his colleagues asking him if he'd had a good weekend. Would he really want to say he had been to the Mothers' Union?

Hannah, under instructions from the CCA, sent us a big envelope with a poster and tickets for a forthcoming Curry and Quiz Night. We had to send the money or return the tickets (which we did). I was a bit fed up of this kind of marketing, and I wrote to Hannah asking her in future not to send tickets we had not asked for. She got the message, and we had no more unsolicited tickets. I knew that by now I would have a reputation as an arch misery, but so be it. In the event we did go to the supper, and it cost us £27 for tickets and £30 for a taxi home at a rather late hour. Jessica had enjoyed it, which was all that mattered to us.

The Maundy Thursday foot washing was much as last year, but Father Steven was now the foot-washer (still one foot only) and as he dried the foot he kissed it (well it was clean). If the washing was perfunctory, at least the drying was thorough. Then Tracy had to wash the fluffy white towels again.

I bought four Beany Boo toys for the Children's Chapel, but I didn't like to put them there without asking. I gave them to Father Kevin in a carrier, and asked him if he would give it to Father Steven. He smiled broadly, though he didn't know what was in the carrier. I wondered if he thought it was a chocolate cake from a frustrated spinster of this parish. I know unmarried priests get a lot of those.

The Good Friday service began at 2 o'clock, but at 1.50 Gordon ushered as all outside for "an act of witness". We assembled in the square under Queen Victoria's impassive gaze, and the clergy gathered round a wooden cross. The choir sang. Jessica asked me later if I knew how Mr Norrey gave them the starting note. A tuning fork, perhaps? No, an iPhone! We all trooped into the nave behind the cross, which was set up on the crossing dais in a socket. It was very gloomy – no organ, no lights, no candles. Tracy told me she had locked the candles away this morning. I was sorry there were no candles as any person might come in to light a candle to pray for a loved one. Are they to be given the impression that God has gone on his Easter holidays, or is dead or otherwise unavailable and cannot deal with their prayers? After the service we left in silence. Gordon almost locked us in, and had to send Tracy with a key to let us out. The thought of being locked in for the night was disconcerting. I still did not carry a mobile phone. Why didn't we leave with everyone else? Well, when you gotta go, you gotta go! It occurs to me to mention a very good thing about the Cathedral. The votive candles are free. A polite little notice invites a donation of 20p to help keep up the supply of candles, but it is clear that it is not demanded. This is good, because people in distress do not always have money for a candle. I have noticed that in other Cathedrals it is most common to be asked for 50p as a price, not a donation. The tea-lights cost between 5p and 10p, so that is blatant profiteering and "making my Father's house a house of merchandise". Well done, St. Nix!

On Easter Sunday we treated ourselves to hot chocolate in the Vermont while we waited for the service. The Bishop preached today. He had been there to do confirmations at the 8am service, and Dominique Hewitson, a chorister, was confirmed. I can't help wondering why such an important ritual was not performed at the main Eucharist so a larger number of people could welcome Dominique, but mine not to reason why. There was a big congregation with lots of children and most of the little ones played in the St Margaret Chapel and seemed to be having a very good time. I hoped the Dean and Chapter, especially the Dean, would observe what a good idea the children's corner was working out to be. At Peace time I went and shook hands with all the babies, which I always intend to do. Afterwards chocolate eggs rolled around in abundance. However, Jessica had a disappointment. I had under-stood, from an email from James, that the choristers were to help make an Easter garden at the east end of the church at 10.30 (it seemed an odd time) and afterward they would go out for lunch to a pizzeria (for £10). Roger and I had planned to go somewhere for lunch ourselves while we waited. Oh dear, I had got it all wrong. That was yesterday and poor Jessica had missed a treat. But I was shocked that these pious Anglicans, who had been so inconsolable on Friday afternoon, forgot that poor Jesus was dead as they feasted on pizzas. Ah well. The best thing about this Easter Sunday was that when I arrived at church Gordon kissed me. Wow!

In May the choir returned to the Alnwick Garden to sing under the cherry trees for the Duchess. I had asked if I could go too, but the answer was no. Michael told me he had been informed that only invited guests could go. Fair enough. Presumably the Duchess had spotted me scoffing one of her cupcakes last year. I had planned to go under my own steam, but at the last minute I asked Michael if I could go on the coach and he was happy for me to. He was even happier to be given a donation towards the cost of the coach. I spent the evening in the Alnwick Playhouse, first having a very nice ploughman's and coffee, then sitting half-way through a terrible film and worse trailers. I was due to collect Jess at 8.45 for 9, but in fact they had delighted the Duchess long enough by 8.20 and were thrown out. They were waiting in the coach. Elisabeth very kindly stayed with Jessica till I came. Jessica was pleased because the Duchess had spoken to her. Apparently the choir were given very nice sandwiches before they performed. I don't think the Bishop went this time, nor the Japanese Ambassador.

Next day the Cathedral was celebrating twenty years of women in the priesthood. That is not something I would wish to celebrate anyway, but I always support anything Jessica is involved in. As we went in tables were being prepared with glasses, bottles of the stuff Tracy had said was not allowed in the Cathedral, and lots of trays covered in foil. It was obvious the women priests did not intend to go hungry. For whatever reason the event attracted a good crowd and the nave was pretty full, though with gaps where a few more could have been squeezed in. Most of them were women, but there were quite a few men as well – no doubt proud fathers, brothers, husbands and sons. There was quite a lot of kissing in the Peace. It seemed to me that we had at least three sermons. The Bishop gave a reflection of "The Present and the Future" (is that possible?), two lady canons gave a hotchpotch of people's memories of 1994 and their ordination, and a lady archdeacon preached for over 15 minutes. A Scandinavian lady bishop presided. She wore a splendid cope but happily no mitre. Most of the readers were female to suit the occasion, but we heard at least two male voices. And of course the girls' choir sang very sweetly (that was the best bit). I did not care much for the service, but I took great pleasure in half-watching two children playing quietly and purposefully in the Children's Corner (or Children's Area as it was described in the service sheet – recognition in print!) They were the only children present, and to the best of my knowledge their mum is not a priest. I suppose most women priests rapidly learn to organise their family life so it doesn't interfere with their Calling, and their children would be where they usually are when Mummy is busy. On her way out Jessica managed to grab a handful of crisps and a small samosa from the buffet table. She did well – there isn't usually a gap.

This year the Regional Sports Day was at Ampleforth. I was quite looking forward to chaperoning Jessica to that. However, it didn't happen. There weren't enough participants from Newcastle.

An email came with information about the proposed summer school. It provided for "core time" for people like Jessica who might just want to go for a fun time and not to be minded, but core time cost the same as the whole day! It has now been reduced to £25 a day (so you can choose, mix and match) but a minimum of three days must be booked. Therefore we should need to commit £75 without knowing whether she was going to like it. Anyone who wants their child to go every day (as no doubt some do) has to pay a block fee of £120, and if they book immediately they get a further £10 off. Big deal. We showed Jessica the letter, and she agreed that it wasn't worth it.

Tonight she came out of choir loaded with stuff. She had won a prize of a pot mug with a music motif and a spoon that fitted through a slot in the handle. That was for getting the most reward stickers, and Rachel and Amelia also won mugs. It isn't quite clear what the stickers are awarded for. In a little envelope was a nice card clearly organised by Hannah and signed by all the team (the Michaels, James and Hannah), praising her for doing well and hoping she would continue to do well, etc. This never happened again, so presumably the idea did not appeal to everyone.

Then there was a letter for Jessica and one for us, worded differently, from the Dean and Chapter inviting us all to a tea reception between the Choir concert and Evensong on June 15th. That was quite good for us, because otherwise we would have had to kick around bored and starving between events. I planned to eat lots. Then there was a huge C4 envelope containing an unfolded A4 letter about *Be a Chorister for a Day* and general promotion of the choir, and some small cards for giving out to anyone who was interested. The letter could have been folded into a much smaller envelope. With the mugs and posh envelopes I felt someone was being extravagant. It seemed that the choir was raising money with one hand and squandering it with the other. But that person's heart was in the right place.

On Saturday May 17 RSCM produced a Great North Organ Day. I had booked for it weeks ago, and as accompanied children were free I booked Jessica too, though I didn't really expect her to want to come. I had been intending to just sit and listen, and I hadn't booked any of the workshops for Jessica as she was probably not coming. A few days beforehand she suddenly said she would come, providing we had lunch at Kingdom World Buffet at the Hub. We had been planning to go for weeks but had not managed it yet. Well, that was fine. I eat anywhere! On our way through town I said to Jessica, "If you should see or hear anything today that inspires you to want to learn to play the organ, don't hesitate to say so. It could be arranged, and we should be delighted." To my amazement she responded that she would like to play the organ, but had never thought it worth mentioning because she didn't think it would be in question.

At the Cathedral a rude man on the reception desk demanded our tickets. "And good morning to you, too," I said. He looked just slightly embarrassed, and accordingly processed us and gave us a programme for the day. It seemed that the first port of call was the Refectory where Jean Graves and friends were doing a running coffee'n'biscuits all day, so that was nice. I had three coffees altogether, and enjoyed the first one. The second one I suddenly had to leave to go somewhere else, and the third one got too tepid to enjoy while I was roped in for something else. But I expect I enjoyed all the biscuits. I was urged to put Jessica's name down for various workshops which I did.

When the event began formally Father Kevin made a gracious speech of welcome. I don't think we saw him again after that. Jessica and I sat at the back and knitted quietly. Gordon Stewart, the special guest for the day, gave a very short introductory talk to tell us what he hoped was going to happen, and then Rosemary Field of the RSCM gave a longer talk on "Yes, you can play the organ." She did not always talk in the right direction for her lapel mike so we missed some of the things she said, but it sounded encouraging. Gordon Stewart spoke again at greater length and told us that his church near Manchester had advertised for an organist a certain number of years ago and had 85 applicants for the one job, whereas very recently they had advertised again and got only one applicant, and that person could only play hymns. This sounded very hopeful to me – if Jessica could play the organ there would always be work for her. Gordon said he could live on the weddings and funerals he played for.

Back in the Refectory Jessica took part in a workshop where a weird gadget had been set up with lots of plastic piping, cardboard tubes and a bellows. I suppose it was to illustrate the basic working of an organ. It was certainly interesting, and very hands-on. From there we followed on to St Mary's (Roman Catholic) Cathedral, which has a super new organ. As we went in I wondered where this organ could be as there was no sign of it, then I realised we were standing under it. It has a platform round it that can seat twenty or thirty people. I hoped it was strong. Gordon Stewart showed several rather small boys (one of whom had his teddy with him) how to play the super new organ there. I think Jessica would have liked to have a go, but it was not offered.

Then it was lunchtime and we made our way to Kingdom Buffet. It was a lovely place to have lunch, but sadly closed not long afterwards. In the afternoon we sat in the nave of our Cathedral for a while listening to someone rather boring, then went back to the Refectory because we understood the pipe man was to be there all day. He was, but with no customers. He set up his act for Jessica and roped in some adults (Tracy, me and the tea ladies) to help with an exercise where we all had a pipe to operate and a music sheet to follow. It was quite fun (and this is probably where my third cup of coffee got cold). I suppose it gave children an idea of what went on inside an organ, and why kitchen pipes gurgle.

Back in the south transept we listened to a representative of Harrison & Harrison playing my kind of music on one of their small organs. This one, he said, was about £10,000 (oh good, we'll have a dozen). Lastly we went back to St Mary's where we heard the second half of an autobiographical talk by Gordon Stewart, and finally he led us in a Songs of Praise with five hymns from a sheet. St Mary's is a very beautiful church with lots of colour and clean, bright windows. It was nice to sit and admire their east window, a pleasure denied to us at St Nicholas's where the east window has been largely obscured by a ghastly Victorian reredos which is of no inspirational value at all. And that was the end of an interesting day for both of us. On the way home Jessica told me again that she really would love to play the organ, and it was not because of anything she had seen or heard today. This made me very happy. It would increase my chaperoning duties for years, but it would be well worth it. I love listening to organ music, and listening to Jessica playing it would be one of the best things I could imagine.

Some of the older choristers were coming up for their exams, and their parents seemed to be encouraging/coercing them to spend more time studying. One Sunday evening about now only five girls turned up for Evensong. I don't think any of them had sent apologies, and Michael had to quickly reconstruct the service to include what the five already knew well. He chose two of my favourite pieces, *Locus Iste* and *View Me, Lord* so I was well pleased. Michael naturally gets upset if people don't tell him they can't come, or give him insufficient notice. The following day Jessica stayed off school with a bad cold and sore throat, but she wanted to go to choir. I rang Michael and told him her attendance was in doubt, but as the day wore on she felt well enough to go. Michael said for someone who nearly didn't come she sang very well, and he wished everybody was as reliable.

Towards the end of May Michael forwarded an email from the RSCM about a Cathedral Course for Choristers at Lincoln Cathedral in August. It was probably just a courtesy and he didn't expect any interest, but for Jessica it seemed a very exciting prospect. I replied to Michael "That's more like it!" The course involved staying in Lincoln's choir school with pastoral care in the company of others aged between 10 and 22. It sounded a packed and exciting singing programme with the odd fun activity thrown in. Jessica was very keen. You didn't fill in an application form, you asked for an audition and you got a place (or not) on merit (and for £475). I sent off a request for an audition at 4.15 and had an appointment fixed up at Durham by 4.30. A few days later Mrs Coulson gave Jessica a singing lesson in preparation for her audition and said she would sail through it. She asked what Jessica was planning to take for her two chosen pieces, and Jessica said "Nothing heavy!" She knew she had to take two copies of both, and wisely didn't want to weigh herself down. One of her pieces was Faure's *Pie Jesu*. Michael let her borrow Cathedral music.

On the first Sunday in June Roger and I started a custom that was to continue throughout Jessica's choir life: we decided to have breakfast at the Vermont. Our taxi got us there with well over an hour to spare, and it seemed a good idea. The breakfast staff were very nice and looked after us well.

Jessica began to get nervous about her forthcoming audition. Would I be very disappointed if she didn't pass it, she asked? I said no, it wouldn't bother me in the slightest. She is in a peer group where competition and success matter, but we are happy to take life as it comes. When one door shuts, another opens.

I knew that the summer before Jessica joined the choir they had enjoyed a week-long trip to Winchester Cathedral with whom Newcastle Cathedral were sort of twinned. They had sung with Winchester choir, and had various fun activities. I hoped something similar would happen the following year, but it didn't. Nor the year after. I was pleased she had this RSCM opportunity, and hoped she would enjoy it.

The audition was fixed for 4.30 at St Giles's Church in Durham. This was a most inconvenient time and I had no idea where St Giles had his church, but I did not want to make a fuss about it. Jessica and I would be there. Either I had to ask for time off from school or we had to get a taxi. I felt she was having more than enough favours from the school, so taxi it was. It worked out very well till we got to Durham. The driver had no idea where St Giles's Church was, but I had given him the postcode that I had been given, and he assured me he was in the postcode now. It was called Gilesgate, so that almost proved it. We said we would get out, thanks, and find our way as it could not be far. Oh couldn't it! Across the road was a church called Christchurch and its doors were open. We went in. It had lots of tables set around in what I suppose had once been the sanctuary, and one or two people were sitting at them doing what looked like craft activities. A young man jumped up and said "Welcome!" and was perhaps a wee bit disappointed to find that we had only gone in to ask directions. He looked dismayed when we told him where we wanted to go, and said it was a long way, up a long hill, over a roundabout by a footbridge, then up another long hill. I asked if there might be any taxis anywhere, but he said no, not in the daytime round there. We thanked him and set on our way. We had well over half an hour to spare, but hadn't wanted to spend it climbing hills.

We found we were quite a way along Claypath and we walked about a couple of hundred yards before we came back to Gilesgate. When we finally got to the top of the first hill we found the flyover bridge. I have no head for heights and that bridge was very high and narrow. I hated it. Jessica held my hand and we walked across it as fast as we could. Down the other side we asked a pedestrian where St Giles's church was, and he said it was at the top of a hill we were now at the bottom of. It seemed a long drag, but we finally got there. I was more peeved than puffed, and I think I did well for a septuagenarian.

The church looked locked and deserted. We could see a car parked quite near, and wondered if Andrew Robinson, who was to audition Jessica, was inside waiting for us, so we gave a good bang on the ancient oak door. No answer. A few minutes later I banged again, but still no answer. Jessica went round the building and banged on a smaller door, but still no answer. We sat on a damp stone wall and fumed. At last, about 4.25, a rather posher car drew up, and to our relief it was

Andrew Robinson. He introduced himself and took us into the church. It is a mediaeval church with a glass extension to one side. He gave me a short and unsolicited lecture about the church's history, and I tried to look polite. Yes, there was a toilet, and he led us to it. Meanwhile I could see that there were two or three people in the various rooms of the glass extension, and I was peeved that none of them had come to let us in. May their socks rot. Andrew said Jessica should go to the music room at the top of some stairs. I sat in the beautiful church and waited. It was quite warm. I could see Jessica and the back of Andrew's head. She could see me too, so I moved to a spot where she couldn't, more or less underneath her. As I listened to her singing *Pie Jesu* I felt I had not heard anything so beautiful since Aled Jones was a boy.

I gather she did not excel in all the tests he gave her, but he said he was impressed by her singing and overall she had done OK and "there was no reason why she shouldn't go on the course." Jessica wondered what that meant, but of course choosing who goes is not his province – he just reports. Now we waited on events. But if there were no events by tomorrow lunchtime I meant to email Sarah King at RSCM to remind her that we wanted to apply. Applications closed on Monday.

Andrew offered to take us to the station in his car, but I thought we would still like to have our planned feed in Durham and mooch a bit. He drove us to the centre, which was kind and most welcome. This time we went under the flyover. As we drove he asked how much the taxi fare from Morpeth had been. I thought that was an unacceptable question and paused, and I could feel Jessica's vibes too. "Pass," I said, and he did. I defused the moment by saying that we took a lot of taxis now because when you give up your car you find you have an astonishing amount of cash left.

In Durham we waited around for a while, looking at shops Jessica fancied, but the only one we went into was Waterstone's. Then to Bell's Fish Restaurant where we sat at a window table. The fish and chips were very good though neither of us could eat all we were given. After that we mooched a bit more, but the shops that Jessica liked were all shut by now. We went to the taxi rank near the Gala Theatre at about 6.40, then we saw the new City Library and popped in for twenty minutes or so to case it out. Jessica found a new Caroline Lawrence Western Mystery, the third, and I determined to buy it. I loved the first two. The hero has Asperger's Syndrome, though of course the word is not used (or known then). It was time to go home so we taxied to the station. Durham Station is much more pleasant than it used to be but you have to go through ticket barriers and when you're on the northbound platform you realise the treats you might have had the other side the barrier – in this case a vending machine and a Costa bar, though we didn't need either. So that was Jessica's audition. In time we learned it had been a success and she could go to Lincoln.

Another Be a Chorister for a Day was held in early June. We had to catch the 8.03 bus, which is tough on a Saturday. After I had dropped Jessica I had a second breakfast in T. J. Hughes and then went to the Lit & Phil for a while, where Roger met up with me later. Today there were three small new children, and they hadn't liked it. One cried and wanted her mummy. Michael, James and Hannah (and I've no doubt Jessica) between them did their best, but to no avail. James told the children to wait ten minutes to see if they liked it better and then if they didn't he would ring their mums, and he did. One little girl was taken home, but the mother of another child came and told her to stay. It seemed a joyless business for a small child.

Next day was a boys' choir day, but girls were invited along to support them and Jessica did. A party came from our twin Winchester Cathedral, and this was celebrated with a "bring and share" lunch. A lady gave a presentation about seating. She invited us to donate £150 for a chair, or £160 with a plaque. They were folding chairs, rush-bottomed, made of oak and quite comfy at a quick test. Oak, of course, lasts a lot longer than rush-bottoming, but nobody (including me) said so. We needed them, apparently, not for services but for occasions like speech days and concerts when lots of extra seating had to be provided. It was already planned that, when we finally got funding for it, we should be clearing the nave of pews to make the space "more suitable for twenty-first century worship", whatever that meant.

The "bring and share" lunch was held in the Refectory. When we went in it was all nicely laid out with puddings on a separate table. A huge blowfly was flitting from cream cake to cream cake, and we hadn't even said Grace! Left to himself the fly would probably have con-centrated on one cream cake, but the lady organisers were flapping furiously at him and he hopped from one to another polluting them all. I made a mental note not to have pudding. The food was excellent, but we only got a small half-glass of fruit juice each, so it didn't do to be thirsty. At night the Quire was full of Winchester visitors which was so nice.

Father Kevin told us the Dean and Chapter were thinking of moving the time of Sunday Evensong forward to perhaps 4 o'clock. There were no plans yet, goodness no, but he was just putting a toe in the water. I felt it would cut both ways for us. If it was earlier Jessica could get to bed at the proper time, but if it was only a little bit earlier, like 5 or 5.30, we would not have time to go home and would have to kill time expensively in Newcastle. In principle I think it would be for everybody's good if it was 4pm because a lot of the younger children, boys especially being younger, are tired by the end of

Sunday. They also need to get home and have their tea and get to bed without rushing, to be fresh for the universally dreaded Monday morning. But the mills of God grind slowly, especially at the Cathedral, and we did not expect to hear much more about it for ages.

There was usually a short period of rehearsal after weekday Evensong, but on Monday June 9th the parents were told that children would be leaving immediately after the service. Why? Well, it was Blaydon Races, and the roads and carparks would be clogged. Parents were warned to make what arrangements they could. Funny, the pavements were quite clear and we got to Haymarket with no trouble or congestion whatever.

Jessica got a response from the RSCM to say she could go to Lincoln, and she could have a bursary. Roger and I decided that as we had missed our Golden Wedding we would donate one of the rush-bottomed chairs with a plaque. It would last longer than a celebration dinner would have done.

On Sunday 15th in the service I saw a boy walking towards me and realised it was Hugh Beney. He whispered, "I've been sent to sit with you. I had to go out of choir because I feel faint." I asked him if he would like some water, but he said he had just been given some (by Michael as I later learnt). I gave him a quick hug of solidarity, and found him the unopened bottle of water I had in my bag in case he wanted more. I thought to ask him if he had had any breakfast, and he said yes, he had. As an afterthought he added, "Only two crumpets!" Well, we should be over the moon if Jessica ate that much in a morning. One crumpet would be a triumph! I scrabbled quietly in my bag and found him a respectable-looking cereal bar which he ate. After the service he asked me a question about the acolytes which I couldn't answer. I told him I was a Methodist and not *au fait* with all the frills of Anglicanism. He asked me what the difference was between Anglicans and Methodists. I was a bit stumped to answer. I said we both believed exactly the same but Methodists were much less liturgical. Did Methodists have stained glass windows, high up, he asked. I said no, not very high up, because Methodists couldn't afford to build such high churches, though that is not always true. Later I asked Roger, and he gave me a long lecture about bishops and John Wesley. Well, it may be about apostolic succession or the lack of it, but to me it is basically about poor people taking part in worship. If the Church of England is, as has been said, the Conservative Party at prayer, the Methodist Church is, or was, the workers at prayer. Nowadays Methodists are a well-heeled lot, but they stem from days when few could afford to build chapels and worship was conducted at house meetings. So Hugh's question got me thinking.

The same afternoon was the long-awaited tea reception with the Dean and Chapter. First we had a short concert in the nave where various choristers did their party pieces. They varied in length and excellence. One girl seemed to take a very long time tuning her instrument, and Michael looked as if he shared this opinion. However she was not tuning, she was playing, as we realised when she stood up, bowed and walked off to less than hearty clapping. Some children did very well, but I think it was stressful for most of them. After that we all went to the Refectory for the reception by the Dean and Chapter so that they could get to know us better and express their gratitude for our commitment etc, but although the Dean and Father Kevin were there we never got recepted, which was fortunate for me because I am allergic to formalities of that kind. Like at a wedding line-up, you know you have to kiss the bride whether you know her very well or not. Does one kiss the Dean? I suppose not. The tea consisted of plenty of tea or coffee, plenty of good thick sandwiches in white or brown, and plenty of small cream scones, It was more filling than elegant, which was just as well, though I remembered someone saying, when the Wilson Labour Government got in, that from now on it would be beer and sandwiches at Number 10 instead of wine and canapés. Looking back, that tea was definitely for the Unions. But it was very good, provided you weren't gluten-intolerant. I had about nine nice sandwiches but no scones. Jess, who was probably doing a lot of talking, told me she only had scones. I hoped she had plenty.

June 29th was Ordination Sunday, when the regular congregation sit in the naughty corner, or maybe stay at home. Roger and I went to the Vermont for breakfast. Should we hurry back, I asked him, as the church would be filling up with visitors? No, he said. If they hadn't got room for us we would go and spend our collection money elsewhere. I agreed. Back in the Cathedral we were "welcomed" by being asked if we had tickets. This annoyed me. They should have said "Have you got reserved seats?" It made it seem like a concert, and people who had not got tickets would feel surplus to requirement. Roger said "No, we are congregation," and we were directed to the humble grey plastic stacking-chairs at the back of the north aisle. Thinking I might need a loo visit in a long service I sat at the aisle end of the short row but this didn't please the bouncers for some reason. One of them asked me if I would mind moving along, and I said yes, I would mind, because I might need to go out. She accepted this (maybe she had a similar problem herself) and we were not harassed further.

Today the Bishop ordained six deacons and seven priests – ten woman and three men (a sign of the times indeed). The service was a full two hours long and quite boring, but at least there was no incense. I trust all the ordinands and their families will remember the choir who sang so beautifully on their special day.

Afterwards we were again welcomed to 50 Moorside South by the Stoddart family for the Choir lunch. Celia had just acquired three Indian Runner ducks called

Sebastian, Gwendolen and Olivia. They were very charming. Gwendolen and Olivia, we were told, provided the family generously with eggs. I was very pleased to see that Michael and Elisabeth had a new kitchen extension. Why was I pleased? Well it meant they were probably staying for the foreseeable future! Elisabeth showed me a tiny teddy bear she was knitting on very fine needles, for a special baby who was due. By the following week Michael and Elisabeth were proud grandparents to Sophie Elisabeth Harper.

One night, as I waited for Jessica to come out of choir rehearsal, I heard an unusual spat going on between Celia and Harriet. Celia was saying, "It's not your problem. It's his business." I wondered what it was about, and as we walked home Jessica told me that Ermintrude had been driving other choristers mad because she sang out of tune all the time. Jessica said it had made her feel dizzy with the effort of trying to follow her own part and trying to ignore the off-key notes assaulting her from the side. Tonight Harriet and Jessica had stood one each side of poor Ermintrude, and were nearly driven crazy. No one dared to approach Michael on the subject, so Harriet asked Celia to tell him. Well of course that was not the right thing to do at all. Celia rightly resented being expected to act as a go-between, and refused. Jessica said it if didn't stop she would have to leave the choir, as she couldn't put up with it any longer. I felt it was a serious problem, and I wrote to Michael about it myself. He replied that he would deal with the matter before September, and he did. Sadly Ermintrude was not the only chorister who seemed not to be musical. Some of them just stood there, quietly fidgeting or miming, and most of them left eventually. By September Ermintrude too had left. She was a very nice girl, but just not choir material.

One Friday evening in early July Michael took the choir to Norham to sing Evensong. I had replied to two different emails from Hannah, who had since left, to say that we would all three like to go on the coach, but there had been no response from her. She was never famous for replying to emails. I assumed the message would have been passed on. We were not 100% sure we'd be welcome, but we turned up. Being quite early I went up to the Thomlinson Room with Jessica where all those who were travelling normally congregate. When Michael came in he looked surprised to see me. I said "May we come too, please?" He looked embarrassed and said "Well … er …" I said obviously we couldn't, so we would disappear. He perceived our various problems (wanting to go because we are loyal choir supporters, and we should either have to go home and come back again or else hang around in Newcastle for six hours) and he said if we waited till the bus came he would see. I asked if it was a problem of the coach being full, but he said no, it was other considerations, from which I assumed he meant safeguarding. It might have been most tactful for us simply to disappear, but we had so much been looking forward to it. Eventually the children got on to the coach. We passed Jessica a couple of juice cartons in case we could not go and she hadn't got enough refreshment. When everyone was loaded and Michael came he said, with some anxiety in his voice, that we could go and we must sit at the front. He ejected a little boy called David who had bagged the front seat behind the driver, and we sat one side at the front and Michael and Elisabeth sat the other. It was comforting to know that the choir, sitting behind us, did not know we were under house arrest.

It was some time before we discovered the reason, and I forget who told us. Michael had been to a big organ conference where organist were strongly advised, nay ordered, not to take parents and other adult hangers-on with them on choir trips because of the difficulty of controlling children in such circumstances. Michael knew we would behave ourselves and recognise his authority over Jessica, but it was a general rule which he had to observe. We, of course, did not know this, though we sympathised.

It was a lovely drive. There were not as many trees as there used to be, due to the depredations of Dutch elm disease and ash die-back, but modern trees in the form of wind turbines proliferated around Wandylaw. They are not an asset to the landscape, but they are nicer than the pylons we have got used to, and infinitely better than sending boys down the mines to dig coal. At Norham, which is very close to Berwick and a 90-minute drive, we found a large church that reflected the activity of a more Christian age up here in Northumberland. It was attractive inside, and had a modern kitchen and (one) toilet. The choir were able to get robed in a modern room over the kitchen at the back of the church. As we went in we were warmly welcomed by the vicar. It was a lovely service, and Father Kevin had come to read the lessons. The choir sang very well and were obviously appreciated. Afterwards a very nice buffet supper was laid out, and the organisers told us all firmly that the choir were to get first pick! They did full justice to the spread, but there was enough left over for the congregation. Andrew Robinson was there in an RSCM capacity, and he thanked the choir and saw them off on the coach. We had a very pleasant drive home. I tried to give Michael £20 towards the cost of the coach, but he wouldn't have it.

Now the summer holidays were fast approaching, and Jessica wanted to go to the Cathedral summer school week. Michael said she still could, although the list was closed some time ago. We planned to go from about 10 to about 4. This would cost us £110 for the week, so it was getting a bit cheaper as time went by.

It began on Monday July 27th. Jessica and I left home to catch the first bus I could travel on with my pass. On our way through Marks and Spencer we collected items for her packed lunch. We were at the Cathedral well by 10 o'clock. Gail Davis, a lay clerk who Jessica was very fond of, was presiding over the coats and lunch boxes in the Thomlinson Room, but the main activity was currently in the Song Room. I left and looked for things to pass the day. First I went to the Lit & Phil where I read and drank cocoa, then to the Lantern café for lunch and more reading. Back to the L & P, then back to the Lantern for a last cup of coffee before they closed at 3.30. I sat in the nave after that, but got nobbled by the duty chaplain who greeted me and asked me what brought me to the Cathedral. She catechised me a bit but when she could see I didn't need her ministrations she went off to pester someone else. At 3.55 I went off to look for Jessica, and a horde of kids came running in. They had been walking over the bridges to the Sage, and had apparently had a wonderful time. Jessica was very pleased with her day.

On the Tuesday I had to dash back to Morpeth to wash up after our church Toddler Group. Back at the Lantern café for a cup of coffee I found they had the cheesecake they used to have 20 years ago when I was a refectory volunteer. It had a biscuit base, cheesecake mixture and a dribble of jam. It was undoubtedly a packet mix, and perhaps nicer than it should be, but I loved it and had a slice with my coffee. Michael said that on Thursday there was to be a picnic in the park and we should send the children with hats and sun cream. I said I might take Jessica out somewhere else. I generally deal with hot sun by keeping out of it, and although I have no objection to hats I don't care for sun cream which I know often has some very nasty ingredients. Today's treat had been a trip round the Castle which had been a great success. They had also done quite a bit of musical theory. One little girl, who was only 6, found theory hard going, and Jessica wanted to help her, but she was not allowed to. The week still seems to be a success.

On Wednesday the Dean spoke to me when he passed me in the Cathedral! He is not famous for socialising with the lower ranks, so I was quite chuffed. I had relented about Jessica going to the park on Thursday, but begged her to stay in as much shade as offered. I looked in the Charnel Chapel, or Crypt Chapel as it is more politely called, and it has now been cleared out and furnished with six prie-dieux. One prie-dieu had a box of flowers dumped on it, but they were at least fragrant. The trouble with the Crypt Chapel is that it will always be used as a convenient dump. Gordon told me that someone in the past had whitewashed the walls, which might seem a very sensible thing to do, but it had sealed in the moisture and stopped the stone breathing, so it is a damp little hole. He said the whitewash was due to be removed but it would be a big job and would be done after he retired! Today's treat was a trip up the tower. Jessica enjoyed it, but with slight reservations because her legs still ached a bit from the Castle visit yesterday.

On Thursday a friend offered to do my Toddler Group chores for me so I stayed in Newcastle all day again. It's a bit expensive as I have so many snacks! Ellie explained the reason for the picnic: there was a wedding in the Cathedral at 2, and it was felt the children might make an unseemly noise! When I came back at 3.40 all trace of the wedding had vanished. Tracy said they'd hurried on to the hotel. The children had had another very good day. They'd had a nice time on the park and played rounders, Celia had helped younger children apply their sun cream. There were plenty of shade trees in Leazes Park. Now poor Jessica had a painful hip from rounders to add to her aches and pains.

For the last day the children had planned a concert for such of their parents who would be available to come. Seats were arranged round the grand piano in the south transept, and Roger joined me just in time. It was presented by Michael with the help of Gail and John

Lewis. Jessica said they were the only staff all week. At the end a CCA mother made a quite uncalled for speech of thanks and presented bottles of wine to Michael and John and flowers to Gail and Elisabeth (who wasn't there but had had a lot of input). I couldn't help doing a rough calculation of the cost of these unnecessary tokens and wishing it had been subtracted from the total cost of the week. We clapped heartily because it had at least been a very good concert. So that was another choir year finished.

Jessica missed choir and singing, and had about three weeks to wait before she went to Lincoln. Eventually the big day came. The course began on a Monday morning about 12, but we couldn't hope to get there so early so we booked into a hotel for the night before and travelled up at leisure on the Sunday. This gave us a chance to visit a cousin who lives in Lincoln and who Jessica had not yet met. We stayed at the White Hart because we guessed it would have character. Well, the view from our bedroom window certainly did. There was the west end of the Cathedral, beautifully floodlit, only a few yards away. Jessica nearly cried and said she couldn't believe she was going to sing there!

On the Monday morning, after a good early hotel breakfast, we set off to explore. First we looked in the Cathedral to case it out, then we explored the Mediaeval Quarter to see if there were any shops Jessica liked. There were very few at all, but we noticed a fudge shop she hoped she would find time to visit another day. Back at the Cathedral we found we had to pay to go in – £6 for me and £1 for Jessica – which I found rather annoying, but the lady who served us was so charming and welcoming that my resentment vanished. We visited the café which opened at 10 and had hot chocolate, plain for me but with the works for Jessica and called Cathedral Cloud. And of course we visited the shop! We went back to the hotel to collect our luggage where the staff told us that Eastgate House, where we had to meet, was only about a two minute walk. They were two of the longest minutes I ever remember. We seemed to walk for miles, asking and getting misdirected, guessing and guessing wrong. Most of the people we asked were tourists, but we were hopeful of some local workmen. No, they knew the area well, but they had never heard of Eastgate House either. One of them looked at our RSCM map and showed me how to follow it on the ground – go down here to the end, turn right into Wragby Road, cross it and turn down another road. He was obviously confident with maps. The problem was that on the map, the house was shown as being in the middle of a sort of wood, with no indication of where you entered the wood. As we walked we kept seeing notice boards that told us that the building behind them was part of the Minster School, or the Cathedral This, or the Cathedral That. Each time Jessica felt sure it was what we wanted, but it wasn't Eastgate House so we didn't want it. Eventually we came to a large modern building that looked as if something was happening inside it, but it did not look residential. We went in and asked, and another mum and daughter were doing the same thing though they were not walking. A kind lady told us where to go (another long two-minute walk) and we all set off to follow her directions. As we left the building a man dressed as a janitor said "It's Number 18." That was the most useful bit of information we'd had all day! If we had known an address (number and road instead a house name) we might have found it soon after we gave up the first time. In fact when we got to where we were being directed it was only the Number 18 on the gatepost that told us we had found it. There was no other indication or name board.

We walked down a long drive and came to a seedy three or four storey house. It was deserted, and there was no answer when we rang the bell. Other parents and daughters began to arrive, all looking as mystified as we felt. It was 12.30 when we got there, and we were not due to register till 1, but it was unnerving to find no one in at all. One of the mums rang RSCM at Salisbury, who rang the person who should have been there and rang back to say she was on her way but had forgotten the key and gone back for it (back where, we wondered). Eventually, just before 1 o'clock, three people arrived but not together. One started dishing out name badges. She asked Jessica her name. "And what's your name?" I asked. She was Elisabeth Shaw. Ah, that rang a bell. We knew she was to be the matron. Another lady who seemed to be in charge but did not identify herself said she was Rosemary Field when I asked her. I remembered her from the RSCM Organ Day at Newcastle. We were let into the entrance hall of the building and invited to leave cases tucked by the wall. The girls might go to the loo through that door over there, then they should assemble their robes, music cases and black shoes and be ready to walk to the Cathedral. I'm still quite good at walking and I didn't mind all this but I was glad we didn't have to trundle the big suitcase any further. Some boys arrived too, but they were told to wait in the dining room till the girls had been processed. Then off we trotted to the Cathedral. It was only a two-minute walk. Or ten. Most of the parents, having cars there, and their daughters having been to these camps before, disappeared at this point, but I walked with Jessica till we got to the Cathedral. She seemed to be the youngest by several years. In the Cathedral I said a quick goodbye and left her, hoping that the pastoral care would warm up a bit after I had gone. I was sure she would be alright, but I would have been happier if there was more evidence of motherly care. I would have liked to explore the Cathedral, but it seemed best to get away quickly.

Chaperones do have a life of their own when they are not with their protégées, just as the broom has a life in the broom cupboard, and now I had to get back to the station. I walked down the famous Steep Hill a long way, fearing that I might trip and roll to the bottom, wherever that was. The last third off it had a welcome handrail. I saw a young mother running down with her tot in a buggy, the tot chortling with delight, and I wondered how she would stop. Eventually Steep Hill became High Street, and the cute boutiques gave way to ordinary town shops. I had a quick fish'n'chips lunch in BHS restaurant then I headed for home.

Jessica had a phone now, and she rang us a few times, but it was obvious she was being well looked after and having a good time. She was sharing a room with a girl called Cerys, who was 14 and nearest to Jessica in age. The girls were not sleeping in the elusive Eastgate House but another building. Jessica and Cerys had an en suite room, but the trouble was that all the other girls kept coming through to use their en suite facilities! Yes, the food was good. I was so glad.

On the Friday she rang up in excitement. She was going to sing a solo in the 12.30 Eucharist on Saturday! Could I be there to hear her? Oh dear, I was sure I couldn't. I had been planning to travel down on the Saturday, spend the night in Lincoln again and join the Sunday services, but 12.30 – no it wasn't possible. She sounded very disappointed, so I said I would see what could be done. I certainly didn't want to miss hearing her sing in Lincoln Cathedral if I could help it! Roger and I spent the afternoon looking up train times, and we were able to tell her we thought it was just possible.

On Saturday morning a taxi came at 7.10 to take me to Morpeth Station, where my train was in good time. I had to change at Newcastle where the London train was waiting for me. My next change was at Retford, where I got the Lincoln train. I arrived at Lincoln station at 11.30, and looked for a taxi to take me up to the Cathedral but there were none except those that had been booked. Everyone around me seemed to be lighting up after their smoke-free incarceration, and I was soon in a cloud of smoke. I decided to walk up. I had time, and I hoped I had the energy. As I climbed the foothills of the town I found a nice art shop with a café. Hooray – if it had a café it would have a loo! I was very lucky to find the loo before I found the café, so I didn't bother with the café which I hadn't got time for anyway.

Soon I was at the bottom of Steep Hill. It had a handrail in the lower section, and I missed its security higher up, especially when I had to cross the road. I confess to being slightly terrified in the upper reaches. There were quite a few other people around which gave me some courage – nobody else was tripping and rolling downhill, so why should I? It was a great relief to get onto more or less level ground at the top.

I had to pay £6 to go into the Cathedral. My general policy since has been that if I am charged entry to a Cathedral I shall not give them anything else, but if they leave it to my discretion they might get quite a bit more. I kept a tight hold of my ticket which I should need all day. It was now 12 o'clock and I wanted Jessica to know I was there, so I asked where the Song School was. The ticket-pusher wasn't sure. She asked a passing Treasury official and he didn't think they'd got one. They told me to ask a verger, but the vergers were busy setting up for communion. Then I saw a chorister. Did she know Jessica? She didn't because she was a lay clerk, but here came an RSCM chorister who would surely know. She did, and she pointed to where the choir were assembling. I asked a third chorister to tell Jessica I was there and if she wanted a quick hug she should come for one. She came running and gave me a very long hug. She didn't cry, but she was very pleased to see me and I was so glad to have got there in time to hear her solo because I knew it meant a lot to her.

Now I sat in the Quire and listened to the rehearsal. Jessica had quite a long piece by herself in the Kyrie. At the end Andrew Reid, the Director, said "Well done. Well done. Well done." It wasn't effusive, but its repetition enforced its sincerity. As at Newcastle they rehearsed on until five minutes before that service. I sat on in the Quire. I had trouble finding the least uncomfortable seat, but I wanted to be well within sight of Jessica. All their normal services are held in the Quire which has enough seating for about 200-300 apart from the actual choir stalls. Jessica sang well. I gather that she had "lost her voice" earlier in the morning and had been told not to sing at all till it was time for her solo, which sounds odd. How would Andrew know she wasn't going to crack up and disgrace him? But she bore up well and was a credit to Michael and the folks back home.

I went to the Refectory and had a very good lunch, but was a bit embarrassed because Elisabeth Shaw and some of her RSCM cronies were on a nearby table. Why wasn't she eating with the children? I booked into the White Hart where I was spending two nights, and disposed of my meagre luggage. I would have liked to make myself a cup of coffee, but the little tubs of UHT milk put me off. I went back to the Cathedral where I expected evensong to take place, but Jessica chanced to find me and said the boys were singing Evensong and the girls had two hours or more free time. She wanted to stay with me, so we asked Elisabeth if she could. Elisabeth said yes, so long as I presented Jessica back at the boarding house at 7 for supper. I had just been intending to go to the Refectory for a cup of hot chocolate and a sit, so we both went, but Jessica was not hungry which was good in the circumstances. They obviously weren't starving her. We went back to the hotel and she liked our room better than I did. She played on her iPad from which she had been cruelly separated for so long. We talked to Roger on the phone. She gave me a packet of fudge that she had bought for me from the Fudge Shop on Steep Hill. There was a packet for Roger too. Secretly I thought it was more like icing than fudge, but I pretended to like it. I probably needed the energy anyway after walking up the hill earlier. I walked her back to her digs about 6.30. It seems quite a long way from the Cathedral, and they have to walk it several times a day in all weathers. She should be fit!

After a short Sunday of services Andrew bade farewell to the choristers who were free to leave after Evensong. We were staying in Lincoln till morning. We spent some time in the Cathedral shop, and when Jessica wasn't looking I bought her a sponsorship of a Cathedral stone for her birthday and one or two other bits I knew she fancied. We had a trip on a City Tour bus which was very interesting. Lastly we had dinner in a nearby restaurant before going back to our beds in the White Hart. Again we had a super view of the illuminated Cathedral to say goodbye to. Next morning home.

A few days later the postman brought us a letter from the RSCM offering Jessica a place on their course next year – at Durham. There's always lots to look forward to!

2014-2015

For a long time I had been worried about the use of incense in the Cathedral. On more Sundays than not, it seemed to me, incense was carried and swung about as if it was going out of fashion (which I hope it is) – down from the Vestry to the Font, then back up the centre aisle, and then swung around liberally at different points in the service. The Holy Gospel (but fortunately not the other scriptures) had to be drenched in smoke before it could be read. At communion time they seemed to go mad with it at the crossing, and the fumes naturally drifted straight into the Quire and into the choristers' lungs. I have no liturgical objection to incense, and it certainly smells nice, but I felt quite sure the smoke was carcinogenous. I plucked up my courage and mentioned it to the Dean. His response was derisory. As a risk, he said, it was insignificant. The Cathedral was a huge, well-ventilated building, and the smoke disappeared into the roof. That was true, but it must have gone through quite a lot of little chests before it drifted upwards. I felt helpless about this. I couldn't alter the traditions of thousands of years of Jewish and Christian worship, but I didn't want my child to get lung cancer. The simple solution was to take her out of the choir, but naturally I wasn't going to do that because it would have broken her heart. She lives in a world where all manner of toxins have to be tolerated, and on the way down to the Cathedral from Haymarket we passed many smokers and inhaled a lot of stale smoke, but surely a Cathedral should be a safe place as far as possible.

One of the first engagements of the choir this term was to sing at the wedding of two priests who we don't know. Towards the end of the service Roger and I went in at the back to listen to the music. There were about 800 guests and they took communion, so it went on for a long time. Tables in the aisles were groaning with food and drink for afterwards, but it seemed no provision was made for the choristers. However there was extra pocket money for such events, so they were worth it.

One Thursday night early in the term the choristers were delighted to have a visit from Rachel Dodd, their former Head Chorister. Rachel had been badly hurt in a fatal car accident some months before, and it looked as if she would not be able to go to university this year, but her fortitude and determination had speeded her recovery and it was now hoped she might be able to go after all. Jessica was so happy to see her.

We had asked Michael if he would give Jessica organ lessons when she was ready, and he was very kind and said he would be happy to. He said she must get Piano Grade 4 first, so that gave her an extra incentive to practise her piano. He thinks bursaries are available from the RSCM. Well, a bursary would not come amiss!

On Saturday, September 19th, the CCA held a sports day on Nuns' Moor, starting at Stoddarts' house. Chaperon-age was needed, but Roger and I did not want to take part. We went equipped with something to sit on, and sat demurely pretending to be interested. They had the traditional races – wheelbarrow, egg-n-spoon, sack, piggy-back etc. I was very nearly hit in the face by a flying welly hoyed by a CCA committee member's child. I suppose it demonstrated his skill that he missed me. We all took food, but the promised BBQ didn't happen.

A particularly tedious chaperoning session came in early October on a Thursday. The choristers had to go to Hexham Abbey at 5pm to rehearse for a Hadrian Festival event on the Saturday. Jessica left school a bit early and we got there as quickly as we could, but it was a bit after 5 when we arrived. We were graciously received however. Now I had to get lost. I could have stayed in the Abbey, but I didn't think Jessica would like me to. Of course I fancied a nice café, but it was not the right time of day. I did some shopping in Hexham's excellent Waitrose, then I went to Tesco who were open for several more hours but whose café appeared to be closed. Finally I found a free table in the waiting area of the Wentworth Leisure Centre where I was able to get some hot chocolate and surreptitiously eat a sandwich I had bought in Waitrose. I did not ask permission to eat my sandwich, I just ate it. Then back to the relative comfort of a pew in the Abbey. I heard the tail end of the rehearsal, then we made our way home. Day events usually manage to incorporate rehearsals, so I wasn't impressed with this one.

Back to Hexham bright and early on the Saturday. The choirs involved were Newcastle, Hexham and Carlisle, and Durham had been invited as guests. The concert was in the evening, so I am still puzzled as to why they couldn't have done their rehearsing in the day. I dropped Jessica off, then went to seek my fortune. Hexham is much more interesting in the daytime. First I visited the new Abbey Refectory and had coffee there. It is quite nice with a folded woollen blanket draped over the back of each chair. It wasn't clear what the blanket was for. Was it to soften the back of the seat? Was it to tuck over your knees on a chilly day? Was it to wrap yourself up in on a very cold day? Was it for children to wipe their sticky fingers on? It looked nice anyway, and softened the general ambience. The coffee was rather strong. A particular treat was the new loos. Our visits to Hexham Abbey over thirty years have always been frustrating because of the lack of such civilised amenities. We felt sure there must be one somewhere, but we were always told there wasn't. Once I managed to find a tiny Gents in an obscure corner of the Mason's Workshop, and availed myself of it, but not being a gent I was reluctant to do so very often. Officially we were directed to the Queen's Hall across the road. It was usually open, but not always. One night at a concert the snooty party on the ticket desk, when I asked the usual question, knowing the answer, told me to go to the Queen's Hall. I said it was shut. "Is it? It shouldn't be. Well, there are plenty of pubs. Next please!" she said. Now there is a lovely suite of loos. The only trouble is their lights are on a time-switch, producing results I won't go into. Suffice it to say the Abbey is moving slowly into the 21st century, and not before time.

Then I spent about 45 minutes in the town library, in the aforementioned Queen's Hall. I was surrounded by lovely books, but I had brought my Kindle and was already immersed in one of my own. I can't remember what it was, but it was gripping. When I thought it was lunch-time I made for the Golden Dragon, an excellent Chinese restaurant whose only fault is that they don't warm the plates. I think they keep them in a fridge. But the food is very good. Along the road from the Golden Dragon is a selection of charity shops, always good for browsing. One way and another I had a happy time. At 3.30 I went back to the Abbey Refectory for a final cup of coffee before they closed at 4, then I sat and read in the nave. One of the advantages of a Kindle is that if you come to the end of a book you can click up another. Hard pews not-withstanding, the Abbey is a very pleasant place to sit.

Roger came and joined me and we sat near the front. The concert, when it began, was very good indeed. Each choir sang a selection of their own with some joint efforts in between. I had cheekily written a note in Jessica's homework book telling her form teacher, Mr Morton, about the concert if he was looking for something nice to do on Saturday evening, and to Jessica's joy he came. Alison Russo was also one of his old pupils, and she was equally delighted. He brought his sister with him, and she said she had been enraptured!

I was particularly impressed with the good conduct and hearty singing of the little boys from Durham. Later I sent Mr Lancelot an email to say so. He was pleased, and early next morning replied to say he would read it to the boys at breakfast. Jessica told me, however, that the little boys had in fact been very naughty and difficult all day, and Mr Lancelot had had to shout at them a great deal. Well, one can only suppose they had run out of steam by the concert!

Helen Robertson, who was in charge of Sunday School and especially Godly Play, asked Father Steven to put out an appeal for old pillowslips for storing the little Godly Play figures in. I took a few, and went to find Helen in the Education Suite on the north side of the church over the Refectory. I had been there once before for a meeting, but I had not had the opportunity to look around. Now I found it had a kitchenette! When I admired it Helen told me I was very welcome to go up there and make myself a hot drink any time, although there would be no milk. This sounded very convenient and would save me having to carry flasks of cocoa, but I felt I would be embarrassed if Father Steven, who was Canon for Education, caught me there. I explained this to Helen, and she said Father Steven knew, and she would explain the matter to Gordon so that he knew too. I was really delighted about this. It made a tremendous difference. Sadly I still had to wait on the cold back stairs afterwards. Gordon liked to lock the Cathedral immediately after Evensong, and I wouldn't want to be locked in the Education Suite all night by accident!

Christmas was on the way again. An early engagement was for the choir to sing at a big craft exhibition at the Racecourse, with the purpose of raising money. I handed Jessica over to Michael, with her packed lunch, and got lost. I soon regretted this, because the seating accommodation in the bar where they were to sing filled up very quickly. I wandered in and out a few times, but there was never a chair. Was there no gentleman present who would stand up and offer a little old lady his seat? No, there was not. I explored the possibilities, and found a box! Not a matchbox or a cereal box, but an enclosed private viewing room, with all mod cons and comforts. There being no racing I didn't think anyone would be coming, so I set up camp on a comfy chair behind the door. I read quietly for an hour or more. I went down again to see if I could find a spot in the bar and listen to the choir, but it was more congested than ever. I stood and listened for a while. I went to try the restaurant, but it was packed. After a very long time I saw some people in the bar getting ready to leave, so I scooted across to be first in the queue for their seats. I was lucky. The table they vacated was right by the bar and I was able to get a nice cup of hot chocolate. The choir had a break and went off for their packed lunches somewhere. I decided to go back to my private box, but the real box-holders had turned up. Curses. I heard later that Jessica had sung a solo, so I was very sorry to have missed that. Apparently Michael said she did well and he must give her more solos. By the time we left it was raining. I had hoped to get a taxi, but as usual I had not got a phone. I saw a lot driving past, but they never seemed to come back. I suppose I was the victim of a one-way system for taxis. In the end we decided to walk down the long drive. Just then John Lewis came along and offered us a lift. He didn't have wings or a halo but to us right then he was an angel. We said we would be so glad to be taken to the nearest bus stop. He was very kind and I think he would have taken us back to Morpeth if we had let him, but we only wanted a bus into town. It was good to be out of the rain for a minute or two. I secretly hoped my chaperoning duties would not include the racecourse again, and I don't think they ever did. I think the clientele preferred backing horses to choristers.

On the last Sunday of the month there was another faith lunch. It coincided with an installation of six choristers. On these occasions new choristers usually seemed to have at least a vague idea of what was going to happen, but not today. The Dean asked them, as a group, if they wanted to serve God to the best of their ability, etc. He waited for their response. None came. After a short silence he said he would ask them again, and he did. This time there was a low, half-hearted joint growl with which the Dean had to be content. I rather sympathised with the children. Some of them wanted to be in the choir, but some had been pushed into it by their parents. I felt it was wrong to ask them to make vows. They were required to turn up and sing, and if they did that the Dean and the congregation had to be thankful. Later one of the boys stayed to the lunch with his family. He refused to eat and sulked in a corner. He wanted to go home. He had been out all morning to please his mum, he said, and now he wanted to go home. I chatted him up a bit and asked him if he liked being in the choir. No, he didn't! Eventually, probably from sheer embarrassment, his mother rounded up her brood and left. We never saw him again. I sympathised very much. Choir is hard work, and takes up a lot of time when other kids are relaxing. It isn't right to force a child into it.

In the evening we had the Advent carol service, and I read one of the lessons which was quite exciting. During the service, or perhaps at the end of it, the CCA launched an appeal for a new "Sponsor a Chorister" money-raking scheme. The Duchess of Northumberland and a top man from The Sage came and said a few words each. Afterwards the choir stayed in their robes and mingled for refreshments. I don't think poor Jessica got anything to eat, but she was chuffed because she had a chat with the Duchess. The BBC had been in the morning to take some photos and interview one or two people and the children were excitedly speculating whether they would be on the box,

A hymn commonly sung on Advent Sunday is *Hills of the North, Rejoice!* That is one of my all-time favourites, so I was looking forward to singing it. I was horrified to see that it has been totally politicised and sanitised so that only the tune is recognisable. It shouldn't be called *Hills of the North* any more, nor attributed to C. E. Oakley. You see we're not allowed now to suggest that any country is pagan, or in any way needing the light of God. Goodness, that might offend their ambassador! To my mind, if any adaptation was needed, it would be an extra verse about the UK and how they lived in Darkness and needed Light. I sang the proper words.

Michael hosted monthly Friday lunchtime recitals in the nave. Sometimes it was organ, sometimes a singer or an instrumentalist. Now we were to have a small violinist called Leia Zhu. She was to come on December 5th. I gathered later that this was James's project. Leia was 7. She was well advertised in posters around the Cathedral and in the Sunday notices, but I am told that James woke up at 4am on the day and worried himself sick in case nobody came. The usual audiences for these lunchtime events were not much better than the Evensong congregation.

I was anxious to attend, not because I am besotted with violin music which I am not, but to find out if this poor child was being exploited. It sounded as if she must be. On my way down I bought a Beany Boo giraffe in case she would like one. I think I had an early lunch in the Lantern café. I'd be surprised if I didn't!

James need not have worried, there was a good gathering. They were mainly retired people (well, who else is available at lunchtime?) and perhaps many of them were people who came to the recitals sometimes, but there were plenty of them. From the beginning I felt that Leia was not being exploited. She looked as if she was thoroughly enjoying the whole business. She played very confidently and it was most enjoyable. At the end she played a duet with Bradley Creswick who is her friend and mentor. As she thanked her audience she said she hoped they would all go and hear her little brother play at Gateshead next week. The said little brother was sitting snuggled on his mum's lap looking anything but the genius he must be. Afterwards I gave Leia a little carrier with some chocolates and the giraffe, and thanked her for giving me so much pleasure. It was a relief to me that she seemed a very normal little girl.

Next day was the Patronal Festival, with the Bishop of Lincoln as guest preacher. It was the custom at Newcastle Cathedral to appoint a Boy Bishop for the day (or a Child Bishop as we must now say, because recent legislation allows a girl to hold this position). He was dressed up appropriately, and took an active but vocally passive part in the proceedings. This year it was Marco, a faithful acolyte, who was about 11. He did his job well. Later, when the Dean reminded Marco that he was on duty as Boy Bishop all of Sunday as well, Marco calmly replied that he was playing Rugby tomorrow. To the best of my memory we have not had a Boy Bishop since.

There was the usual tasty buffet lunch, in the Eastern Chapels for the congregation and in the Refectory for the Newcastle and Durham choirs. I rather got the impression that Newcastle and Durham choristers didn't socialise any more than eating necessitated. But at least they didn't fight.

On Friday, December 12th, as a sort of spin-off from chaperoning, I went to Gateshead to hear Leia's little brother Leo give a violin recital at St Mary's Heritage Centre. This was a very small event with a tiny audience and not much room for a bigger one, but as it was Leo's first solo performance it was undoubtedly the right scale. I think Leo was 6 years old. He was obviously only a beginner-genius, but he did amazingly well. I gave him a Beany Boo monkey. Leia had her giraffe with her and apparently takes it everywhere. She has called it Georgia. The family are going to China shortly for the children's first visit. It occurred to me that although it was Leia's first visit to China, Georgia was born there in a toy factory! Their mum said she had always planned to have four children, but the careers of the eldest two took so much time and effort that she thought the youngest two would be unlikely to happen.

Crisis at Christmas always have a carol service in the Cathedral, and the choir sings. Service users, as they are tactfully called, take part in the service. This year a man of about 30 read the story of the coming of the magi from Matthew. He found it difficult and read slowly and haltingly. We all sweated for him, but he persevered and read all twelve verses. One or two brave sprits clapped, and within a few seconds the whole congregation were clapping heartily, as much as anything in relief for the young man who had finally succeeded without giving up.

A few days before Christmas the choir gave a concert in the Castle Keep. The Castle has no heating and no toilets, so a sadist might consider it an ideal venue. It was certainly atmospheric. Going up the worn and uneven outside stone staircase to the doorway half way up was a feat in itself, then there was a narrow spiral stone stairway inside. The Great Hall was set out with chairs and candle stands. We saw on the backs of our tickets that we were advised to wrap up warmly, but until that moment we had not read the backs. Well, you don't, do you? It was a mild December night and I was only wearing a waistcoat, not a cardigan, under my anorak. I soon felt quite cold. The candles were pretty but whatever heat they gave out didn't reach very far. The concert was very good and we enjoyed it, and almost felt it was worth getting cold for. Emily Stoddart was home from college and she sang with the choir. At half time we were led down to the hall below and given wine, fruit juice and mince pies – all very cold of course, but we hoped the calories would warm us. This, I suppose, was a CCA project. I remember it was quite expensive, and that it got more expensive with every passing year, but those who gritted their teeth and paid up generally thought it was worth it.

On the 22nd the choir went to Sainsbury's at Heaton to sing to the shoppers. This was certainly a fund-raising event. The original idea had been bag-packing, but singing was a much better idea. The choir can sing very well, but it is doubtful if many of them have a clue how to pack bags efficiently. And singing spreads the Gospel story to people who may not have heard it. We had to be there at 9am, so Jessica and I had to leave home about 7.15 to get there. It was to be a long day as the girls had to be back at the Cathedral at 2 to rehearse for the Crib Service at 3. They were told to take a packed lunch, but I gave Jessica £10 so that she could either eat in their café or choose something she liked in the shop. I sat in the café, which is on a gallery, and read my Kindle and drank coffee. The carols sounded beautiful. At first they were competing with canned music, but I asked the café lady if she could fix for it to be turned off, and she did. The other parents who came were busy shaking buckets in the foyer, but I did not volunteer for that. I am allergic to buckets. At the end of the day when the buckets were emptied I believe the CCA would have reason to be well satisfied – if they ever were.

At the end of the morning session I believe the lay clerks stayed on, but we had to go back to the Cathedral. After waiting for what seemed like ages at a bus stop we gave up and called a taxi. Simple innocent soul that I am, I went to the Lantern Café for some lunch. "You can only have soup and sandwiches. We're trying to close early" snapped the representative of the Ministry of Welcome. I took my appetite elsewhere, and had a pukka Christmas Dinner in T. J. Hughes. I read for a while, then went back to the Lantern for a cup of coffee to show there was no ill feeling. I had a nice quiet read till it was time for the Crib Service. Alan Edington, the Assistant Verger, gave me a lovely photo he had taken of me, sitting reading in the nave, at a recent flower festival. I hope he will let me use it on the cover of this book. This year lots of families turned up for the Crib Service. I wondered where Father

Steven had got them all from. This time the mini-tableaux were already set up at the various stages, with lay clerks, clergy and various Cathedral staff. How he did it I don't know, and on a weekday too. No volunteering was necessary. Poor Roger never did get to be the donkey. The angelic host of choristers did very well and their singing was inspiring. It was a truly Christmassy occasion.

On Christmas Eve Jessica and I made our way to the Vermont and set up camp there. At 4.20 I took her across to the Cathedral and we met Roger in the south doorway. Back at the Vermont we ordered tea and sandwiches on room service, but the sandwiches included a pile of salad and a basket of chips. We hoped such a filling "snack" would not sap our appetites for the supper we knew we would want later. Roger kept the jug of milk he didn't want in his tea so that Jessica could have a Malteser nightcap with it. It was a very comfort-able way to spend a winter evening.

The Cathedral was full for the service of Nine Lessons and Carols. Bishop Frank White, the assistant Bishop, preached. It wasn't memorable but, as Revd David Peel once quoted to me, "Sermons are for receiving, not for remembering". I have certainly received far more sermons that I have ever remembered. For the choir, this night and morning was the high spot of the year, and they were a great credit to Michael. It was very tiring for them, but they kept going. Of course a lot of the carols had been sanitised, but I knew them well and sang them as they should be sung. It didn't matter because nobody was listening to me. At the end the youngest girls and the boys could go home for a good sleep (if anybody sleeps when they are waiting for Santa) but the older ones had to keep awake.

Back in our room Roger and I still felt full, so we decided to have something light. Roger had scones with jam and clotted cream, and I had soup and a roll (donating my roll to Jessica). She had haddock and chips with mushy peas that came very elegantly in a silver basket lined with pretend newspaper, and the peas in a wee saucepan. As last year, Roger very nobly insisted on sitting on the carpet so that we could sit on the chair and the stool. Now we all had to stay awake till 10.45 which was easier than we feared.

At 10.45 we took Jessica back to the Cathedral for rehearsal, and we sat in the hotel lounge with orange juice to save having to go back up five floors in their lift that always gives me the bends (or that's how I feel). It was still mild, dry weather so the frequent trips between Cathedral and Vermont were no hardship. Midnight Mass was very well attended. There were no children in the congregation except the odd baby who was too small to know it didn't like being there. Or perhaps it did. Bishop Martin and his wife, now retired, had given us a beautiful olive-wood crib scene and tonight it was blessed. I asked Roger, in a whisper, why Bishop Martin couldn't have blessed it himself to save trouble, and he opined that it might have been blessed several times on its journeyings. Well, now it was blessed again. It had always amused me, and it did tonight, to hear the episcopal couple referred to as Bishop Martin and Marlene. It made her sound like his floozy. Why not Bishop Martin and Mrs Wharton? After all, she was probably Mrs Wharton to far more people than she was Marlene. She would not be Marlene to me (though, if the truth were known, she might be Cousin Marlene, because I do have Wharton ancestors). This is the service when we sing "Yea, Lord, we greet thee, born this happy morning!" It's nice to sing that, and maybe again later. Before Jessica went to bed I used the rest of the Maltesers to make her another drink with the milk. We were in bed soon after 1 o'clock. With a bit of luck we might get six hours sleep.

Roger had a new alarm clock and he brought it with him. He hadn't tested it. It woke us very rudely at 7.45. Guests in many nearby bedrooms must have thought it was the fire alarm. It took Roger some time to assemble his faculties and remember how to turn it off. By 8 o'clock we were down for breakfast. We all found we had good appetites, our late suppers notwithstanding. It's important to eat a good breakfast when you're paying for it.

Bishop Frank both preached and presided. In his sermon he told us about an obscure fresco in an obscure church in Italy, where a Nativity scene shows a cow licking Jesus's face and a donkey licking his hand. A silent "Aah!" enlivened the faces of the congregation. In The Peace I tried to shake hands with all the little ones, and all but one responded. I suppose that one had been well trained not to talk to strangers. A few minutes later I saw Bishop Frank go into the St Margaret Chapel and not only exchange The Peace with the children but also stay and have a little chat with them. I said to Roger, "He's a nice man. I shall vote for him."

I saw Gordon and thanked him for coming back to work, on the heaviest weekend of the year, when he had been ill, and he said he was glad to be there because he didn't like to miss what was going on. "I love this place," he said.

Then home by taxi to see if Santa had called. He had.

Jessica worked out how much free time she had in her evenings in the week between school and bed, not counting Fridays. It was nine hours. I asked if choir was getting too much, but no, definitely not! She wasn't complaining, she said, she was just working it out.

This year's Christmas treat, when it came in January, was a trip to a bowling alley on West Road, with pizza afterwards. They were to meet at the bowling alley, so I took Jessica on a couple of buses. Externally it was a very seedy-looking place. Inside it was physically respectable but all I could see in any direction was gaming machines and a bar. Further on we came to a rather small bowling alley. It was clearly geared up as much to gaming and drinking as to bowling. Amy Leach, our new Music Assistant, was there. I asked her whose idea it had been to go there, but she didn't know. I said, "Well, pardon my language, but I think this is a bloody awful place!" She looked a bit embarrassed but assured me she would make a note of it and pass it on. I would have liked to take Jessica away but it would have embarrassed and disappointed her. Michael arrived and I left. Father Kevin came too which suggested the treat had been provided by the Dean and Chapter – we had not been asked for any money. I mooched around the shops till it was time to meet her. They had finished up at the Pizza Express, and everyone seemed to have really enjoyed themselves. Oh well. I suppose I'm just getting old.

In response to an appeal I volunteered to help out as a second adult at Sunday school. Father Steven sent me a schedule. My turn will come about once a month. The function of second adult is to take children to the toilet if they want to go, and generally to satisfy the safeguarding regulations. My first stint came in mid-January. The class consisted of Pumza, who I knew already, as the teacher and one little girl. The Education Suite was set out with little tables and chairs, floor cushions, crayons and felt pens in tubs. On a side table was a tray of juice and biscuits. It looked cosy. The little girl didn't seem to mind being the only child with two adults.

Pumza asked us to be very quiet for a minute, and I thought it must be silent prayer. No, it was to see what we could hear (so to speak). The little girl could hear birds. I could hear breathing. Pumza told us a story about listening from the lesson book about a little boy called Samuel and an old man called Elly. I was a bit em-barrassed because I knew if I mentioned the old man I would have to call him Elly too, so as not to embarrass

Pumza. But then, do any of us know now how the ancient Hebrews pronounced Eli? Later, during colouring, I remarked that we might wonder why God spoke to Samuel and not directly to Eli, but maybe it was something Eli didn't want to hear. From the look on her face I concluded that Pumza probably did not know the rest of the story. Few people do. We weren't long because we had to get back for communion.

At the end of the service we had to say goodbye to Alison who was leaving, and install Bella and Celia and Head Chorister and Deputy Head Chorister respectively.

There was supposed to be a meeting in the Education Suite at 11.30 for any interested parents and children to find out about Sunday School, but on my way up I met Father Steven who said no one had turned up so there wouldn't be a meeting. I went back to look for Jessica and heard strains of plainsong coming from the south transept where coffee was being served. It was the lay clerks, now back in mufti, singing all about choir and the CCA and what was planned and when we should be paying our subs. I think it was piously hoped all members of the congregation would want to become members (fully paid up, of course). I missed quite a lot of it, but it was very entertaining and the coffee drinkers were enchanted. It ended, "and see you all at the Epiphany Carols Service tonight at 6. Amen." I think John Lewis would have written it.

Michael, with CCA input, was trying to plan an autumn choir holiday. He didn't know yet where it would be, but when I asked if it would be in the UK he replied "Probably not." I told Jessica this, and that she would not be able to go because, for reasons unnecessary to relate, we did not want her to go out of the UK. I said I was just as disappointed as she was, which she didn't believe, but it was true. I was really sorry it wasn't a trip on home ground and that such a wealth of cathedral heritage is being undervalued. I strongly suspect that the CCA committee, some of whom would be planning to go along as chaperones, were consulting their own interest. With predictable lack of originality they eventually chose Paris.

Now we had the Epiphany Carol Service which seems to wind up Christmas for Anglicans (everybody else's having been wound up on Dec 27th). It began with an introit being sung invisibly from the Eastern Chapels. It sounded so lovely. Then a nice candle-lit service with no sermon. Once I got a shock because I thought the roof was leaking right over my head, but then I saw the Dean was walking down the aisle throwing holy water over us all. Better than incense anyway.

One Thursday night when we arrived at the Cathedral we saw two people hugging outside the north door. One was Tracy. She told me an interesting story. The other person was a Russian student who had a very important exam next day and was very worried about it. She had come in to the Cathedral feeling very anxious and seeking spiritual comfort. She noticed Tracy, and had a funny feeling that she had seen her somewhere before. Tracy, as was her custom, went over to say hello to her and got the same funny feeling. After a puzzled search of each other's faces they eventually realised they had met before in Moscow two or three years ago. Tracy was then working as a missionary on the Mercy Ships, and she had been introduced to the girl and her mother. They were so pleased to meet again and, as Tracy said, the girl went out of the Cathedral in a much happier state of mind than when she came in. Either she or Tracy left a prayer request because we prayed for her in Evensong. God moves in a mysterious way.

Towards the end of February we heard that at half term the RSCM were running a two-day course called Sing4Joy at the Cathedral. I asked Jessica if she wanted to go, but she said she didn't and she would rather I didn't mention it again! I didn't, but Michael emailed to say he hoped she would go and the leader was very good. Celia was going. Maybe that clinched it, because Jessica grinned and said maybe she would go. It was £20 for the two days, and included lunch and drinks. The perceptive reader will notice that this was much better value than last year's CCA summer camp! On the following Sunday Michael said he was so glad Jessica was going. He sounded quite sincere.

At this time there was a Sunday after-service meeting called Red Wine and Tomato Juice. Stupid name for a group? Yes indeed, but all the more stupid because no tomato juice was served. The group had started in the Vermont, and the participants had all ordered drinks. I dare say one person went to the bar to order for everyone, and the order seems to have included a tomato juice (I'd love to know who had that). Someone must have said that Red Wine and Tomato Juice would be a good name for the group, and it stuck. Not a very good name, but "People Who've Got Nowhere Better to Go After Church" was a bit longwinded, even if abbreviated to PWGNBTGAC. After a few months it moved its venue back to the Cathedral and met in the Refectory. Katherine Govier, one of the Readers, was in charge of drinks and served red wine, white wine, orange juice and apple juice by the half-glass, and we all put something in a saucer to cover the cost.

Roger and I started going when there was an interesting talk about prisons. I think there were about twenty of us, which I gather was better than usual. It was, as it sounds, very drink conscious. I was interested to see what various members of the clergy drank. Suffice it to say none of them seemed to be teetotallers. And of course they had already knocked back the left-over communion wine. I hoped they weren't driving. This was quite good for me and Roger because we had to hang around for Jessica to finish rehearsal anyway. When she was finished she joined us and sat and read at the back. I asked why we couldn't have tomato juice. I am very fond of tomato juice. This was passed over with a laugh, but I insisted that I would like to know the reason, and if there was no reason, could we have it? Next time we met I was told that the Café Manageress had been consulted, but as tomato juice is not on the café menu she didn't know what she could do with the rest of the carton. How pathetic. I could think of several things to do with it. The clergy could have done what they did with the communion wine – slurp it down till it was all gone. Our family put more on the saucer than would have paid for one carton – we could have slurped it down. Or the café manageress could have put it in the soup. Anyway, the answer was clear: no tomato juice. But the name stayed. Eventually the group fizzled out.

In choir, Michael was having a lot of trouble with some little boys who didn't behave. He tried sandwiching them between big girls who could keep them in order. At one point, in Evensong, one of the little boys appeared to be hitting Celia! Naturally she couldn't hit him back. I suppose that was one of the unexpected duties of being Deputy Head Chorister.

At the end of January in Evensong I suddenly noticed that Jessica was wearing a blue ribbon with a senior chorister medal. How exciting! No one else had one, except Harriet who had had one for ages. Afterwards I was told that there had been no ceremony at all. As the choir were walking downstairs from the Song School to the Thomlinson Room, only a couple of minutes before, Michael said "Oh, wait a minute," and turned and rushed back upstairs for something. He came down with the medal in his hand, and Jessica tried to look as if she couldn't imagine who it was for. Michael said, "This is for Jessica, because she has been with us for so long and is always regular and sings so well!" Harriet (I'm told) said, "Oh, that was Celia's. It will have her germs on!" Celia, of course, had now been promoted and had a green ribbon. This meant Jessica would get a higher rate of pocket money, but she didn't yet know how much. The current Choristers' Handbook did not give this highly sensitive information.

Even Cathedral choristers must have some other life, and Jessica was involved in NETBA (North East Teenage Book Awards) which took place mainly at school in the daytime. Once a year there was an award ceremony at the Life Centre when panels of children presented their favourite (living) authors and made awards to them. Horrors – this year it was a choir night! Help! What should she do? She couldn't be in two places at once, but she must be! Now Jessica, let's take this calmly: when do you have to be at choir, and when do you have to be at NETBA? As W. S. Gilbert so rightly said, "Quiet, calm deliberation disentangles every knot". The NETBA award ceremony began at 6.30 officially, though it started with a pop'n'crisps fight. Choir ended – well, it all depended, but before 6.30. It was fluid, depending on how long the service of Evensong took. Perhaps Michael would let her leave at the end of the anthem? We were pretty sure he had let others do so in the past. She asked him. Yes, that would be fine! So on the night Jessica duly stepped out of the choir stalls, bowed to the altar (why?) and slipped out quietly. At the same time a large percentage of the congregation did the same (without bowing to anyone) and slipped out after her. All went well, and would have gone even better if the said large percentage of the congregation had been able to walk a bit faster. Geriats are such a drag.

Gordon often read the lesson at Evensong, if there was a shortage of clerics. One night he had to read a very long passage about Jacob's carryings-on with his two wives, Rachel and Leah, and various maidservants (he had clearly learned nothing from Grandfather Abraham's folly), and what each female begat and how. Gordon did well, but it was a pretty awful passage to have to read to a bunch of little girls. Afterwards Rachel was excitedly telling everyone that the reading had been about someone with her name! This coincidence seemed to excite her much more than Jacob's conjugal complications, which had hopefully passed over her head. Just as well.

One evening I was sitting alone on the stairs when the door banged and Mrs X came in. She wanted to see the Dean! Perhaps she could ask me, she said, about something she wanted to discuss with him? She wanted the choristers to come out as soon as Evensong was over, and not stay for more rehearsing till 6.30. It made it so difficult for parents! She was sure if people could collect their children straight after Evensong more parents would come to the service. She could not stay for the service herself because she had other children. What did I think? I clumsily and Aspergically replied, "This is a huge organisation and it can't be changed for the odd parent." She began to get cross and expanded on her subject as I clearly didn't understand her problem. Eventually, after letting her ramble on, I asked, "How old is your daughter?" She was 15, 16 in a fortnight (goodness, nearly old enough to be married!). I asked if she couldn't now travel home by herself (I knew it was only a short trip on a frequent bus service). Mrs X nearly had apoplexy. Of course not! The poor child would get cold! It was *very* cold out there now! It was freezing! (In fact it was a very mild evening for February.) Mrs X was clearly not used to being disagreed with, and did not like it. I have no doubt the Dean gave her a kinder hearing, but the system was not about to be changed.

At half term Jessica attended the RSCM Sing4Joy two-day course. As soon as we got to the Cathedral we met Eleanor Wathey so she and Jessica went off together. It's fun to meet new people, but it's comforting to have regular friends around too. I saw Eddie keeping warm by a big radiator, and I asked him if he would like some coffee. Yes, he would love some! I went to the Lantern

Café to get some. Knowing they served coffee in large, shallow cups at that time I asked if I could have a mug which would be easier for me to carry and would stay warm longer. I explained that it was for Eddie. One of the café ladies pulled a slight grimace and got a polystyrene cup and plastic spoon. "I don't encourage Eddie to come in here because of his coat," she said. Yes, I could see his coat would offend all the laws of health and hygiene, but he would probably still offend the café ladies if he was stark naked. And they charged me full price! After I had taken Eddie his coffee I went back and had one of their excellent breakfasts. Chaperoning is such a hungry business.

Now I had to fill in the day before I met Jessica out at teatime. It wasn't worth going all the way home to Morpeth so I jumped on a bus and went to Durham (maybe two miles further). Naturally when I got there I made straight for the Cathedral. Cathedrals grow on you somehow. It's a pleasant walk from the bus station, passing a few itinerant musicians and enjoying a beautiful view. A current fund-raising project in Durham Cathedral was the building of a model of it in stone-coloured Lego. This took place in the Undercroft between the shop and the café. Some "architects" sat at a table assembling a small section of the building to a plan, and if you gave them £1 you could place one Lego brick exactly where they told you to. Then they give you a sticker which said something like "I helped build Durham Cathedral in Lego." Of course if you wanted to see your brick in all its final splendour you would have to come again, and again. The model, in a huge glass case, was about a third completed, and looked wonderful. Stained glass windows and flowers in the surrounding lawns gave it relieving colour. It was beautiful as it already was. What was assembled so far must have already raised tens of thousands of pounds. I was so pleased to have seen it.

All this bricklaying made me hungry, so I went to the cafe and had a very good lunch. With all these breakfasts and lunches I made a mental note that I would probably not need much supper. Walking back down Owengate to town is more risky than walking up because you can lose your footing if you're not careful. Traffic uses the hill, limited mainly, I think, by its difficulty and people not wanting to do it. It is mainly used by residents. But such traffic as there is presents a great risk to the unwary walker who, if he is a visitor, forgets he is not in a pedestrian street.

Back in Newcastle I ended up at the Lantern Café fifteen minutes before they closed. They made difficulties. Yes, I could have coffee, but I must drink it before 3.30. I could only have instant coffee because they had washed the coffee machine. Oh dear – hadn't I got the right change? They had cashed up! By now I had the coffee and I didn't plan to let it go, but the nice lady said if I was going in tomorrow I could pay then. I was grateful.

At 4 o'clock there was an unscheduled evening service by the children. They were busy getting ready for it. It was official, but the parents had not been invited to it. I spoke briefly to Jessica to let her know I was there, and they were all intrigued by my sticker. Celia said she wanted to go and lay a Lego brick. I hoped someone would take her. The children sat on the crossing dais, and the tiny congregation sang the hymns and tried to do the right things. Jessica had been very pleased with the day and had had a nice lunch. Hooray for the RSCM. The leader who Michael had commended to us was none other than Andrew Robinson who gave Jessica her audition last summer.

My second Sing4Joy day was less exciting. I had obligations in Morpeth so I had to go back directly when I had delivered Jessica. I was back about 3 o'clock and made for the Lantern for coffee (what it is about coffee? Oh yes, caffeine I suppose). I had my own sandwich that I had just picked up in Marks and Spencer. I politely asked if I might eat it. No, the manageress said, she was sorry. I said I bet she wasn't sorry at all, but she said yes she truly was. The annoying thing was that there was nothing else to eat except some packets of biscuits. I couldn't have had their sandwich because they would not have wanted to make me one then. Goodness, they were closing in half an hour! I wished I hadn't asked. At 3.25 the children came running into the Refectory for drinks and pancakes. Pancakes had been served to the public today (they didn't offer me one) and there were a lot left. I heard one of the welcomers (taking a break from welcoming) asking the café ladies what they were going to do with all the left-over pancakes, and one of them said "Give them to the kids" rather derisively. However a table was set with a cloth and covered in bottles of syrup and Treat sauce, and the children all got two pancakes and had a good time eating them. In fact I suspect Andrew had ordered the pancakes. I went out then because it was closing time for the likes of me.

Today the service at 4 o'clock was well attended by parents and carers. I sat in the Quire but others sat in the nave. We had a printed order of service. There is no Evensong in the holidays, and Evening Prayer would be at 5.30, so this little service was not intimidatingly circumscribed by canon law. It was very good. Jessica sang a couple of cantor lines at the beginning but sounded slightly hoarse. I think it was the result of pancake syrup lining her throat. She had very likely had nothing to drink. Celia croaked very briefly in one of her turns. Father Kevin presided, and it was a joyful service. At the end the choir came back for a photo call, and Andrew gave them all a certificate. Someone also gave them all a little poster about a two-night residential course in Whitby in May. It cost £230. It sounded good. Jessica's general verdict of Sing4Joy was very positive. It seems Andrew has promised another for next year. I emailed him to thank him. Michael, in our next communication, said he was so pleased Jessica had done the course, and I think he really was.

My second Sunday School stint was on February 22nd. Today Helen was doing a Godly Play session. She warmly welcomed me. I had seen Godly Play once before, and I was looking forward to it. Helen told me about what would happen, so that I knew. If choirboys fidgeted I was not to hit them (a joke, of course. This was a temptation we always knew we had to resist for legal reasons). Godly Play continued uninterrupted till the leader might indicate participation was welcome. She would perhaps say "I wonder …" which was an invitation to us to make any contribution we thought of. She allowed me to make contributions too. It was riveting, but not inspiring to me because I didn't like the topic. It was all about us needing six weeks to get ready for the Mystery of Easter. I think the Church of England overdoes misery in Lent. We know, after all, that there is everything to be joyful about because Christ is risen, once and for all. We should remember his agony, but not wallow in it. But it was a very interesting experience and I looked forward to being Helen's second adult again. I earned my keep this time by taking a little girl to the toilet. Michael came up to collect his choirboys and was very nice to them. Father Steven told me he was grateful, and that Helen had been grateful too. There is not much to be grateful for, but the importance of a second adult is that without one Sunday School could not be held at all. At the end of the day, the leader or second adult might be required to testify in court against allegations of mischief by the other!

We were told the new organ would be installed next day. The speakers were already in situ. They were not beautiful but I hoped they would do a good job. James would be performing on it on Friday lunchtime and I planned to go to hear it. I asked him if there was to be any consecration ceremony, but he said no, it was just an interim measure for a few years – perhaps five. Well, considering the importance of an organ in any church, and considering the inanimate objects they do consecrate (new copes, new lighting, sleeping bags for the homeless, Yvonne's knitted blankets) I thought this was very poor. But perhaps it was an economic matter. Blessings are usually conducted by bishops, and we were currently in an interregnum. Bishop Frank could have done it, but then it would have been an occasion for drinks and nibbles and fuss. Better leave it.

Jessica says they have been told by some optimist that there will be a new organ (the old one rebuilt?) in 2018. They will need a few million, but maybe that is in the pipeline. Millions often are. Now we no longer had the nice little organ console sitting by the north Quire gate. I liked seeing it being played, and I often left a small bar of chocolate on it "for the next person who plays the organ". I wouldn't be able to do that any more because the organ loft is kept locked. I was going to miss it. Now the organ loft was to have two consoles in it, which must have been rather cramping.

At the end of that service the Dean told us what he called "bittersweet news". Father Kevin was leaving. He had accepted a post as Priest in Charge of St James's Church, Vancouver (in Canada, he added helpfully). He would leave on May 10th. He would be sadly missed, not least by us. He did beautiful services, and often quoted Charles Wesley hymns in the prayers. As a Methodist I have great respect for Wesley, but to the C of E he seems to be an also-ran among hymn-writers. *The New English Hymnal* contains only 26 Charles Wesley hymns, but the Methodist *Hymns and Psalms* contains almost 200. I hoped the Canadians will appreciate Father Kevin.

We had heavy rain that afternoon, and a homeless person came in and draped his wet sleeping bag over one of the big radiators where it steamed happily. They wouldn't get away with that in many cathedrals. Hooray for St Nix!

Next night when I went I to the Cathedral Eddie was there sitting in his favourite pew, and he had a pal with him. The pal had a gin bottle sticking out of his raincoat pocket. I remembered Tracy firmly telling another homeless person that alcohol was not allowed in the Cathedral. Mind, there is nothing wrong with gin. In his sermon yesterday the Dean raised a chuckle by admitting he was very fond of gin and had given it up for Lent. I suppose it's all a question of whether you drink it from a crystal goblet out of a mahogany drinks cabinet in your sitting room or from a bottle in your raincoat pocket.

In mid-March Jessica and I were off to Durham again. In the RSCM's *Network* magazine she had seen an item about a session at St Giles's Church to introduce candidates to the Silver Award. Jessica had never heard of this, but she wanted to take it. We rang up and asked if she could go, and a nice lady called Joan Johnson promised to book her a place. It was to be held on a Saturday in mid-March at 10am. This time we had no difficulty getting there, but as before the church was tightly locked. However a kind lady who said she was a retired priest was busy organising Mothers' Day daffodils in a nearby shed, and she had a key and very kindly let us in. Then George Barber arrived and was very nice and welcoming to Jessica. He told her that only one other girl was expected. Last year, he said, there had been about twenty participants, but this year only three had registered and one of them couldn't come. Joan Johnson came and made very welcome coffee. I told her that Jessica had found out about the event from *Network* but that we really knew nothing about Silver awards (or any other colour). I set up camp for myself in another room, but the other girl's mother stayed with her. I didn't know which was best, but Jessica is very confident and I think it's right to let her manage her own affairs where she safely can. Joan said Jessica was not in the Durham area but she was welcome to do Silver from Durham. It is done by diocese, whereas *Network* made it look as if it was regional. It will cost about £45 plus £20 for the actual medal. It will be on Wednesday, May 20th, at 6.30. Jessica will need an accompanist, but when I blenched Joan offered to accompany her herself which was a very welcome offer. I was really glad of the coffee. It could only be described as warm and wet, but I needed warm and wet very badly. The heating was on, but the church was still very cold because it had not had time to warm up. I sat close to a good radiator but still felt cold. I heard George telling the vicar, who dropped in, that he had planned to end the session at 12.30 but as there were only two girls it would be 12. This was good news. Two and a half hours sitting in a cold place is not good for an elderly chaperone. At the end Joan very kindly offered to run us back into Durham, where we had a lovely lunch at the Café Continental (sadly no longer there). Jessica had a big pack of information to digest. She would need a referee and we hoped Michael would do that for her. I emailed him to ask.

Next day was Mothers' Day and the choir distributed daffodils. Jessica hoped to give me a posy but another chorister got in first and gave me one with scant grace. Father Steven announced at the beginning of the service that two of the Readers had special birthdays today – Katherine Govier was 50 and Marjorie Wood was 80. I can only suppose he had their permission to divulge this sensitive information. On our way home I gave my posy of daffodils to an eastern European Big Issue seller. She seemed very touched. In the afternoon Jessica began sorting out the music she would like to offer for her Silver exam. She was somewhat daunted by all the liturgical stuff she has to find out for it. It is not just to test your singing ability but to ensure that you are an informed chorister. She had hoped to go for Gold, but the RSCM rule is that you have to start with Bronze and suffer all the way with no short cuts. However they allowed Jessica to start at Silver because she is a

Cathedral chorister and a certain level of expertise is assumed!

On the following Thursday I might have found myself in Durham again, but it was not to be. It was their Patronal Festival and our choir was going in a coach. I didn't really expect to be allowed to go in the coach with them, but I thought I'd try my luck. When I asked Michael he said no. He was sorry, he said, *so* sorry. I think he really was. Ah well. Now I had to spend four or five hours occupying myself in a city that is not very hospitable to elderly female teetotallers after hours. I spent the first two hours in the City Library till they closed at 7, then I went to the Theatre Royal and bought the cheapest ticket they had for *Shrek the Musical*. They could only offer me a seat in the middle of the back row of the gods, but I wasn't going to sit in it anyway. I was going to read my Kindle. I know from bitter experience that the usherettes are very nervous about anyone who sits in the bars during the performance, and having inspected your ticket several times they watch you discreetly to see what you might be planning to get up to. I'm sure I don't look like a terrorist, but they can't be too careful! However I found a nice, bright, warm, comfortable place (never mind where) and read happily till 9 o'clock.

Back at the Cathedral I stood in the deserted darkness of the west door, waiting for the coach. Few things are less welcoming than a dark, locked Cathedral. Eleanor Wathey's parents came about 9.20, and they were comforting company. The Howard Snaith coach arrived at 9.30 and disgorged its cargo of sleepy-heads who had had such a long day and worked so hard. Parents appeared from nowhere, or probably from their cars. We went home by taxi.

I had emailed Michael to ask if a special dispensation could be made for the parents of choristers with a 95% attendance record over the previous year, especially if the parents were over 70, had no transport and were willing to make a contribution to the cost of the coach. I hadn't had a reply, but tonight Michael promised a reply would be coming soon.

Next Sunday I was second adult at Sunday School again, and Helen was doing Godly Play again. There was one little girl and four little choirboys. It all went very well. Part of a Godly Play session involved a Feast, when Helen gave us all a serviette to keep the floor clean, a biscuit to go on it and a tumbler of juice. It was rather formal. I think there is always juice and biscuits, but not always this formality. One little choirboy, M, said he could not have a biscuit because he had a gluten allergy. Helen was really upset and apologised profusely and assured him she would get some biscuits for him next week. I asked Helen if I could tell M what I did with biscuits I couldn't eat for any reason. I took them outside and fed a pigeon. It didn't go down very well. I suspect M had been brought up to regard pigeons as vermin. But ever after that occasion there was always a carefully labelled tub of gluten-free biscuits. Helen was very caring.

Amy emailed us all to say that Father Steven would be so pleased if as many choristers as possible would go on Holy Saturday to help him make an Easter Garden, and then he would take them out for a pizza. How nice! This was the treat Jessica missed last year so she was keen to go.

On Palm Sunday, as we left the Vermont after our excellent breakfast, we saw the choir and clergy coming towards us waving palms. We remembered that on Palm Sunday the procession starts in the Castle Garth and goes back to the Cathedral singing. In fact quite a bit of the service took place there. It was held in the open on the footbridge between the Castle Garth and Black Gate, and the followers, 20 or more, huddled under the railway arch where it was not raining. In fact it was hardly raining at all, but it was trying to. Back in the Cathedral we had a very nice service. As we are being sad for six weeks we did not have incense, so that was a relief. In the evening the choir sang Charles Wood's beautiful *St Mark's Passion* which had taken quite a bit of rehearsing. Jessica complained afterward that they had not had a chance to sit down between 4.30 and 7 o'clock.

I don't know what the church celebrates on the Monday after Palm Sunday, but Evensong had a larger clerical presence and a bigger congregation. James arranged the psalm so that each of the nine little girls got a solo line to sing. It worked very well. Jean Skinner was the preacher, but her sermon was listed as a Reflection which I think means a short sermon with visual aids. Jean's visual (or olfactory) aid was to sprinkle what she said was spikenard onto a pad and pass it round for us to sniff. Frankly it didn't smell all that exciting. Later I wondered if the choir had had a sniff, as I didn't see the pad being passed to them. I decided I would buy Jessica a little bottle of scent tomorrow. The things you think of in a sermon! Next day she told me that the choir had been given a sniff, but she was still delighted to browse for EDT in the Body Shop.

Michael sent the promised reply to my query. It is official policy now, after consultation with the Choir Schools Association and the Association of Organists who have found serious problems can arise when supporters are present, and they can be very difficult to deal with. Fair enough. Now I know that, I have no complaint.

On Good Friday Jessica and I set off early for a special children's service at 11. Some weeks ago Father Steven had sent out an appeal for helpers with this, and we had offered, but had no response. In the event it was a very small do, with only four young children and about ten adults including me and Jessica who would count as an adult height-wise. Sandra Hood, one of the wardens, had brought her five year old granddaughter Isabel with her. She introduced Isabel to Jessica and asked if they would like to go round together. Isabel and Jessica seemed very pleased with each other and stayed together till the end. We were walked round the Cathedral seeing a few mini-tableaux done mainly by one of the lay clerks and Father Kevin. Jean Skinner read a commentary. It was not well done, because the age of child they had in mind knew little or nothing about the Passion and did not understand what was being talked about. At least once Jean used the expression "If you remember … ", and the children would have been unlikely to have even heard of what she was talking about, let alone remember. At one station in the South Quire aisle the lay clerk was being Jesus washing Peter's (Father Kevin's) feet and serving the last supper. Jean told the children they might get a bit of bread. The lay clerk said "This is my body" and broke a pancake and gave bits to us all, which we ate, then he said "This is my blood" and passed a chalice of red juice round, but there were no takers!

Afterwards everybody was given nice buttered hot cross buns and cartons of decent juice in the Refectory. I urged Jessica to eat plenty of bun because she would not get anything else to eat till about 4 o'clock. She seemed reluctant, but kind Sandra told her that the left-over buns would only be thrown away (which was not strictly true), so she ate up. At 12.30 she had to go to a choir rehearsal for the 2pm service. I went to TJH and had a nice lunch of fish and chips with vegetables. The server asked me if I would like to "upgrade from pollock to haddock for 99p". She seemed hurt when I said pollock was quite good enough for me. In fact I think it has a better flavour. Eating fish and chips is definitely one of the more satisfying aspects of chaperoning. And I can feel virtuous for supporting the urban economy.

I went back to the Cathedral to wait for the Good Friday service. I knew that it started outside the north door with a procession forming around a life-size (or I suppose one should say death-size) wooden cross. It was raining and I hoped the choir would not get wet, but happily they did not have to go outside. Very properly the clergy and their retinue did the dirty work themselves – after all they had got themselves into it, the choir hadn't. The service progressed with some very nice singing, then the crucifer carried the cross up to the front where it was lowered rather noisily into an iron socket set up for the purpose on the crossing dais. Later the congregation were given the opportunity to go up and pat it or kiss it or do whatever they felt disposed to do to it. There was a sermon and communion, and it all went on for rather a long time, but that's what's proper in a Cathedral on Good Friday. The crucifixion is, after all, pivotal to our faith, provided we don't forget the resurrection.

On Easter Saturday (or Holy Saturday as it should strictly be called) I accordingly took Jessica to meet with Father Steven to set up an Easter garden. As this was the saddest day of Lent, when to all appearances Jesus was dead forever, it seemed a bit of a liturgical slip-up that the Cathedral flower ladies were busy doing the flowers for tomorrow. There were flowers everywhere, just as if they were anticipating the joy of tomorrow, which they may have been for all I know. We made our way to the Chapel of the Resurrection where the garden was to be set up, and there was no one else. Shortly David and Gill Lawrence arrived, and as they were obviously in charge I disappeared. Jessica was wearing a new pair of Nike trainers and I had been alarmed to see cans of paint among the equipment left out. It was supposed to be wash-outable paint, but I didn't want to have to wash trainers. Happily the paint and Jessica never collided. We had gone armed with five little decorative birds that our minister's wife was throwing out, and some glass pebbles Jessica could spare. Now I had two hours to get lost. I sat reading my Kindle with a glass of juice in Wilko café, then I read some more in TJH's café where I had lunch. I was now reading *The Kindness of Strangers* by Kate Adie. It was very absorbing. On a nearby table were four "young" geriats having a binge. I felt they were giving me occasional pitying looks. I suppose they were thinking, "Poor old dear, all on her own. How sad." It's true, you tend not to see many old biddies reading at a table for one, but that's chaperoning!

When I got back to the Cathedral a couple of policemen were escorting an old man out. They were being as kind as they could be in the circumstances. I went after them to give him a chocolate egg, but I didn't catch them up in time. Alan told me the old man had been asleep, drunk and lying on the Vestry floor and would not leave when asked. It would not have been in Alan's interests to manhandle him, so he was obliged to call the Police. I don't think the old chap was being aggressive, and Alan would have left him to sleep if he had been in a pew, but the Vestry is definitely not for that purpose.

There was no sign of Father Steven and the children. I guessed I was early, but another parent told me she had just had a call to say the children had only just started their lunch. They were at the Herb Garden, an interesting restaurant in a railway arch in Westgate Road where herbs were grown under artificial light. I heard later that they had all had pizza. I sat reading, but first I had a look at the Easter Garden. It wasn't impressive. There was a tomb of sorts, but it hadn't got a stone and it was festooned with bits of coloured print fabric. Around the edges of the patch were some potted primulas. But I was spoilt. The only other Easter Garden I had ever seen was in Hartburn Church a year or two before. Hartburn Easter Garden is a hard act to follow! When the children came back I thanked Father Steven, knowing that Jessica would have done so but wanting to express my own gratitude. But he pre-empted me and thanked me for taking Jessica and saying how lovely it was to have her with them! I was greatly touched.

The Easter morning service was happy. Bishop Frank presided. When he shouted "He is risen! Hallelujah!" he threw his mitre in the air! Father Steven took an early opportunity of retrieving it, which was a pity because it wasn't needed. There was a very good congregation, but of course Easter is the principal Holy Day of Obligation when the superstitious join the faithful. At the end of the service Jessica told us she was very impressed with Bishop Frank because, when he sprinkled us all with holy water at some point, and he had sprinkled the choir, he turned and gave a very hefty shower to the younger choirboys who had apparently been misbehaving something rotten. This seems to have taken them by surprise, as it would, and delighted all the other choristers.

We had booked a table for lunch at the Vermont for 1.30 (the earliest they could take us). When we were thinking of going for a walk to pass the time Elisabeth Stoddart came and asked us to go to theirs for lunch. I said it was very kind of her but we were booked at the Vermont, but I must have wavered a bit because she asked if we could unbook it. I said I thought we could, and I asked Roger and he offered to go across and cancel our booking. Elisabeth said the lay clerks were going too. Some of them were at a loose end between services. I only wished I had brought my knitting because it helps me cope with social occasions. Elisabeth said she would try to get us a lift with someone (she was on her bike), but I begged her not to on the grounds that the walk would do us so much good, and she seemed relieved. On my way through the Quire I met Michael and said gaily, "We've been invited to yours for lunch!" and he said "Oh, I'm so pleased!" He obviously knew she was asking us.

We walked and hoped we should see some flowers to buy for Elisabeth, though of course most shops were shut. Happily we found a small Sainsbury that sold a few bunches of flowers, and I was able to get a big bunch of mixed tulips and scented yellow jonquils. Jessica and I took turns carrying them. It was quite a long walk, as we missed our route a few times, but eventually we found ourselves on the north side of Nuns' Moor and we remembered the way. We arrived just before 1 o'clock and were among the first. Elisabeth had put two biggish tables together and managed to seat fifteen people in comfort. Celia showed us her ducks. The little family of last summer had escaped and she had new ones. Michael told us Celia had been asked to go and help sing Evensong at St Johns' Grainger Street, who rehearse at 2pm for a 3.30 service, and would Jessica like to go too? He had already asked her and she was keen. We were very happy for her to go. Before we had dinner Michael said grace which delighted me as I had not been anywhere for a long time where grace was said. After the first course of a wonderful roast lamb Sunday dinner Michael took Celia and Jessica, puddingless, to St John's. Still, if they had done full justice to the dinner they would not have been able to sing. We felt rather guilty as we tucked into pear and almond crumble and cream. Gail had taken some brownies and she promised to save some for Jessica, which she did.

We left about 2.40 to walk to St. John's to attend Evensong (and hear Jessica and Celia). It is about a two mile walk, but this time more downhill and we knew the way. It was the first time we had attended a service at St John's, though we remembered going to a mini-concert there, in their church hall, the night Terry Waite was released. After the service we found ourselves walking not far behind Jessica and Celia, and as they seemed very companionable together we hung back.

Our own Evensong started at the Easter Garden which was blessed (why? A bit late), then we trooped back in procession to the choir stalls. I could not see any very bad behaviour from the little boys, though once or twice I heard some very unmusical noises. I suppose they were getting too tired to be naughty. So we celebrated Easter by having two Evensongs! It was a most enjoyable day.

Some good news came in an email from Michael. He was making quite a few changes to the choir timetable, and each choir (girls and boys) would only sing once on a normal Sunday. This was very helpful to us because we should no longer have the problem of spending time in between services, and it might reduce the number of morning taxis we had to take.

On April 23rd, after Eucharist, we were asked to go to the Thomlinson Room for a CCA meeting. As we passed the open outside door we saw Amy marshalling children. Didn't Jessica want to go out to play with them, she asked? No, I said, she's coming with me. This was an off-the-cuff decision because I had forgotten that the children, who work so hard to delight us with their singing, were not welcome at CCA meetings. To me, if it wasn't for Jessica it wasn't for me either. Jessica made no objection. Bella Dalliston was also at the meeting, so they sat together which was nice.

We were given posh drinks and nibbles, which was in itself suspicious. What were they after? Michael made a speech, welcoming us and thanking us all for our support and saying the choir could not exist without it (true). Then he told us about two exciting forthcoming events: Sports Day at Wolverhampton (by train) in the summer and a three-night trip to Paris (by air) in the autumn. Now he would hand over to the CCA. One of their ladies told us excitedly about some of the fun things they had been thinking about to raise money – all the thrills and spills – they had even talked about singing a mass on bicycles! Good grief. It may have been at that point that I accidentally dropped my empty juice glass and it broke into a thousand pieces, but the excitement was reaching fever pitch and I doubt if anyone noticed except James who discreetly brought a brush and pan and swept it up from round my feet. I felt confirmed in my opinion that the CCA were trying to create fun opportunities for themselves on the backs of their children. After we had been indoctrinated we were urged to stay on afterwards for more drinks and nibbles and chat, but we were anxious to get away.

I feel strongly that the choristers work hard for their living and should not have to raise money as well. Parents, similarly, put in a lot of time and transport and should not be dragooned into fund-raising because other parents are looking for social opportunities. If the Cathedral want a choir, they should find some other way of paying for it without further exploitation. Few people seem to realise how hard the children work. Of course CCA membership was open to anyone in the congregation, and those non-choir congregants who took up this offer and paid their subs were doing the right and proper thing.

The next stage of the painting of the Forth Bridge was the repair of the Song School roof which was leaking. For months all choir activities had to take place in the Thomlinson Room. The outside of the area east of the south transept was clad in scaffolding. Choir personnel used the west door, which was quite an improvement. Mrs Coulson, the current singing teacher, usually gave lessons in the Thomlinson Room while the choir were in the Song School, so now she had to teach in the Refectory. The Education Suite was above part of the Refectory, so when I was sitting there having my cocoa I could hear the lessons below me. The first time I heard Harriet, then Bella, then Jessica. They were all strong singers and I enjoyed hearing them. On other occasions I sometimes had to try very hard to hear little mouse-voices trying to compete with the piano which was drowning them out. I remember Father Kevin's last Evensong with the girls' choir. James asked them to try to make it memorable for him. I don't know if they did, but it was memorable for me. I left a prayer request for Jessica's Nepalese relatives who were struggling to cope with life after a violent earthquake, and Father Kevin prayed for them. He would have prayed for Nepal anyway, but it gives more significance if it has a connexion with a member of the Cathedral community.

At the end of April posters appeared all over the building asking for volunteer vergers. They could be male or female, and of more or less any age. Now parading up and down at services in a black gown carrying the St Nicholas Mace might sound like fun, but doing the donkey-work, like putting out 200 chairs for a special service, might soon pall. I mentioned it to Gordon, who said rather grumpily that if the idea worked he and Alan might get their hours and their pay cut, and it would adversely affect his pension. I asked if he was in a union, and he said no, but now he wished he was. I don't know which union caters for vergers. I fear cases were beginning to come to light that showed up some churches often to be the most inconsiderate and even dishonest employers. No, I did not volunteer! I don't think many other people did either.

One Sunday night in Evensong, when Father John Sinclair was presiding, we sang a hymn that referred to a "sultry glebe" wherein "I shall not faint". I whispered to Roger, "What's a sultry glebe?" and he whispered back "A vicar's farm". I actually knew what a glebe was, but hadn't heard of them being sultry. It so often happens that the congregation are called upon to sing, and often sing heartily, words that they are most unlikely to understand (for instance, like the first-born seraph trying to sound the depths of love divine in Charles Wesley's *And can it be*). After the service the Dean and Father John went to the west door to see people off. "Can I ask you something?" I said. "Yes, yes!" they said eagerly. "What is a sultry glebe, and why might I faint in it?" I asked. They responded immediately. I found their explanation as clear as mud, but I said they had done better than some Methodist ministers of whom I had asked the identity of the first-born seraph. Father John snorted.

"Oh, you don't want to ask Methodists. They don't know anything. Always come to us!"

About now we decided take advantage of a scheme called Arriva Teen Card which allowed a person up to their 19th birthday to travel for £1 outside school hours. This was rather a business, having to fill in forms, get two passport photos and make a copy of her birth certificate. On a weekday her journey into Newcastle was still in school time so she couldn't use the card, but coming home she could. On the whole return journey she only saved 10p, but it was very useful at weekends. Some very kind drivers, when they got know her, let her use it on the outward journey too.

The following Sunday in Eucharist we sang *And can it be.* Canon John was the President, and I wondered if he had chosen it because of our conversation last week? We get all too few good rousing hymns at the Cathedral. Suddenly Gordon appeared at my side and whispered, "This is a Methodist hymn. Peace be with you!" After the service we had a short farewell to Father Kevin. Wine was served as well as the usual coffee. The Dean said a few kind words, Timothy Wigglesworth gave Kevin an envelope from the congregation, and Bishop Frank said a few kind words on behalf of the Diocese. We felt sad to think he was going so far away. Just before we left we bumped into him in a corridor, and Jessica gave him a big hug which seemed to touch him deeply.

In mid-May a little boy was expelled from the choir! He was a particularly naughty child, and I gather the lay clerks may have given Michael an ultimatum. This action would enhance the prestige of the choir by showing that there are standards of behaviour which must be met.

On a Friday in May the Headmaster phoned me to say that a lady from the BBC had phoned to ask for his permission for Jessica to take part in *Hadrian's Wall of Sound* which was being televised the following Friday. It was not in school time, and Mr Johnson had no idea why his permission was required. He was ringing me to check if it was genuine! I assured him it was, but that I knew very little about it. Michael was not always good at sending out practical information, but we had complete confidence in him, and we more or less just let things happen. This was not Jessica's first involvement with the BBC, but it was exciting!

On May 16th Newcastle held an event called *The Late Show* when various arty local bodies put on displays. The Cathedral decided to take part by staying open till midnight for anyone to come in and look round and have a cup of coffee. There was to be Compline at 10pm, and Michael asked some of the bigger girls if they would go and sing. Jessica was keen, but the only trouble was that we had to be back the next morning by 9, and after getting home on Saturday night there wouldn't be a lot of time for sleep. I decided to take Jessica to the Vermont for the night, as we do at Christmas. We set up camp there and had some supper, then we went to the Cathedral for rehearsal at 9. I mooched around to fill in time, and I saw some labyrinths chalked on the floor in the Eastern Chapels with people walking through them. They seemed a big hit. At the other end a short queue of people were waiting to be taken up the tower. Someone was dishing out glo-sticks which I fear I detest. To my grief I did not realise, till too late, that refreshments were being served in the Refectory! Only four girls turned up to sing, but there were some adults too. It was a beautiful little service with lovely music, and a bigger congregation than we would normally hope to get at Evensong. I felt it was worthwhile. As we walked back to the Vermont we found ourselves behind a little group of lay clerks who were making for the same place. Thirst after righteousness! Our bedroom overlooked Side where there are several hostelries with chairs and tables on the pavement. We had to open our window for air, but the noise from below was deafening with merrymakers merrymaking like billy-o. I wondered if it was like that every Saturday night, and I dare say it was. We did not expect to sleep, but we did. I woke up at 3.30 and all was quiet.

Next day after a good breakfast we were back in the Cathedral. As I went to my usual seat by the south aisle the Dean came rushing towards me. Oh, was he going to bid me good morning and tell me how pleased he was to see me? Was he perhaps going to say he had heard about our noble gesture in staying overnight so that Jess could sing both Compline and Eucharist? No. He asked me to move back a row! It put me in mind of the parable of the bloke who overestimated his own importance at a feast, and the host had to ask him to budge down to a lower place. I was annoyed and a bit sorry for the Dean who no doubt felt just a twinge of embarrassment at having to offend his regulars in favour of people who rarely darken the door. My order of service revealed these important people to be the Lord Mayor and Freemen. Important enough, certainly, but are we not all equal in the sight of God? Obviously not. It was clear that the civic party rarely went to church as they had no idea when to stand or sit or face the font. One thing I was glad about. I had assumed they would be funnelled out to the Refectory at the end and regaled with wine, but no. They had to scramble for coffee like the rest of us.

In Evensong Jessica sang a solo part in Howells' *St Paul* setting of the *Magnificat*. I heard her rehearse it and it sounded very beautiful. I heard Michael say "Brilliant. Brilliant." But he said it as if he was talking to himself and I'm not sure if Jessica heard. Roger joined me and we had the pleasure of hearing the solo again in the service. Moments like that make it all worthwhile.

On Wednesday, May 20th, the long promised Sports Day took place in Wolverhampton. Jessica and I got up at 4.30 and had a taxi to Central Station where we arrived just after 6. Amy and Michael arrived within a few minutes. There were only three girls going – Clare Asprey, Jessica and Lucy Che – but Lucy had not yet come. Having handed Jessica over I left. I couldn't get a concessionary bus ride home before 9, so I wondered how to spend the time. I planned to sit and read in an early café, but then it occurred to me that my coffee and snacks would probably cost as much or more than my busfare, so I went straight home. I stopped briefly at the Cathedral to use their facilities as they open at 7. In the loo I heard hearty gospel singing, and I found a cheerful black lady cleaning. She apologised for disturbing me, but she made my day! I forget what she was singing, but it wasn't from *Hymns Ancient and Modern*. More like Sankey and Moody. It was the first time I had had the pleasure of bumping into the people who keep the Cathedral clean. I supposed the cleaning staff would leave before the end of the morning, so I would be unlikely to see them often. I later learnt that this dear lady was the only cleaner, and that her name was Assi. She did a great job.

Now I was off duty for about fourteen hours, so Roger and I went to Seahouses on the bus for a treat. In spite of my early start I managed to keep awake all day. I had to go back to meet Jessica when they arrived back at Central Station 9.30. They had had a very good day and were really tired. They had played hard and sung hard, and had met new people. It was a very good spin-off from being a chorister.

About now James had some saddening news for the choristers. He was leaving and going to London. We understood that he had not got a job to go to but he knew various options that might soon be coming up and he wanted to be in the right place. He had always been very nice to the girls and they liked and respected him, and he would be sadly missed. Next time we heard of him he was organist at Rochester Cathedral.

In early June came Jessica's long-awaited RSCM Silver exam. She was allowed the day off school. Yet again we had cause to be grateful to Mr Johnson, but headmasters like to have Silver Medallists among their pupils. We set off early to Durham so that we had time for a nice lunch at the Café Continental. When we got to St Giles Church Joan Johnson was just arriving with Christine Alder who was to be the examiner, so we did not have to wait outside. George Barber came, and he gave Jessica a warm-up session in the music room upstairs. The exam began at 3.20. I could hear her singing and it sounded lovely. I was standing at the back of the church near the font where she could not see me through the glass screens. After the singing part was over the theory part began and George came out. He whispered to me that Jessica had done well and sang beautifully. That was kind. I learnt later that he had also lent Jessica some of his own music because hers was illegally copied! He really saved her bacon! The other candidate, whose name was Faith, arrived and they swapped over. When Jessica came out she was quite pleased. It seemed to have been a happy experience. It had been happy for me too, because I loved overhearing her singing and it was a much warmer day than last time!

This time there was no one to offer us a lift into town, but we knew the way. We'd had lunch and I offered tea in the same cafe if she liked, but she said she would rather go to Starbuck's for a Frappuccino! A few days later Joan sent Jessica a nice little card to say she was impressed that she had prepared for the exam entirely by herself.

Friday June 5th was the occasion of the BBC *Hadrian's Wall of Sound* which I had heard about through Mr Johnson. We still had very little idea what was going on, except that we had to go to the Cathedral on a non-choir evening. Apparently a baton was passed from Bowness-on-Solway to Wallsend. It passed the Cathedral where the choirs were outside singing, and then they trooped down Side to the Guildhall and the Tyne Bridge, still singing. Michael led them, and I am told he walked backwards all the way without incident. What happened to the baton, which I never saw, I don't know. It was televised, but no one seemed to know when it would be shown, if ever. Certainly there was nothing on tonight though we let Jessica stay up late in case there was. That's the BBC all over. They make you sweat for hours for a few seconds on air, and they don't tell you when those few seconds will be. But it was fun.

Next morning was another *Be A Chorister for a Day*. Jessica had to be there at 9.30 to welcome people. I spent the morning at the Lit&Phil. At 12 we had a nice little service There was one hopeful little girl recruit who sang heartily, but Michael was having to spend much of his time glaring at a little boy who was very naughty – even naughtier, I'm told, than the boy who was recently sacked!

That evening we had a CCA Curry and Quiz night in the Refectory with Glyn Evans as quizmaster. He began by booming out, "I am the Revd Canon Glyn Evans and I am Vicar of St Andrew's!" I suspect that's what he'll say when he gets to the Pearly Gates, and he was probably practising. Oh well, we can't all be modest. He was a good quizmaster but his main hobby was trying to be funny, and every question was interspersed with at least one joke (all clean, I'm glad to say). When it was time to eat he said grace. It was in rhyme. It asked God for blessings on various things including the curry. The penultimate line was something about "this feast to which we are invited," and I guessed something awful was going to have to rhyme with "invited". It did. "And Lord, if you've any blessings left, bless Newcastle United!" He is their chaplain. Indeed I gather it is because of his services to football that he was made an honorary

Canon of Newcastle Cathedral. God moves in a mysterious way. The curry was very good.

Next morning Helen Robertson came to my pew and asked me to be her second adult because the scheduled one hadn't turned up. I was very pleased to. I loved listening to Helen's Godly Play stories. In this one she had to show around a number of little figures of people who come to the communion table. The first was a black man, and I heard an audible and very impressed "Wow!" from Kasie to her little sister Soochi, followed by a whispered "Black!" I watched them and as the figures were shown round they exchanged delighted looks whenever the dolly had a dark skin of any shade. I wondered if the girls attended an all-white school and didn't see many other black people. They seemed so delighted to realise that there were other black people in the world who even merited a place in a Sunday School lesson!

On the following Thursday evening I went up as usual to make myself a cup of cocoa in the Education Suite, and I saw the back of Father Steven's head. I didn't know if he was alone, but I scuttled off anyway. Later I saw a group of dignified-looking people in the Refectory having coffee, but I didn't go back upstairs. In Evensong there were lots of extra people who seemed mainly to consist of churchwardens and unfamiliar clerics. Later Jessica told me that three of them had been candidates for the position of new canon to replace Father Kevin and the rest were interviewing them. Michael had told the choir to sing extra well for them because the new canon, whoever he/she was, would have power to fire them! Well the Dean and Chapter could fire Michael, but I think they would leave him to fire the choristers. The candidates sat opposite me in Evensong. There was a man and either two or three women. None of them impressed me, though at that point I still didn't know what they were there for. When I knew I hoped the man would get the job. I don't like women priests. Some are excellent, but more are not. And I know St Paul agrees with me, though the idea would have been so outrageous that he never even mentioned the matter. It's an odd situation. In theory God calls a person to the ministry and to higher levels of it, but mere mortals have to make the final decision after a quick prayer. At best you might say the Lord has sent us a selection to choose from. Anyway, the choir did indeed sing well, and I'm sure Michael was proud of them.

A few days later Joan Johnson rang to say Jessica has passed her Silver Award exam. The medals would be presented at a ceremony in Durham Cathedral in the autumn. But I think she will get it before then, and hand it back to have it presented (like the Queen opens a road bridge that thousands of people have driven over). I knew Jessica was hoping to wear it at the RSCM summer course at Durham in August. She is very anxious to do Gold next year. Well, said Joan, she'd need help with that. She couldn't *possibly* prepare for Gold on her own!

Unlike Mothers' Day, which has been recognised by the church for centuries, Fathers' Day is a more recent and purely commercial celebration, so it would be surprising if the CCA planned their mini-concert on that Sunday deliberately. The purpose seems to have been to showcase their children and to raise money. A father, perhaps for his Fathers' Day treat, was detailed to sit at the back and take money as people came in. I forget how much, but the CCA would have carefully calculated how much they thought they could get away with.

In addition to some choral singing, individual children were invited to entertain us by playing their instruments. Nine children took up this opportunity and played party pieces – maybe eagerly, maybe reluctantly. Who knows? Only Jessica, Bella and Eleanor refrained, and I'm sure we were all grateful to them. The performance was sometimes enjoyable and sometimes painful, but we all sat and smiled and clapped. Jane Austen's Mr Bennett's words came to mind: "You have delighted us long enough."

Just before the end Michael told us all that the Dean had something very important to announce. Goodness – what? Was he closing the choir down? Was he sacking the Director of Music? Were we all to make our way quietly to the nearest Fire Exit? No. He announced that a bald-headed gentleman, in front of me, who was a Freemason, was giving us lots of sponsorship money from his Lodge (it turned out to be £1,500). There was much clapping and photographing (some officially by Amy). Indeed many of the parents had been snapping and videoing ever since they came in. I found this information underwhelming.

After that we were invited to go to the Refectory for tea as the Dean's guests. Sadly it was all cake – very nice cake and plenty of it, but I don't much like cake and try not to eat it. Last year it was lovely doorstep sandwiches. I love sandwiches. But the tea and coffee were good. It was a good social occasion for people to mill round each other saying "Oh Millicent, I didn't know you could play the triangle! And Jeremiah, you really made that bassoon speak! Oh Doris, you must be so proud of Jimmy! How on earth did you get the double bass into the car?"

Next evening, at choir rehearsal, Amy had all the left-over cakes to give to the children, who fell on them ravenously. I hoped they had been covered. Identical cakes were also offered to them on Thursday evening, but I'm sure there must have been another catered event. I'm sure they would not still have been Sunday's cakes. Well, almost sure.

 One night I saw Gordon stacking the plastic chairs after an event, and I noticed the stack was higher than his head. Lifting above chest level puts a greater strain on the heart, and I hoped Gordon would not damage himself. Of course there was no one else to do it. I wanted to help, but no gentleman in his sixties would accept manual labour from a lady in her seventies. I thought Gordon was seriously overworked, especially since Tracy left as she had not been replaced.

At the end of June the girls had a small excitement when they were asked to sing a world première performance of Nicholas Wibberley's *Newcastle Service* which he had apparently dedicated to James Norrey and the girls of Newcastle Cathedral Choir. Well, they certainly didn't get anything else for singing it as it was Evensong. Mr Wibberley himself came to hear them. I have to say it didn't sound anything special to me, but maybe it was challenging. Bella's mum and sister came and were hugging her afterwards, so presumably it was a triumph for Bella. There was a photo-call at the end.

One of the last excitements of this choir year was the interviewing of the candidates for James's replacement. Candidates would need a choir to practice on, so the children were involved. Michael emailed parents to ask if they would stay behind for a buffet and meet the candidates and talk to them. I love a buffet, and we were there anyway so we offered. There was a great deal of coming and going of choristers and clergy between the Education Suite and the Music Department, and we tried to dodge the groups when we seemed to be likely to get in their way. The candidates were eventually asked to play the organ while Michael conducted the choir. I suppose this was not to test their organ playing so much as to see how they interacted with Michael though the mirrors. Then everyone disappeared again. Alan told us he was locking up, but that there was "a nose-bagging session" in the Refectory (I'd never heard that expression before and I loved it). Were we going to it? Yes, we supposed we were! We wandered around, and found the two candidates in the Refectory looking a bit lost. I introduced myself and shook hands and they responded effusively. They were Kris Thomsett and (shall we say for delicacy) A.N. Other. The former had a small Mephisto-phelean beard. There should have been a third candidate but he/she had not turned up. Fancy not turning up for a plum job at Newcastle Cathedral! I didn't feel drawn to either of them, but I knew one of them would be sure to get the job. Aspergers don't make small talk easily, but I did my best. At length Michael appeared with his retinue of parents and children and a few clergy. Roger and I "nose-bagged" then rounded Jessica up to go home.

Naturally the first thing to do when we got home was Google these two hopefuls. There was not a great deal about either, but what we found about A. N. Other left us trembling. Kris Thomsett, on the other hand, seemed OK and looked much nicer without his beard in some photos we saw of him. He was quite young, and probably adopted a beard to give him an air of maturity and gravitas. Jessica told us she and the choir had liked Mr Thomsett best and thought they could work with him. I took the liberty of emailing Michael to that effect, and he expressed himself grateful. We heard a few days later that Mr Thomsett had been appointed. Now we had the whole of the summer holidays to wonder what he was going to be like.

Jessica attended another RSCM Summer Choral Course, this time at Durham. It was uneventful for us as it was only a short way to go to take and collect her, and we quickly got the impression, on the phone, that she was enjoying herself. My only input this year was to give permission by email, in response to an urgent telephone appeal from a leader, for Jessica to go up the Cathedral Tower in a group. I had signed all the usual indemnities and assumed she was covered for anything up to a trip to the moon, but apparently it was not so. I didn't hesitate, but rather her than me! This year Andrew Reid took his eldest daughter Sarah with him, and she and Jessica became great friends.

2015-2016

An email from Michael told us all about the various changes in the staffing. Kris Thomsett was our new Assistant Director of Music, Emily Stolting was the new Music Assistant, and Clare Maclaren was the new Canon for Liturgy and Music. We also had a new Operations Manager called Kate Sussams, but she would be in the offices next door and we should not see very much of her. The offices in Cathedral House were much more comfortable than the Cathedral, and the people who worked in them tended to stay in them. I replied, "So many changes, and so much consequent insecurity. I trust we can rely on you to stay put for at least ten years!" He replied, "Hope so." A rumour has been going round, courtesy of Celia, that as soon as she has left school her parents will go back to France. Who could blame them if they did? Michael started his musical career in Westminster Abbey. Would he really want to end it at Newcastle?

On Wednesday, May 9th, we had a special service to celebrate the Longest Reign. Our Queen had beaten George III and was still going strong. I think she had become the longest reigning monarch in the world. It was certainly worth celebrating. I had asked Michael if Jessica might be a bit late as it was the occasion of her very first Latin lesson and she didn't want to miss it. She might have missed some essential information that would have held her back through the course. Michael was very understanding, and said he was very pleased she was doing Latin! But as it was an important night, I promised to get a taxi as soon as she came out of school. We did, and were not very late. It was a lovely service. The Lord Lieutenant, Lord Mayor and several local mayors, with their mayoresses, graced it with their presence. Yes, I had to agree that this was also of great civic importance. The choir sang superbly (though most of them were too young to fully appreciate what we were celebrating). Kris played the organ, with some super dramatic pieces like the National Anthem and *Crown Imperial* which he wouldn't get the chance to play all that often. He is a brilliant organist. I was glad of this celebration. For 63 years, since I was ten years old, Elizabeth had inspired and encouraged her country and the commonwealth and made a worthy focus for our national pride. She has been a great blessing to us and it is right to thank God for her.

From the sublime to the ridiculous, our next service was dominated by the Great North Run. We had a very small congregation, and the Dean told us that must be why. As I look around the Cathedral on a normal Sunday morning I don't see many people I would identify as runners, but maybe a lot of them had decided to stay at home so as not to get confused in the disrupted traffic. In the middle of the service there was a slow, deafening rumble of massed aircraft just above the roof, and I hoped it was defence rather than attack, but in fact it was the Red Arrows paying a courtesy call in honour of the Run. More comfortable excitement was provided by the news of twin daughters born to the Adigwe family who already had three girls, and the installation of Harriet Watts-Wiliamson as Deputy Head Chorister. Celia, who was 17 today, is not going anywhere at present so we shall have two DHCs. This was presumably to ensure that Harriet, a faithful chorister, would not miss out on a deserved privilege if she left before natural succession. Jessica was watching her chances. She felt she was bound to be next for promotion!

Kris Thomsett seemed to be shaping up well. He left the organ loft door open when he was playing, rather than locking himself in secretly as so many organists do. I am told (in confidence) that when Michael called to him in rehearsals he often shouted back "You what?" which would probably not go down well as Michal is very formal. I also heard (in confidence) that he was a bit bossy and told people off – and once even told my informant that she was dragging! When Kris took his first girls' choir rehearsal there was a very audible sigh from one of the younger girls when the anthem ended. Apparently when they got back to the Song Room Celia immediately asked Kris (in her capacity as DHC) if she could say a few words. She mentioned the sigh and made a few other criticisms of behaviour in a very nice way. Kris thanked her and said he had been going to mention them. It may have been out of order, but she probably taught Kris a valuable lesson which he obviously did not resent. As time went by he seemed to establish very good rapport the girls.

Jessica was very pleased to report that the new singing teacher this year would be Gail Davis, one of the lay clerks. Gail was very popular and would be an encouraging teacher.

Sunday, September 20th, was the CCA AGM after Eucharist. We were told how much money the CCA had raised, and what they were going to do with it. They were going to pay half the cost of the forthcoming trip to Paris! Mind, they warned, they could not afford to do that every year! They could only do it alternate years. We were all supposed to look solemnly grateful. I wished they could think in lower-budget terms, so that the choir could have a modest UK trip every year, visiting our own wonderful cathedrals of which I suspect many of the CCA were largely in ignorance. But there we are. And oh – excitement – there was to be a binge on October 17th when the adults could meet at the Cathedral and have a "good drink"! How the committee ladies' eyes sparkled! But in case anyone had babysitting problems the children could come too and "watch a film somewhere else". Big deal. I wondered who would pay for the good drink? Would it be cocoa? Horlicks? Ovaltine? No. I fear a lot of the CCA were very alcohol minded. We had no wish to go ourselves, but it was nice to think we had something much better happening anyway. That was the evening Jessica was to receive her Silver Award in a ceremony at Durham. I was sad to notice the meeting neither began nor ended with a prayer. As usual, God never got a look in. If it wasn't for printed orders of service and the prayer books I doubt if he often would. I would have preferred Jessica to be at the meeting, but it had been arranged that the choir should rehearse for another hour with Kris. I don't think it's right to leave children out because it's all about them and what they are going to be expected to do.

One Thursday at the beginning of October the choir were required to be at the Cathedral from 1 o'clock. I cannot remember why, and I suppose it must have been a wedding or funeral. It was necessary for me to write to Jessica's school and ask for permission for her to leave at 12, which was graciously granted. A few days later I got an email from Emily Stolting to say that plans had changed and the choir must be there from 12. This would mean asking the school to mess up the plans that had already been made, and I wasn't prepared to do it. We were totally dependent on the good will of the school, and they have always been most helpful, but I was not going to muck them about. I replied to Emily to that effect, politely but firmly. Later, thanks to the complications of technology, I saw an email she sent on to Michael, which I wasn't supposed to see, saying "How should I respond to this?" It seems Michael told her to pass it on to Kris, probably on the principle of "Don't keep a dog and bark yourself". Kris duly phoned me and said it was absolutely vital that Jess should be at the Cathedral for 12. I said "OK, but will you ask the school?" Yes, he certainly would, and he did, and they kindly agreed. I was relieved.

One Monday, after Jessica had been quite ill all weekend with a sore throat among other things, she insisted on going to school (for her first Chamber Choir rehearsal) and choir. After I had made myself cocoa in the Education Suite I went back down and heard the most amazing singing. I didn't recognise it at first because the timbre of the voice was different from Jessica's. However, it was Jessica. She was practising for Rose's *Risen Lord*. She did very well. Michael said, "Oh, you've got a sore throat, haven't you? I forgot. But that was fine!" I was anxious she might lose her voice before she got to the anthem. It was a long service. There were 30 verses to the psalm, then Father Steven read two long lessons: the whole story of Naaman and the whole of Paul's defence before Agrippa. But I could have listened to Father Steven reading for hours. He brought the Bible to life. Later he apologised to the choir, and then to us, for the length of them, but of course they hadn't been *his* choice. Jessica managed to sing her solo very well, and Michael was pleased. He said sometimes a sore throat relaxed the vocal cords and gave you an advantage. Jessica was very chuffed. She went home and resumed being ill. It was not the first or the last time she dragged herself from her sick-bed to sing at the Cathedral.

On October 11th there was a special Evensong service for the installation of Clare Maclaren as Canon for Music and Liturgy. There was a good congregation, including her husband and two grown up children and some of her past flock. My initial impression of her was that we were not going to need a choir any more.

Our next adventure, for which a chaperone was essential, was a trip to Lincoln to hear Bob Chilcott lead a day workshop. It was to be held in the Minster School, and we were pretty sure we knew how to find that! It needed an overnight stop for us to be there in time. We set off immediately Jessica got home from school on Friday, November 6th, and went down by train. We stayed at Lincoln's excellent Premier Inn. It was of course dark when we arrived, and as we looked up the hill we could see the Cathedral floodlit in all its glory. It was a wonderful sight. Later we were to hear that Bob Chilcott, at about the same time and place but from his car, had been similarly enraptured with the view.

I had bought tickets for both of us so that I could stay in a warm, dry building and have whatever coffee was on offer. It turned out to be well worth it. We were among the first arrivals at the Minster School and we presented our tickets. We were asked to take music books from a box. Each was numbered, and we had to sign a list with our name against the number of the book (so if we ran off with the book they would know who had pinched it and could excommunicate us). Coffee would have been welcome but there was none at that point. With permission I tucked our small suitcase into an obscure corner behind a filing cabinet and hoped we should not forget it when we left. Eventually we were invited to go into a large brick-walled hall and arrange ourselves on portable raked seating. Jessica sat at the front and I went to the very back which had a nice black curtain hung behind it for acoustical purposes, visual elegance and imagined security. I would not have liked to be up there at the back without that curtain, although of course if the whole thing had gone over backwards the curtain wouldn't have done anything for us.

The assembled company of RSCM members filled about the front half. Bob Chilcott and his accompanist appeared and made themselves pleasant. Bob told people where he wanted them to sit according to their voice level. I didn't see Jessica again for some time because she was surrounded by tall people. I felt rather embarrassed being at the back. The assembled company couldn't see me, but Bob could, and he must have wondered who I thought I was. Two ladies next to Jessica also wondered. "Who's that up there?" one asked the other. "It's my chaperone," Jessica explained. They no doubt wondered who *she* was. People don't realise how young she is. Later lots of people asked her if she was at university and were surprised she was only 13. There were three young boys there too, who behaved impeccably.

The session began with a warming-up hum. Bob had them humming in four parts and it really sounded lovely. In fact I think I liked that best of all. There were four sessions broken up by coffee, lunch and tea. "Coffee" and "tea" of course meant tea or coffee. I had coffee both times and it was very nice. There were no biscuits, which was perhaps a good thing because biscuit crumbs stick in the throat and are not conducive to good singing. I did not read my Kindle but listened attentively all day to the singing and followed it in my score. Often I could hear Jessica's voice soaring above the other sopranos when they got to a high note. At the first break a middle-aged lady said to her, "I'm glad we're sitting next to you!" by which I suppose they meant she was covering up their imagined inadequacies. At lunchtime we were supposed to have an hour, which is short enough if you have to go out, but in fact it was only 55 minutes. We hurried to the Cathedral where we had a very nice lunch in the Refectory with a few minutes to spare to sight-see. At this point we went our separate ways because I am not as nimble as she is and I knew she would want to see as much as she could and that she could easily find her way back.

At the end of the last session the participants were asked to form a big circle round the piano to sing some of the pieces they had learnt. It was very pleasant to listen to. Afterwards Jessica was lucky enough to have a conversation with Bob that lasted at least a minute. She bought some music at the last minute but forgot to ask him to autograph it, and our taxi for the station was ticking away. I had not forgotten the suitcase! We were both very pleased with the trip. A long way to go, but well worth it.

Michael said he would be happy to start teaching Jessica to play the organ in January. She had just taken her Grade 4 piano and was waiting for the result. She was looking forward to organ lessons. I knew it would increase my chaperoning time, but hey-ho. I was looking forward to listening.

Nobody bothered too much when Michael was away for a few nights in mid-November. Things went much as usual, except for one Evensong when an innocent expression in one of the prayer requests had a possible rude meaning and several of the lay clerks found it impossible to control their urge to giggle. Sadly the Assistant Director of Music also found it difficult. I did not know what the joke was, but I knew Michael would not have descended to such indignity.

Then one Sunday in mid-November the Dean made an announcement before the service began. He said he had "bittersweet news". He had used that expression when he told us Father Kevin was leaving, so I knew someone was leaving, and there were not many old hands left. Yes, it was Michael. He was leaving at the end of January to become Director of Music at Holy Trinity Cathedral, Auckland, New Zealand! His absence last week had been to fly there for interview. I gather he had already told the choristers last thing before they came down from the Song School, and they were all sad. I was very sad, but not much surprised. Now who would teach Jessica to play the organ? Oh well, we should see. Maybe she could take a musical break for a bit. The new chap (or as Jessica points out it might be a woman) could hardly be expected to take up post earlier than May. We could ask Kris, and I thought it would be appropriate, but Jessica was not sure, although she liked him. In the afternoon Michael sent an email out to all the chorister parents in case they had not been at church (as indeed most of them hadn't). We Googled Trinity and it looked super. We also understand they have a brand new organ!

Saturday, December 9th, was a very special day for the Cathedral and Diocese. It was the Enthronement of our new Bishop, Christine Hardman. Like me she had a very nice husband called Roger, but there the similarity ended. The event was for invited ticket-holders only, but when I asked Ellie if there were any spare tickets she gave me one. As they say up here, shy bairns get nowt. Jessica and I got to the Cathedral about 9.50. The bouncers — sorry, welcomers — were assembled in strength at the west end, but I had my ticket and instead of being sent to the naughty corner I got a warm hug from Yvonne Hall. That was a nice start to the day!

I took up a seat at the aisle end of the back pew, in front of a nice warm radiator. I had an hour to wait, but there was plenty of interest going on. Along my half-pew were six orders of service. There would normally be four, so it was obviously a cramming job. Behind me there were several rows of plastic stacking chairs, and more filling the south aisle. The Dean gave out that bored children (there were a few) might go and play in St. Margaret's Chapel, but they couldn't have done because there was no access. They would have had to push past six tightly packed people, some of whom might not have been amused. By the time we started at 11 the place was jam-packed. I was lucky to be there!

The service proceeded cheerfully. The clergy and all the important people (a huge number) processed with great dignity. A children's choir from the Church of England Academy sang twice, and there was some dancing to inspire us in the prayers of intercession, which I strongly disapproved of because dancing is a performance art and therefore a distraction and not an aid to worship. It was chaste and dull, but inappropriate.

The new Bishop Christine gave the traditional three raps on the outside of the west door and was admitted and duly installed. I hoped someone had dusted the inside of the carved canopy over her throne. It must have been full of spiders.

The whole event had been choreographed by Canon Clare with the aid of the Music Department. It would have been challenging enough for anyone, but she was so new. She did brilliantly. The whole event, as far as I could see, went off without a hitch. And of course the choir sang beautifully!

On a cold winter's day it was necessary to refresh people before sending them out to freeze, and that was quite a problem. I already knew, from an earlier loo visit, what to expect. Tables in the Eastern Chapels and the side aisles were loaded with glasses of warm, spiced fruit juice and hundreds of little brown paper carriers with "locally produced" goodies. Some of them were labelled as being gluten-free! The idea was that everyone had a picnic, either taking it away or sitting in a warm pew. I had not intended to take part in that. I knew the choristers were going to be fed, and I had errands to do.

As I waited to leave I could see through the open west door that the rain had turned briefly to snow. I heard a lady behind me, who would either be a clergywoman or a parish representative, snarl to her companion, "It's snowing! Oh my God!" I supposed at a later stage in the year she would be heard heartily singing "*He sends the snow in winter …* " without a thought. I saw some posh cars waiting and I think they were to spirit the Bishop and her retinue to a more elegant lunch. I don't think she had a paper bag.

I walked up to T. J. Hughes and had an excellent turkey lunch, then I went to Poundworld to see if I could get sachets of cocoa powder, paper cups, biscuits etc, to make hot chocolate for the choir when they came back later from singing carols at the Metro station. There were not many and I only managed to get thirty sachets, and hoped that would be enough. In the event it was. I also bought two £1 umbrellas for me and Jessica because we had not taken any with us.

Back at the Cathedral there were still lots of paper bags so I helped myself to one, but the warm spiced fruit juice had been cleared away. I went up to the Thomlinson Room as the choir were leaving, wearing only their robes, and I asked Michael if umbrellas were allowed. Yes, he said. I gave Jessica the second one as well, as I was not going to need it, to lend to someone else, and she lent it to Rachel. Then I sat and enjoyed myself while I waited for them to come back. I washed up all the mess in the little kitchenette cupboard, as no one ever cleaned it up but just piled dirty crockery on top of more. I was quite proud of it when I'd done. Why is other people's washing-up always so much more exciting than one's own?

The picnic bag contained a pie, a cupcake, a large muffin, a Satsuma and a bottle of Fentiman's fruit pop. I tucked in to it as I waited, but it was rather disappointing. The pie was awful. It was supposed to be cheese and potato and I suppose it was, but it had no perceptible onion in and it was quite tasteless. I noticed that there were several half-pies in the bin. Jessica later told me hers had gone in the bin too. I was not surprised, but I was sad to see that many of them had also left most of their Fentiman's pop which was so delicious and good. The muffin was too sweet, and I did not get a cupcake at all. Happily I had taken lots of biscuits!

The snow did not last long but the choir still got a bit wet and cold and were glad of the hot chocolate. Elisabeth and Michael, separately, were very kind about it. Roger had joined them and shaken a bucket. It had been a great day for the choir, and we now had a Bishop to look after us again. It was too soon to say if this was Clare's finest hour, but it had been a triumph.

Christmas came and went as we now expect it to do – without much variation year on year. The candlelight concert in the Castle Keep was more financially ambitious this year in that there were two consecutive concerts, without interval or refreshments. The first audience were tipped out without ceremony to make way for the second one. Michael announced politely that if we very badly wanted to keep our programmes we could, but it would be appreciated if we left them for the next person who sat in our seat. I kept mine. Goodness, I had paid a lot for it!

I remember on the Sunday before Christmas Canon Clare was the president at Eucharist. She addressed us briefly from the lectern before the service began, as was common. "Good morning!" she said, with a bright smile. Silence. The congregation was used to this weekly greeting, and ignored it. "You can say good morning to me, if you like!" said Clare. A few people did. We did, because we are Methodists and use to such cheerful exchanges. I think the Church of England regard enthusiasm as being in questionable taste.

On Monday 21st the choir went to Sainsbury's again to sing carols, and again I chaperoned from the comfort of the gallery café. At the beginning there was a slight hiatus as the manager decided that a large, prominent display of a certain kind of potato crisp, which the choir had been singing in front of, should be moved. This was not, I think, as a courtesy to the choir, but in order that the crisps display should not be obscured. Goodness, if Sainsbury's did not sell the projected amount of crisps, what would their shareholders say? It was a lovely experience listening, and many of the shoppers said so as they left. Jessica had several solos, but I couldn't often hear well enough to know it was her. People were very generous as they passed the buckets. They probably thought it was for a good cause. At the end the buckets contained £882.51, €10 and a Duracell battery! On the following Wednesday the choir sang there again. After another much appreciated performance the buckets held £797. Megan Kelly's dad, Mike, gave us a lift back to the Cathedral. I was expecting to have to get a taxi, so I told Mike I would put my taxi money in one of the buckets, and he seemed pleased.

This year Father Steven had recruited more people to help with the tableaux around the church at the Crib Service. The youngest "volunteer" was a real baby boy, a few months old, taking the role of Baby Jesus. He smiled at us! Again the "heavenly choir" of the younger girl choristers, who we could not see from the Eastern Chapels, sounded eerily beautiful. Then hot drinks and mince pies in the Refectory to reward us all for turning up. Poor Father Steven was very ill with a terrible cold and its complications. But he told me he was not as ill as he had been the day before when he had to conduct a communion service, with a congregation of one, and wondered if he would get through it to the end. Clearly it was God's intention that he should, and he did. He should have been in bed, but priests don't go off sick at Christmas or they would be very unpopular with their colleagues. I gave him some Werther candies, and they must have done him good because he survived.

Over Christmas our new Bishop was prominent. She was involved in all the services and took the Christmas Day Eucharist entirely, both preaching and presiding. She had her children and grandchildren with her, and we understood they were all staying with her. She would have had her own turkey to cook, but she didn't let it get in the way of the day job. She was quite a good preacher, though I can't remember what she said. Now, apart from a few essential services held in St George's Chapel, the clergy – and the staff – could have a rest. Certainly the choir could. They had worked very hard, and they deserved a holiday.

At some point, probably at Durham in the summer, Jessica had become involved with a choir called Northern Cathedral Singers which was a branch of RSCM. It involved two winter rehearsals at a place called Gildersome which I had never heard of before (or since), then day events at about half a dozen or so cathedrals between Peterborough and Durham where they would sing Evensong. At first it seemed a bit challenging, but we decided it was all part of life's rich tapestry and we must go along with it. I exchanged letters with one David Rothwell who was the organiser.

Our first date was at Gildersome on Saturday, January 9th. I looked it up in the atlas, and on Google. I wondered, but didn't like to ask, what its attraction was. It was remote (to more people than me) and seemed to have no shops or cafes or anywhere a chaperone might amuse herself. I just hoped the good people of the church (St Peter's) would tolerate me camping out on them all day.

We got up at 5 and took a taxi to Newcastle Central Station to catch a train to York at 7. We were in good time and kept warm in the Pumpkin Café till our train was ready. At York we caught the Blackpool train to Leeds, then got a taxi to Gildersome. The driver knew Gildersome well, but he naturally didn't know St Peter's. I have discovered that taxi drivers are not too hot on finding churches.

We were about one minute late, and the event had already begun which was good. A kind lady welcomed Jessica and registered her. Pastoral assistants would be taking care of everyone, on the assumption that their parents were bunking off. I was told I was very welcome to stay and make myself comfy. Jessica was shown to the hall where Jonathan Eyre was training the girls (about twelve of them) and doing warming-up exercises.

Andrew Reid was training the boys (I think nine) in the sanctuary. Between the two areas was a banana-shaped foyer with three or four tables and chairs and some easy chairs. The kind lady showed me a little kitchen when I could make myself tea or coffee whenever I wanted. That was nice!

St Peter's is a beautiful modern church, built to replace one that burnt down (I think). Outside at the back was a nice lawn with a bit of the original church on it as a memorial. The sanctuary has lots of big windows and is accordingly very bright and cheerful. From the notice boards I got the impression that the church was evangelical with a strong social conscience. I knew Jessica would not want me listening to her, but I thought Andrew might not mind me slipping in and sitting at the back to listen to the boys. I had taken knitting to pass the time. Three mothers and a couple of small children had set up a rather exclusive camp at one of the foyer tables, and I took over another. I got stuck into a crossword, which is another way I like to pass the time. David Rothwell came and had a chat. I made coffee from time to time, using my own decaf sachets. There was a little saucer for donations. When it was about to be the lunch break I made up Jessica's Pot Noodle and unpacked her drinks and other bits. She brought a new friend and joined me. At one point Jonathan and Andrew walked through. Jonathan patted Jessica on the head and said "Superstar!" which surprised me. Apparently Andrew had called her that. Jonathan seemed pleased with Jessica and he gave her a substantial solo to sing at York Minster on May Day. Wow!

During the day I had about five cups of coffee and some Cuppasoup. There were some nice biscuits too. At the end when I was washing my last cup a little boy came into the kitchen and asked shyly if I knew who the biscuits were for, and did I think he could have one? I said I was just a visitor like him, but I was quite sure they were there to be eaten and whoever put them there would be delighted for him to have as many as he liked. I phoned for a taxi to meet us and we had a good trip home, catching an earlier train at Leeds which gave us a longer period to wait at York but I think I like York better. Our train went to Edinburgh and happily for us it stopped at Morpeth. It had been a good day. Certainly it had been expensive, but that is Jessica's life now and we want to make it as comfortable as we can, both for her and for us.

One night in January Andrew Robinson was at Evensong with what might have been either a large briefcase or a small suitcase. I wondered if he had come for an interview, forgetting that nothing happens that quickly. Afterwards Clare was chatting to him. As I passed them I said, "I hope I can guess why you're here!" They looked puzzled, then Clare said "Do you mean – are you thinking about the succession?" I said yes. She said "Oh, that would be lovely!" and Andrew said "Well, it *had* crossed my mind!" Having opened my mouth and put my foot in it I scuttled off.

About now we had an email from Emily to tell us about a surprise party the CCA was arranging after Evensong on the 21st to say goodbye to Michael. It would be fab, she said, if we could all bring food, and the CCA would provide wine and balloons (good grief). Michael is being said goodbye to officially on Sunday 24th, and that will be good enough for us. Jessica has school the next morning and there was no question of us staying for parties. Today a card came in the post from the CCA asking us all to creep into the Refectory before 6 on the night, using the carpark side door. After Evensong the choir would process as usual, but instead of going into the song school they will carry on processing to the Refectory. When Michael followed them into the Refectory "we will all jump out and yell 'surprise!'". It all sounded very silly and undignified to me. Why should we creep? Why would we jump out – and out of what? And why would we yell? I couldn't help thinking Michael would have been happier if all the partygoers had attended Evensong instead.

One night about then Clare was leaving the vestry to go home after Evensong and found a load of parents waiting at the bottom of the stairs for their children. She wanted to make us feel more at home and comfortable and wondered if we would like to have some place where we could sit and make coffee and chat. Where could it be? Emily was present and said there was a kitchenette in the Thomlinson Room and she could buy in coffee and biscuits. Wonderful, said Clare. No one said "We just want to get our kids and go home!" though I think they all did. And the vergers would not have liked the idea at all – they wanted to lock up and go home. Nothing came of it.

Two weeks after our Gildersome trip we had to go again. This was when the choir prepared all the music they would sing at Cathedrals during the following year, so it was important. I only wished it was on the main London-Edinburgh railway line! This time I found another little kitchen, a few yards from the first one – why did they have two? Today a nice lady from the church was sitting on duty behind a little counter, and she would make our drinks. She sat there all day. As I had my own decaf in sachets she let me do my own, and at lunchtime she kindly let me go in and make Jessica's Pot Noodle. It was much busier today because the adult singers were there too. I spent more time sitting in the church listening to the boys. Jessica practised her solo for York, and the adults clapped her enthusiastically which was very encouraging. Again it was a pleasant day, but I was glad I wouldn't have to go again for a year. It was such a long way to go. Goodness, I didn't realise what was coming to me!

On Sunday January 24th we had our official farewell to Michael. Clare preached, and four choristers were installed. Michael presented Celia and Jessica to the Dean and requested that they be made Head Chorister and Deputy Head Chorister respectively. The Dean gave them some wise words and asked them to promise something, which I think they would both take very seriously, and he hung their new medal ribbons round their necks – Celia's yellow and Jessica's green. For Jessica this was almost the culmination of her dreams – now she knew she would graduate to being Head Chorister in the not too distant future. We were so happy for her. We felt sure she and Celia would make a good team, and they did.

Afterwards, as the choristers left the song school, I am told Michael stood at the door to shake hands and say goodbye to each one personally. When it was Jessica's turn she said, "Do you do hugs?" and Michael said "Oh, go on then!" and she hugged him. I dare say he would like that. In the south transept the congregation, now imbibing coffee with wine and nibbles, were entertained to a plainsong rendering by the lay clerks of what John Lewis called Psalm 151, which was all about Michael. It was very entertaining. Presentations were made, and nice things said by the Dean and others. It was, in the Dean's words, bittersweet, especially for Jessica for whom Michael had been a guide and mentor for over three years.

There were quite a few more people than usual at Evensong which was not surprising. Kris played *Pomp and Circumstance* as a recessional. In the hallway at the end a lot of parents were hugging Michael, but we left because Jessica had done her hugging and we would see Michael again on Wednesday when he had promised to give Jessica one organ lesson, so that in years to come she could say he was her first organ teacher. We bumped into Michael Haynes later and he said "It's the end of an era!" Yes, it was. What would happen now?

It was perhaps not our business, but we wondered what would happen to Michael's family. It had all happened so quickly. Elisabeth would naturally go with Michael, but not immediately because someone had to wind up their affairs here and sell their house. Celia was the only daughter who was under age, and she was to be looked after by one of her sisters. I think we all worried for them. I remarked to Elisabeth on one occasion, "It's supposed to be children who leave home, not parents!" She said her eldest daughter had said exactly the same thing. I sympathised because our own children had to be transplanted at a tender age to fit in with their father's career, but New Zealand was such a long way away!

The following Wednesday Jessica met Michael for her lesson. He was wearing casual clothes and glasses instead of his normal contact lenses. He was pleased to see her. We had arranged for him to give her an hour, and I went off to sit and read in the choir stalls. They spent a lot of time examining the organ's guts, especially the main organ which was an unknown world. They looked at the console and talked about stops and pedals and such. Jessica found it all fascinating. At the end of the hour I asked Michael how much it was, and he said oh, nothing. Yes, he was quite sure. I asked when he was leaving and he said as soon as his visa came. I said I hoped it would never come, and he said "Yes ... " as if he had got slightly cold feet. Into the euphoria would have been creeping the sad realisation that, geographically at least, he was breaking up his family for ever.

Sunday 31st was Candlemas, and Jessica had Evensong only. Clare blessed a lot of little candles in glass holders and invited us to go up and receive one with a prayer card. I didn't because I don't do gimmicks. Kris was now in charge of the choir but was very low key. They did well. At the end of the service we had a farewell to Bella who was being decommissioned as Head Chorister. The Dean got quite emotional and hugged her (well, she is his daughter). Jessica and Bella had an emotional parting too, though they knew it wasn't goodbye for ever. But one way and another it was the end of an era.

At Monday Evensong I was a third of the congregation. There were 13 girl choristers but only Jess and Celia were singing with any real power. The rest were rather like little mice, but they did bravely. In the prayers of intercession Clare prayed "for elderly people: for our parents and grandparents and those who have looked after us and now have to look after each other in their old age and find it a struggle, and might feel lonely and forgotten." I was afraid the choristers would look at me, so I kept my eyes averted.

In the weeks ahead we had quite a few visiting organists come to help out so that Kris could train the choristers. Michael Haynes was often around, and sometimes Andrew Robinson came. The Music Department seemed to continue seamlessly. Kris was very young and he had only recently taken up his post as Assistant Director of Music, but he rose to the challenge bravely. He sometimes looked as if he was having a little difficulty keeping a serious composure, but he managed.

On Saturday February 6th we were off to Hexham again for what had become known as Hadrian Three Choirs Festival. It began at 2pm, which was more sensible. We were early so we had a browse in the Abbey Gift Shop, which is a lovely place to be "just looking" but a very expensive place to be buying. I don't think we bought anything. I left Jessica when other Newcastle people began to arrive, and went off to seek my fortune. The Abbey Café was full and very busy, and it was now raining, so I went to explore a little place I had often seen, called Number 4 The Deli Café. It was a former fish shop opposite the Abbey, which had been turned into a little delicatessen downstairs and a tiny café upstairs.

They had about four tables, and the waitresses had to run up and down the winding stairs with everything. I had a sufficiently substantial snack to entitle me to sit and read till 3.30 when I went back to the Abbey Café. Now they had tables free and I had a scone and hot chocolate and read till they closed, then I went to sit in the nave to listen to the choirs rehearsing. At first I sat where they (especially Jessica) couldn't see me, but later moved to a better seat. The concert was charmingly presided over by Canon Dagmar Winter, and the choirs sang beautifully.

I often have a look at the memorial slabs in the Abbey, and one on the south wall of the quire always catches my attention. It says,

> *"God, thou art love. I build my faith on that.*
> *It were too strange that I should doubt thy love."*

I believe it comes from Robert Browning. It is my sentiment exactly. Afterwards Mike Kelly was kind enough to offer us a lift back to Morpeth, and we gratefully accepted.

Next morning Jessica had had hardly had enough sleep to be ready for another busy Sunday, but she coped. Just before Eucharist Clare went to the lectern and told the assembling congregation that she was not sure if we knew one of the hymns we were going to sing, and she wanted to teach it to us. First she sang it herself, very powerfully, then we had to sing it back bit by bit. It wasn't a very attractive tune and it wasn't easy to learn, and if anyone had wanted to indulge in silent prayer they'd had it. I think by and large people are happier singing hymns they already know. New hymns become familiar from hearing them, perhaps, on Songs of Praise or similar programmes, and thinking "That's nice!" Personally I was glad when the lesson was over. Jessica had several solo parts today, mostly quite short. It was easy to tell when she was singing as Celia was not there today, and there is no one else who could be confused with Jessica now. We are told Michael flew off to New Zealand today, hence Celia's absence.

Today was the occasion of one of the bring-and-share lunches the Dean had instituted. It was scheduled to begin at 12.30, and before then we either had to get lost or make our coffee last for an hour. I had forgotten the other big occasion of the day: the CCA meeting. Megan came and asked me to show her dad where it was to be held. Thanks for the reminder, Megan. I should hate to miss a CCA meeting.

Upstairs in the Education Suite a very few chairs had been arranged. For the next fifteen minutes someone had to keep jumping up to find a chair for late comers, one after another. It was very disruptive. The Dean introduced the meeting in the absence of the Director of Music who by default was always the chairman. He told us that the advert for the new Director would be in the *Church Times* this week and that the interviews would take place on Wednesday and Thursday March 16 and 17. A choir would be needed on the Wednesday afternoon for the candidates to practice on, so please would as many as possible of us send our children. He told us that three of the six members of the committee had come to the end of their term of office. He handed over to one of the ladies who ran through the things that the committee had done, were currently doing and would be doing. Meanwhile the sounds of merry laughter and general mingling were floating up from the Refectory below us where the lunchers were assembling. I wondered if Roger was there as he had not appeared and had probably forgotten. Since I had forgotten myself I naturally couldn't remind him.

When it was mentioned that one of the regular activities had been a pooled lunch at Stoddarts', the Dean said that we were welcome to use the Deanery next time. That was greatly appreciated. Clare came in and stood at the back. Whether any gentleman stood up and offered her a chair I don't remember, but I dare say she would have preferred to stand. At some point, the CCA lady having been bragging about how they had provided new cassocks for the little kids, I asked if they could buy some new blazers. I knew one senior chorister, whose name I did not mention, had been given a huge blazer that she found embarrassing to wear. Clare's voice from the back said that was being dealt with – she and Emily were dealing with it. Then we discussed the vexed question about jolly coffee gatherings while we waited for our kids. It had been reported that there were safeguarding issues with the idea of using the Thomlinson Room. Another member of the committee said that problem could surely be solved by not letting the children go into the Thomlinson Room. I exploded that that was the choir's special room and they should not be turned out of it, and again Clare said she was looking into it (so shut up Christine). Another of her ideas is that we should use the Vestry. That would make life very difficult for the vergers who are anxious to lock up, and the locking up is done from the Vestry. Anyway the Vestry, while used by all sorts of people, is still basically a clergy preserve and should not be invaded by – I was going to say the ungodly but that would not be polite – people whose interest in the Cathedral does not extend to attending services. And who would be responsible for clearing up any cups, tidying the mess away and seeing everybody out? It seemed to be agreed at the end that the present committee would email us all, asking who would like to be on the committee and who would like to do various jobs from time to time without being on the committee. The Dean brought the meeting to a close but did not say a prayer. The whole meeting proceeded, as usual, without God's blessing being invoked.

Those of us who were staying for lunch repaired to the Refectory where people were sitting scoffing. I don't know if anyone had said grace. I suspect they would have, because although the Dean was upstairs there were other dog-collars there who were well qualified to speak to God on our behalf. Roger was sitting on a settee at the far end, by himself. He had decided to do that so I would easily spot him. I think he had been getting worried about me. The serving table, much smaller than usual, looked as if the vultures had finished with it. Having contributed £15 worth of nosh I was a bit peeved at getting very little to eat. I decided that if this clash of activities ever happened again I would skip the CCA meeting and just go to the lunch. I think Jessica, when she arrived, was the only chorister who came.

Before we left I had a word with Clare who was not busy at that moment, and said I thought the choir parents did not want a coffee gathering. I was always among the first to be waiting and I was quite happy and most of the other parents didn't arrive till just before the children came out and then they wanted to get off home. She didn't like it, I think, and said a touch frostily that she was glad of the feedback but she would make further enquiries and discuss it with people.

In mid-February we had another two-day Sing4Joy. As we went in to the first one Andrew Robinson left his station behind a reception table and came to meet me and warmly shook my hand! I spent the first half of the morning reading in the Lit&Phil, and went back to the Cathedral in good time for a Lenten Talk by Father Steven about the Rule of St Benedict. However, before the talk began I had a rather embarrassing experience.

I went to the Ladies, and selected one of the three cubicles which happened to have a baby-changing table and hand-basin. After I had been communing with Nature for barely three or four minutes there came a tap on the door. I couldn't believe anyone was knocking for me. I said "Yes?" and it stopped. A few seconds later it started again, persistently and unmistakeably. "YES??" I responded. A crabby female voice said "Are you alright in there?" Yes, I said, I was. "Only you've been in there a long while!" said the voice accusingly. I was staggered, and said "So?" The voice went on, "There are other people waiting!" Well, I didn't believe that at all. The place had been deserted when I went in, and I had only heard one other person come in briefly. I had not heard any voices or discussion about my supposedly protracted occupancy. I repeated that I was alright, and continued my communion with Nature for another couple of minutes as a matter of principle. When I came out there was a woman drying her hands. "Was that you knocking on my door?" I asked her. No, she said, it wasn't her. It was one of the vergers, she thought. They had worried because I had been in there a long time. I made no further comment, and left. There are no female vergers, and I suppose the woman I heard had been one of the café staff. But why? Who had fetched her? I was quite put out. I knew some of the staff, and in particular some of the café staff, have a down on homeless people who often use the Cathedral loos for drug-taking, and that cubicle, because of its extra facilities, is a mecca for them. Anyway, I felt offended. It was getting on time for the talk I had come to hear, so I did not waste time going to the café to demand to know who had harassed me.

I spent the afternoon in the Lit&Phil again, then when I went back at 3.40 the children were singing round the font. The café was now closed so I sat and read in the nave. Eventually Clare brought me an order of service and said we should begin in the chancel, then move to the crossing, and end up at the font. What larks! It was quite a nice little service, ending at 4.30. Clare led it, and very well. The children, or some of them, had made bread buns during the afternoon, and they were passed round, still warm. Clare encouraged us all to break our bread, and – oh my goodness – there was something inside! Rather like a fortune cookie, each roll had a little slip of paper baked into it with a text on about Jesus being the bread of life (in a modern translation). I did not break mine but slipped it into a clean pocket of my shoulder bag to give to some hungry person on my way through town. In the event we did not see any hungry people. That is, unless they are overtly begging by sitting on the ground muttering "Have you got any spare change?" they could be starving to death and I would never know. It's just not socially acceptable to say to a stranger, "Hello, you look as if you could do with a bread bun!"

Next day, the second day of Sing4Joy, I started off with a cup of decent coffee in the Lantern but it did not have a welcoming feel. I went to the Lit&Phil and had a very pleasant day reading there, breaking off for a lunch visit and returning. I can thoroughly recommend the Lit&Phil to anyone who likes a quiet retreat from the world with a vast choice of worthy literature. It is not an officially silent library, but it is generally quiet except for trains rumbling past, the comforting ticking of a well-seasoned clock and the occasional clink of a teaspoon against a coffee cup.

Back in the Cathedral I waited for the service of Evensong which Sing4Joy were doing. They did it very well. After the recessional the choir and clergy reassembled in the Quire for a presentation of certificates. For some reason this was done without any clapping, probably because parents were so busy taking photos on their mobile phones. Andrew took lots of official photos and I thought he ought to be on them too so I whispered to Clare who took over his camera

Just as Evensong was due to begin a black man in a huge wheelchair came in to the choir crossing with a lady helper. They stayed put, just inside the gate. He was totally shrouded in black covers below his neck, and I guessed it was Clarence Adoo who, in my pre-grandmother days, I heard play the trumpet many times when I was a regular patron of the Northern Sinfonia. Poor Clarence had had a terrible accident as he drove down to his brother's wedding in 1995, and had as a result been severely paralysed. I had not seen or heard of him for years, and I was so glad to see him. I had a very brief chat with him. He told me he sometimes still played with the Sinfonia at The Sage because he had been made an electronic trumpet that he could play. Last time I heard of him some students were trying to design such an instrument, but had not been successful. Obviously they pegged away at it till they were. Clarence is a hero who, with determination and a little help from his friends, has triumphed over adversity and become an example to all of us. It was such a joy to see him. You meet the nicest people in cathedrals!

The children had been given lunch and presumably some cake in the afternoon break because there was quite a lot of it left. I saw Gordon tucking into a piece of sly-cake which he recommended me to go and get. I chose a piece of chocolate cake which was very nice, but later, when there was a general appeal issued to go and eat it up, I helped myself to some sly-cake and it was very good indeed. I am not normally a cake person. I can only suppose the children did not have enough time to do justice to it. Jessica had enjoyed these Sing4Joy days and we felt so grateful to Andrew for organising them.

On Saturday, February 20th, we had the first cathedral day of the NCS year. It was at Chester. East-west travel in the UK, by road or rail, is always more tedious that north-south, and we decided that in order to be able to do the trip in the day we would have to make generous use of taxis. I got up at 5 and woke Jessica at 5.20. Our taxi driver, who we had not met before, reeled off a list of vital essentials his passengers might have forgotten – passports, tickets, wallet, phone, etc. I didn't need passports, but we had everything else. After a few hundred yards I realised I had only got my reading glasses with me. Oh dear! He asked if he should go back, but I decided against it. I suggested he added "specs" to his checklist, and he said he would. I felt pretty sure my main need all day would be reading glasses and that I would be OK without my distance specs. If I couldn't see from one end of the Cathedral to the other, well, tough.

On Newcastle Central Station, in the portico, was an upright piano with a big notice saying "Play a tune for the Toon!" This was the first time I had seen a piano on a station, though they were to become popular. This one had been given by the Rotary Club. I thought it was a wonderful idea and we both had a brief tinkle.

We caught a train which took three hours. It was a pleasant, clean train, but had no buffet or trolley service. I passed the trip doing crosswords and Jessica did whatever choristers do on their iPhones. I was forced to overhear some pretty tedious conversations among nearby passengers, the main part of which seemed to consist of "Jer know wodda mean?" It was hard to shut them out. The main theme seemed to be alcohol – who had drunk how much of what, and where, and what effect it had had. I don't think anyone was bragging. I felt it was likely to be their main interest in life. At Lime Street we got a taxi to Chester. There were trains, but no time to travel on them. We knew we were going to be a few minutes late so Jessica texted David Rothwell. I was beginning to realise that iPhones do have their uses.

In Chester we followed the obvious path round the Cathedral. It seemed a long way round, especially as several doors were blocked by the scaffolding of ongoing work. We passed an extremely ugly edifice that looked like a grey slate twisted windmill with no sails. I later learnt it was a modern bell tower. Eventually we came to the main entrance and were funnelled in to a visitor centre. Some young men told us that entry was free but they would be very grateful for a donation of at least £3. It would have been a brave visitor who went any further without coughing up. I have developed a strategy for this. If I am forced to pay entry money, in whatever guise, that is all they will get off me. If I get in "free", they will get a decent donation when I leave, most likely considerably more than they would have asked for. The young men (who looked as if they would make excellent bouncers) showed us the way to the Song School where David met us and told me the door code number in case I should need it. Bye-bye Jessica! Have a nice day!

I started my day of waiting with a visit to the refectory where I found the only visible radiator and sat near it. I had a cup of hot chocolate and a sausage roll (it was six hours since breakfast!) and read my Kindle. I had a brief look in the gift shop then went out to look at The Rows, Chester's main tourist attraction (apart from the fact that a short walk brings you to a boundary where you can stand with one foot in England and one in Wales). I wasn't very impressed because whereas when I was last there in 1959 there were lots of interesting boutiques, now they are mainly High Street chain stores and you could be anywhere. As I walked in the town the rain fell thickly but not fast, and I was able to keep dry with judicious walking, but I was delighted to see a street stall selling cheap umbrellas. I saw few eateries, and those I saw were full. I went to M&S café but there was a long queue so I came out. I don't do queues if I can help it, do you? I saw a taxi and asked the driver for a card so I would know where to ring when I wanted one later.

I went back to the Cathedral where the refectory was also full, but as time went on their queue diminished and I was able to have lunch. There wasn't a lot of choice now, but enough. Soup, pasta salad (I hate cold pasta), pear tart and hot chocolate. I browsed the large and well-stocked gift shop again and bought a book I thought Jessica would like. I wandered round the Cathedral and noticed that they did not have down-and-outs dropping in as we do. I suppose it was because to get to the church part on a weekday you have to go through the visitor centre. That would not appeal. And they have nice chairs that the bottoms of the Great Unwashed would perhaps not be welcome to sit on. A pity. The Cathedral is even more central to the city than we are in Newcastle, and there must be many who would be glad of the peace, warmth and shelter it might offer. A Lego model was in progress, and I paid £1 to lay a brick. It wasn't as pretty as the one at Durham. I got a sticker, but at some point it fell off my coat and got lost.

When it was time for the choir's dress rehearsal, so to speak, I went to sit in the Quire but was prevented by stout red ropes. Barbed wire could not have made a clearer statement. I spoke to a floating cleric about it, but he said it was nothing to do with him and a verger might be able to tell me why it was done. I asked a verger, and he said it wasn't anything to do with him either (except that he was putting the ropes up) and he was simply acting on orders. I wasn't rude, you must understand. I knew fine well it wasn't the fault of anyone I could see. Once I saw a black-clad cleric firmly locking a wrought iron gate against a tourist. I was going to ask him if he was St Peter or just one of his apprentices, but I couldn't catch up with him before he disappeared. I sat on the front row of the nave and chatted briefly to another choir mum, but after a bit I felt I must walk around because I was cold. I asked a verger if there was a warmer place I could go, such as a radiator, but he said the church had underfloor heating and if I hadn't got shoes on I would probably feel it. Well, I had and I couldn't. Maybe if I had taken my pants off and sat on the floor I would have felt it, but you just don't do these things, do you? It set me thinking. The radiators in Newcastle Cathedral are a source of great comfort to the tramps who come in to get warm. Shall we lose our welcoming warmth when we have our own underfloor heating? Where will Eddie dry his sleeping bag?

Eventually the time came for Evensong and the ropes were removed so that the congregation (mostly choir parents) could assemble in the Quire. Jonathan Eyre who was conducting as usual, has recently been appointed Assistant Director of Music at Chester Cathedral (Chester's answer to Kris Thomsett). It was a nice enough service. Afterwards I went up to the Song School to collect my chorister. It was a beautiful suite with lots of little rooms and huge cupboards – very luxurious. Jessica took a long time changing and saying goodbye to her new friends, but the Cathedral was emptying, the shop had closed and we were clearly all surplus to requirements. She phoned for a taxi to take us to Chester Station. We were no longer in a hurry and a taxi to Lime Street seemed quite unnecessary. When we got on the train we expected to have a shortish run to Liverpool, but we seemed to stop at dozens of places I had never heard of (and they had probably never heard of me either). It was dark outside, and I did not realise we were coming into the underground section of the Liverpool Metro. When we finally got out we were in the bowels of the earth. We had to go up a very long escalator which scared me, and then after walking along a tunnel for a while we had to go up another, not quite so long but still long enough to give me the heebie-jeebies. Then at last we were out in the relative friendliness of Lime Street station. It was only relative. I don't like Lime Street at all. I would have expected it to be Victorian, but it was like a vast Meccano hangar.

We had to wait quite a long time for our train which left at 7.25, but as we were getting on it a tannoy voice was telling us loudly that there were certain disadvantages to boarding – the only one that I clearly heard being that there were no toilets. Well, I didn't want to ride for three hours with no loo, so we got off. This was a mistake. There was another train to York about 8, but that was cancelled. The first one for us, which involved changing at York, left about 8.20 and we should not get to Newcastle till after midnight. I began to wish we had stayed the night. Jessica wanted us to ring Roger, but I said don't ring him till we are on a train or he will worry about us and there is nothing he can do. In the event, when we were quite sure we were about to get on our train, we rang him and told him our situation. He urged me to get a taxi if I could, but that was a bit premature. Our train to York was OK, and we arrived with plenty of time to look for our Newcastle train. York station was very unsavoury with lots of inebriated lads and girls waiting to carry on partying in Newcastle. A couple of mixed police officers kept an eye on them. The kids were as annoying as they could be without actually committing any offence. They knew there was little the police could do. Jessica and I moved well down the platform to where more reasonable travellers were waiting. Our train came to time, and we had a decent trip to Newcastle. I phoned LA Taxis to ask them to meet us at Newcastle, but they said they had no cars for 35 minutes. We were lucky in that we were able to get off the train quickly and scoot out through the foyer to the front of the taxi rank, and soon we were home. All was well, except for the late hour. It had been a good day, but I hoped we would not have to go to Chester again because it is too far. But we were safe. Thanks be to God for journeying mercies. Had it been worth going so far and spending such a long day to sing Evensong in Chester Cathedral? Definitely!

On the first Saturday in March the RSCM were hosting a John Rutter workshop day in Durham. We heard about it from their quarterly magazine, and Jessica was very keen to go. It was held at Elvet Methodist Church. As with the Bob Chilcott day I bought a ticket for myself in order to keep warm and have coffee. I did not plan to sing because I only croak and the RSCM doesn't cater for frogs. We went to Durham on the bus and got there in very good time. It was cold, and we were glad to find the day began with coffee and biscuits. Michael Graves was registering people, and seeing him in an unfamiliar setting I had to ask him where I knew him from! John Rutter is about three years younger than me, but in much better fettle. He was very athletic in his conducting. He has a lively sense of humour and it was very entertaining to listen to him. I sat at the back and did not try to sing but I thoroughly enjoyed listening to the others singing. At lunchtime we went to the Café Continental and planned to have a good dinner, but as the service was slow we did not have time for pudding. Jessica went back on her own while I went to the shops to buy a jumper to keep me a bit warmer. The Edinburgh Woollen Mill obliged, though the jumper was only cotton. By now little flakes of hard snow were falling, so I was very glad to have the jumper. I couldn't find anywhere to change into it till I got back to the church, but then it made me feel a lot warmer. I spent the next session sitting reading in the hall where I looked at the music that had been set out for sale to see if I could afford to give Jessica a free choice. Yes, I just could. At the coffee break she said she didn't really want any music, but she would like to have some so she could ask John to autograph it. She chose *For the Beauty of the Earth* which was sentimental to her because it was the anthem when she first sang with the Newcastle choir. In the third session we all (except me of course) sang the Hallelujah Chorus which was very inspiring. Jessica was really pleased with her day and it was well worth the trip. It's nice, when children are singing, for them to be able to picture the composer, and she was very glad to have met this one.

Next day the girls were doing Eucharist and were doubtless looking forward to a free afternoon and evening. Soon after we got home and were preparing our late lunch Kris rang. He was short of a lay-clerk soprano for Evensong, and would Jessica go? She would get paid at lay-clerk rate! I called her, and she heard Kris's tale of woe and readily agreed to help out. I went back to the phone and reminded Kris that we should have to leave Morpeth in fifteen minutes, and would be sure to be a few minutes late. That was fine, he said. Hmm. We dropped everything and prepared to rush off. Roger, when he heard about it, said it was a great honour for Jessica and we should take taxis both ways! Well, taking one on the outward journey certainly seemed a very good idea and enabled us to calm down! Sunday Evensong services have taken a little longer lately because Clare has decreed we should have the homily that the rubric provides for. These homilies are not full sermons, though to a tired chorister they may well seem like that. On this occasion it was Jean Skinner who homilised for nine minutes (homilies give excellent opportunities to glance at your watch). Poor Jessica had missed her normal meals and had eaten very little all day, so we had to go to MacDonald's and get chips on our way to the bus. God bless Mr MacDonald.

After being second adult in Junior Church for some time I decided to offer my services as a leader, and was accepted. This was my first turn, and indeed the first time I had taught Sunday School in over fifty years. I armed myself with Parry, my glove puppet parrot. The Education Suite was rather grubby as a new lift had just been installed, but I took a duster. It was a very enjoyable occasion for me. There were three little girl choristers and another girl, and a second adult to protect us all. Parry and I said hello to everyone by name. I taught them to sing *Open our eyes, Lord, we want to see Jesus* as a prayer. They are not used to singing in Sunday School, which is a pity. As an ex-Girl Crusader, brought up on choruses, I often find the words come back to me in a way sermons and lessons never do. I had a sequence crib and a story crib, but I didn't need the story crib. It was about Mary anointing Jesus's feet, and I asked Amelia Lewis, a chorister, if she would take my Chanel 5 EDT spray round and give everyone a squirt on their hand. Parry had a squirt on his head. We talked about who Jesus's friends were today, and how they could show their love for him. I had decided not to have games because I had come to regard them as an irrelevant distraction for which we really had insufficient time anyway. My activity was to draw on a printed text which could go home. I tried to teach them to sing *Jesus, Friend of Little Children*, but frogs don't make very good singing teachers. We had squash and biscuits, and soon it was time for one of the big choristers to come and fetch the little choristers down to sing the *Agnus Dei*, so we packed up. Apparently the service had been slightly traumatic for Kris as the new organ conked out. That's the trouble with cheap organs.

Wednesday 16th, as the Dean had told us, was the first day of interviews for the post of Director of Music. I went with Jessica as the choir were required for the four candidates to practise on. For two hours they stood and sang, and at one point kind Clare led them on a "hop" around the nave to get their blood circulating if it had gone to sleep. Canons for Liturgy can do that sort of thing and get away with it. The candidates looked young and pretty similar, but I didn't study them. At the end parents were invited to join everyone in the Refectory for nibbles. I had a bad cold and was losing my voice so I was very glad of hot coffee, and I had two rather dry sandwiches which had probably been exposed since 3 o'clock but were still welcome. I did not attempt to socialise as it is not my strong point and I could see that each candidate had been well and truly nobbled by one or more aspiring parents or CCA committee members, so I read my Kindle. I was glad to see that Jessica was socialising with gusto. I stayed till she was ready to leave, and by then most other people had left. We got a taxi home. Jessica tried to tell us about it, but she seemed to have no special preference. No one seemed to have been outstandingly good or awful! Now we just had to wait and see.

On Friday, March 18th, the choir went as usual to help Durham Cathedral celebrate their patronal Festival. This time there was no difficulty about me going on the coach, which was a relief. Whether Kris was unaware of the dangers presented by hangers-on, or just didn't worry about them, I don't know. I was delighted that the coach took us all the way up to Palace Green. However, now we had arrived, I knew there would be nothing else happening till Eucharist at 7.30 (it being then 5.45), so I felt I had to go off and seek my fortune. Above all I wanted a nice hot drink, and purveyors of nice hot drinks were mainly closed now. As I crossed the green I could smell the most beautiful Chinese aroma and decided to follow my nose to wherever it was coming from, but it must have been from a private building because I never found it. Just as I was giving up hope I found a Cafe Nero where I was able to have lovely hot chocolate and read for half an hour. My taste buds were disappointed of the eastern promise wafted by the evening zephyrs, but the hot chocolate was very good.

Back in the Cathedral, which looked very fine in its floodlighting, I was confronted with the usual mass of red rope to keep tourists out. At the back of the nave I came upon three red-robed backs chatting to each other as Durham welcomers so often do. They looked very, very important. I wondered if any of them would turn round and welcome me. Two ignored me, and the third simply asked me if I was attending the service and gave me a service sheet. I asked if the congregation would be sitting in the nave or the quire for the service, and she said we had to sit in the nave till the choir rehearsal was over and the choristers came out. I knew that, and repeated the question, but she only repeated her answer as if I was deaf, stupid or insolent. I found a comfy spot on a padded pew near the front (one of very few padded pews) and sat waiting for another red-gowned welcomer to come and turn me out, but no one did. I decided to light a candle to cheer the place up, but regretted it when I saw I was asked for a "suggested donation" of £1. Goodness, at Newcastle you could light candles for the whole family and the dog for £1. In due course some more red-gowns told us where in the quire we might sit, and directed us. None of them looked at all friendly or welcoming, but they all looked, and I'm sure felt, very important. As I watched them busying around and bossing people a line from the Immortal Bard (in *King Lear*) came to mind: "*A dog's obey'd in office.*" Woof.

The chap next to me had a terrible cold, like mine had been a couple of days before, and he was trying to be very economical with a tiny packet of tissues. I planned to offer him one of my packets at the end, because I hardly needed them now. The greater suffering of others reminds us of how much better we are getting.

The service, all about Cuthbert (though surely it was Peter's special day?) went well. The singing was super. Our Dean read a passage from the Ven. Bede (I think he's officially Saint Bede now, but he'll always be the Ven. to me). The sermon was about Cuthbert's attention to people and how we needed to pay more attention to people. It was a very good sermon. I was paying a lot of attention to the organist opposite me who was perched on a very high and very exposed organ bench, with his back to the void. The uninitiated might not realise that an organist needs to have a very good head for heights! During communion I rootled in my bag for a Werther candy for the man behind me who was coughing a lot. He looked puzzled, then very pleased. Soon it was time to round up my chorister and go home. I think the welcomers had mostly gone home themselves, there being no one left to welcome.

On Maundy Thursday there was the usual foot-washing service. On my way through Gosforth I saw, from the top of the bus, a biker who had had an accident and was lying in the road, surrounded by passers-by, waiting for the ambulance. When I got to the Cathedral I left a prayer request on the board for him, but as it transpired it was too busy a service to bother with visitors' prayers. I hope he recovered, in spite of ecclesiastical neglect. I was pleased to see that the transformation of the men's toilets, into three unisex cubicles, was complete, and the lift was finished and ready to go. Tonight the Bishop preached, and she and the Dean, with canonical assistance, washed eight pairs of pre-arranged feet. Yes, pairs. Perhaps this common sense procedure was the result of a woman's logic. At the end we were invited to sit in the Eastern Chapels and, if we wished, wait quietly till Compline at 9. Jesus would have wanted company all night, but we probably couldn't afford to pay the vergers overtime.

Jessica told me she wondered why a reasonable God demanded the kind of worship the Church of England pushes down our throats. Well, in my private opinion he doesn't demand worship at all but wants us to be nice to each other. As the hymn says,

> To worship rightly is to love each other –
> each smile a hymn, each kindly deed a
> prayer.

On the Saturday choristers were again invited to make an Easter Garden, but this time there was no pizza lunch. I believe the children who turned up were given hot cross buns in the refectory. We all had an email from Kris to say that the new Director of Music had been appointed, and it was Ian Roberts. This would be announced in church tomorrow morning, and meanwhile Kris hoped we would not tell anyone. Naturally our lips were sealed.

On Easter Sunday Clare came to the lectern well before the service began and taught us a new Easter hymn. This was a noisy business, and it came as an anti-climax then that the clergy processed in silence. I whispered to Roger "Is this a funeral?" and he whispered back, "No, there's no corpse." At the font they turned and told us that Christ was risen (rather like the CCA yelling "Surprise!" I suppose), and we were allowed to say the H word for the first time in weeks. Actually I had said it quite a few times, but always quietly so as not to give offence. I'll say it now – Hallelujah!! The Bishop presided and preached, and did both very well. Jessica sang in a Kodaly trio and later got a lot of praise from Kris. The Bishop, by arrangement with Buckingham Palace, presented Royal Maundy money to Joan Marrs who had not been well enough to go to Windsor Castle to meet the Queen. The Bishop said she knew she was a poor substitute for the Queen, but I doubt if Joan thought so.

 We had lunch in town, and as we finished our pudding Jessica got a call from Megan to say that "everyone was asleep in the Thomlinson Room!" She seemed alarmed, so we hurried to the Cathedral to find out which fairy tale was being re-enacted. Yes, Kris, John Lewis and another lay clerk were fast asleep with their heads on the big table. They had all been up since before the 6am service on top of the Castle, and they were very tired. Kris kindly woke up to receive the girls and start thinking about Evensong. Roger and I went to the Education Suite. I went by the staircase, but Roger insisted on taking the new lift to try it out.

During the rehearsal in the Quire I heard Kris address the choir as "Guys". I hate that expression, and later I wrote to him and asked him not to address my granddaughter as "Guy". He wrote back very diplomatically and graciously, but showing no remorse unless he had personally offended Jessica, which I knew he hadn't. I fear it's just another example of the world overtaking me.

The next Saturday, April 2, we had our second Cathedral visit with NCS. This time it was in Manchester Cathedral. I had never been there and we were both looking forward to it. We got up at 6.15 and our taxi came for us at 7 to take us to Newcastle. We had time to get a hot drink and snack in Costa on the station, which was a blessing because there was no refreshment facility on the Trans-Pennine train. The journey was two and a half hours, and we took a taxi to the Cathedral. It was a very wet day, as one traditionally expects in Manchester. We were about the first to arrive, but David Rothwell was already there to welcome Jessica. Being now surplus to requirement for a while I went off to look for the "Proper Tea" café which was across a little road and appeared to be a concession in a Cathedral-owned building. I had some lovely coffee and a salad. It was a bit early for lunch, but it had been a long time since breakfast! I asked for the loo, and was directed along a lot of corridors and down a lot of stairs that led to a book shop which definitely belonged to the Cathedral. I looked forward to exploring that later. Meanwhile I found the toilets most unsatisfactory. There were three cubicles, of which one was locked permanently. Of the other two, one had no supplies and no working lock, and the other was OK but with a rather dodgy lock. Within seconds another person took up occupation of the other and banged, pushed and squeezed till they managed to lock it. In so doing they joggled the whole structure till my lock came undone. I was not impressed. You may think, dear Reader, that this is not a very elevating topic, but it's very important to a chaperone who's out all day.

I scuttled back to the Cathedral through the raindrops and puddles, and at the door was confronted by a bouncer who must surely have been the grandson of the miserable cleric at Durham Cathedral in the 1960s. He was busy telling a family that they couldn't go in because there was a service on – unless they had come to the service? No, they hadn't. They left, and I doubt if they will ever go back. Meanwhile I ignored the bouncer and walked in. Well, he wasn't having that! Who did I think I was? He called me back and repeated that there was a service on. Was I going to the service? "Well, that's why I usually go to church," I said. "Oh, go on then," he said grudgingly, and let me pass.

Inside I could see that there was indeed a service in progress in the nave. I sat down on the back row at the side, meaning to read my Kindle, but eventually I became interested in the service. It was a hotchpotch of guitar-accompanied singing and odd contributions from people who didn't all look Mancunian pink. It transpired that it was a multi-faith candle-lighting service to pray about terrorism, and in particular for the victims of the Lahore tragedy on Easter Sunday. The Bishop of Lahore sent a message, and several other-faith leaders made contributions. At the end they all lit little red tea-lights. It was very moving, and I was glad to have happened to be there. My *bête noir*, who perambulated between the porch and the nave, did not bring me an order of service, though I eventually saw where they were and helped myself to one. At the end of the service Bully Boy swapped with a colleague who was pleasant but, if he was a welcomer, certainly did no welcoming. He and Bully Boy wore red sashes to show how important they were.

I now decided to visit the bookshop. It sold mainly books, including some second-hand ones, but there was a little bit of gift-type merchandise. I had a quick browse, but there was nothing either Jessica or I would have wanted to weigh ourselves down with. I was offered coffee which I could have drunk at one of three tiny tables overlooking the oldest Roman bridge in Manchester. I bought three second-hand books that attracted me, and returned to sit in the Cathedral and read. It was a very nice place to sit. Occasionally I heard the choir rehearsing. When I felt peckish again I set off to look for food. The rain had eased a bit. The Proper Tea café was now heaving, so I carried on walking. Predictably the centre of Manchester is no place to waste land, and every building was either tall or very tall, with little space in between. Many tall things were under construction, unless they were being given a face-lift. A Premier Inn, which had a fairly small footprint, went up for 28 or 30 storeys. I found M&S and had a cheese scone. Wherever you go in England, from Exeter to Newcastle, M&S cheese scones are identical, and delicious!

Back at the Cathedral I was hoping to find a good seat in the Quire, but it transpired that the choir were singing in the nave next to the organ console. I sat behind them while they had their last rehearsal. I selected a seat in the nave facing the front as is proper, but from where I could see Jessica easily. The bouncer did a few desultory things with hymn books and prayer books, but most people didn't get one and few people seemed to be sure what they should have. I gave mine to someone who seemed clueless, as I pretty well know it all off by heart. I suppose there were 30 to 40 people in the congregation, and their lack of know-how suggested they were the parents, spouses or hangers-on of the choir. At a point while we were assembled and the choir had not come in I heard a bouncer telling people that the cathedral was now closed to visitors unless they were taking part in the service. I felt indignant. Sadly he didn't say it to me because I was ready with a reply. Then he went to the lectern and said it all again: officially they were now closed to visitors unless we were taking part in the service. Credit to Newcastle – any of our clergy would have said "But we do hope you'll stay for the service. You will be very welcome!" And in any case Newcastle does not "close" to visitors or anyone else until the last service is over. The conductor was cantor, but a lady cleric did the readings and prayers. She had a very boring voice, and a total lack of fire in her belly. Afterwards we assembled in the Song School corridor to collect our children and have them crossed off the list by the pastoral ladies. Goodbyes always took a long time, but this time the choristers knew they would met again in a week.

Then we needed a taxi. I had a number, but it wasn't clear where we should ask to be picked up as the

Cathedral is surrounded by pedestrian precincts. We went to stand where we had been dropped off in the morning and tried to hail taxis. Sadly they all seemed to be full. Eventually Jessica rang one of the numbers I had and tried to describe where we were. We were close to the Cathedral and at the beginning of an old bridge that went to Salford. Perhaps all bridges in Manchester go to Salford. We could not identify anything else we could see. Manchester Cars did their best and eventually Jessica got a message to say they were waiting for us at the Premier Inn. The driver was standing under their awning trying to contact us. I gave him a very decent tip. We managed to get a good meal at Carluccio's on Piccadilly station. Our train home would have been very satisfactory if it were not for drunks of both sexes. People have been campaigning for banning alcohol on trains for all the years I have been interested in the matter, but it is a source of revenue to the train companies. We were home before 11. Jessica had had a very good day. Mine could better be described as interesting, but I had done lots of reading.

Only one week later the NCS were together again, this time at Peterborough Cathedral, where the RSCM was celebrating its Golden Jubilee. It was a very easy journey for me and Jessica, the least pleasant part of which was waiting for 25 minutes in a cold waiting room at Morpeth Station. At Peterborough, after a very pleasant train ride, we had some lunch in the adjacent Waitrose, where I urged Jessica to eat as much as she could because she might be stuck for several hours. When we got to the Cathedral at 12.45 we looked around for faces Jessica might know, but recognised no one. We took a walk around the outside of the Cathedral, then as we returned Jessica saw Pam Moore who she knew was a pastoral assistant for the day. I left then. A grandmother can be such an embarrassment to a teenager.

I wandered along Bridge Street which is a cheerful pedestrian street with seats, trees, shrubs, shops, buskers and beggars. The concept of beggars may not sound cheerful, but I was always greatly cheered by the lovely smiles they gave me in return for a small bar of chocolate with which I am usually well-equipped in cities for that purpose. One beggar was a very old man with a bull-mastiff who sat on his knee and gazed at him lovingly. They looked besotted with each other. A passer-by might have said "Poor old chap, he ought to be in a home!" but I doubt if there are many care homes where bull-mastiffs are welcome. I sat on a seat and fed pigeons with a roll I had rescued from some earlier snack. I love pigeons, but the general passing populace seemed not to. I got some disparaging looks. I wandered along looking in charity shops, of which there were plenty. You just never know what you might find in a charity shop.

Eventually, getting tired of walking, I repaired to BHS café. I was happily reading and drinking hot chocolate when an ear-splitting din made me look up. What was that noise? Goodness – it was the fire alarm! Seeing and smelling no evidence of fire I assembled my luggage calmly and strolled across to where an assistant was beginning to wonder if I was deaf or daft. She hustled me through a couple of unmarked doors and on to a gloomy stone staircase. Another assistant was very gently steering us all downstairs (she had gravity on her side), being especially kind to a mentally handicapped boy who was even more bemused than the rest of us. We emerged into their loading bay where a greater imminent danger than fire was a number of lorries manoeuvring and not expecting to have to look out for customers. We were shepherded to a pavement where we could wait and see the fun when the tenders came, if they did, but I felt it was time for me to move on and discover other delights.

Back in the town centre I came upon a church, I think it must have been St John the Baptist, and remembered that the choir were spending much of their day rehearsing in there. The door was open and I decided to go in and sit and listen. No one bothered me, and I took up an unobtrusive seat at the back. Sadly they were just finishing and getting ready to move on, so I didn't hear much. I followed at a distance and went into the Cathedral where I was not charged for entry but £3 was suggested. I had been before, and it was nice to be there again. The toilet arrangements were strange. Just outside the south door was a little stone hut divided into Gents and Ladies, and clearly labelled, and as the Ladies had two rather constricted cubicles I supposed the Gents did too. Later, after Evensong, I patronised the facilities again and this time found that both doors now bore the sign "Gents". An arrow pointed to the Ladies which was a few dozen yards away, and consisted of a modern brick building with much more generous accommodation for a larger number of people. I suppose to reduce the need for cleaning and supervision the small one was available during the daytime to visitors, and the main one locked till it was needed for larger gatherings at services. Sensible really, but disconcerting. Had the Gents sign *really* said Ladies only a couple of hours before? Had I unwittingly trespassed on an all-male preserve? Was I – was I cracking up?

The star of the show was Martin Howe who had founded the RSCM fifty years before, and he conducted some of his music which was sung beautifully in Evensong. He was a gentleman of mature years, and obviously if he had been old enough to establish the RSCM in 1966 he must have been quite elderly. After the service Andrew Reid made a speech about him, thanking him for what he had meant to the RSCM over the years. Coffee was served with lots of nice home-made cake. It was clearly for congregation as well as choir and VIPs, and I appreciated it. By now I felt quite positive to the

Cathedral and gave them a donation considerably in excess of the £3 they were asking for. I respected them for not charging an entry fee. Jessica asked Martin Howe if he would autograph her copy of his Introit, and he did, with apparent surprise. Then home. Whenever I leave a cathedral I wonder: will I ever come here again? At present the chances are good that I will.

One Sunday in April as we took our seats in the Quire for Evensong we found an unaddressed envelope on each seat. It was a letter from the Dean and Chapter to say that they were thinking of changing the time of Sunday Evensong to 4pm, but would be interested to know the feelings of the congregation. Would we write, email, or discuss it in person if we had any feelings one way or the other. Later, as we left the church, we found a stack of Annual Reports on a table by the west door. I took one, and as I read it on the bus going home I saw that the Cathedral had serious financial problems. When we got home I emailed the Dean and said we and Jessica would much prefer a 4pm Evensong. Then I told him about an idea I had for solving the Cathedral's money problem, though I said I knew it would give him apoplexy. I said I thought the Chapter should offer the Hedley carvings for sale on the American market. They might bring in millions, and give people in the New World a chance to enjoy the carvings that have delighted us long enough. He did not reply.

Next day we had an email from Kris. It seems that the Dean had rather jumped the gun by writing to the public before consulting with the choristers and their parents who after all are pretty important. We replied to him, as asked, to indicate our vote for a 4pm Sunday Evensong. I think, however, from the Dean's point of view, the correct procedure was followed. There are two principals in a service of worship: God and the worshipper(s). Of the two it is perhaps more important what suits the worshipper, as he is constrained by time and place and

God is not. The choristers and their parents must fit in. If they can't, they must quit. They are there to serve, not to dictate. If the children did not turn up to sing they would be greatly missed, but worship would go on without them. And we would still have the lay clerks. They get paid, and they do as they're told.

The following Sunday Clare presided. During the responses at the beginning there was a bit that said if we denied Jesus he would deny us. I wasn't happy with that. After the service I asked Clare if she really believed it. She hesitated, then said she wasn't entirely comfortable with it. Father Steven was passing, and she asked him what he thought. He did not hesitate. He quoted the parable of the sheep and the goats. I thanked them both for their time. I have never been entirely comfortable with the parable of the sheep and the goats, mainly because I love goats. And if I love them, I'm quite sure Jesus does.

On May Day the NCS went to York Minster to spend the day preparing to sing Evensong. I was looking forward to the occasion, because it was many years since I had attended Easter morning service there and heard Stuart Blanch preach. It was another very easy train journey for me and Jessica. We walked to the Minster, and were delighted to encounter a pair of geese with a brood of nine goslings, on the pavement by a little shrubbery. They seemed quite unfazed by our presence. At the Minister we found the doors firmly shut. We couldn't understand this as they must have been open for early services, but it was pretty obvious we were not wanted then. It was still not 9 o'clock, and I think we were not due till 10, so we went off to see what we could find. Ah, Betty's – that was a good idea! I hadn't been to a Betty's for years, and Jessica never had. They were still closed, but we would come back in a few minutes. Well, it was 9.15 when we came back, and Betty's was full with a queue! We got the impression it was a coach party having breakfast. Happily we found an excellent breakfast elsewhere.

Back at the rather uninviting Minster we saw David Rothwell strolling around outside. We called to him, but he did not respond. I suppose there are lots of Davids in the world and he was not expecting to meet anyone he knew so far from home. When we caught up with him he found a way in, and got us past the pay desk with some difficulty. In fact I was expecting to pay, but I didn't argue. He led us to the Camera Cantorum, a part of the church that we would never have suspected the existence of. I went too, to find out where Jess was going and to sign her over to the pastoral carer. The Camera Cantorum was accessed by a spiral stone staircase that I found rather alarming, but it only went up one storey. Now I was surplus to requirement again so I trotted off. First I went back to the paydesk and coughed up, as I knew I should not be able to get in and out all day without a ticket. It cost me £9 as a pensioner, and any child with me was free, so Jessica was free twice over. I noticed my ticket lasted twelve months, and I worked out that I would still be able to use it on May Day next year so I kept it carefully. I cased the joint and discovered excellent toilets but no café. Oh well, I would be supporting the urban economy rather than the Church of England when I snacked. The Minster did not look very attractive inside. It was full of scaffolding on which men were working noisily, but I wasn't sure what was going on. It might even have been the erection of very large seating and staging for some forthcoming event. I assumed they would pack up and leave before Evensong and they did but only just. As for the rest of it, I found it a wee bit too ornate for my liking.

Jessica was going to need a packed lunch, and I planned to get it in M&S and take it to her. I strolled round the shopping area near the Minster, and from there found my way to the less characterful High Street shops. I bought Jessica's lunch in M&S and then went to their café. I didn't need coffee or the delicious cheese scone I had, but I wanted somewhere to sit and read. My current book was *The Co-op's got Bananas!* by Hunter Davies. Hunter is a few years older than me, but many of his post-war memories chimed with mine.

Back at the Minster I braved the spiral staircase to slip Jessica her lunch carrier, then after a look round I set up camp for a while in a chapel. Guides were now taking parties of tourists round, and shouting in competition with the background noise. Many of them were shouting in other languages. Some of their victims were listening, some clearly weren't. Most of them had their phones glued to their faces taking photos. It occurred to me that when they got home and looked at their videos they would see what they had not properly looked at in real life. From a pulpit a cleric read a prayer every hour on the hour, but again he had too much competition and probably very few people were listening. I did not find it a restful place, and eventually I went out again. There were doors I could get out of, but I could not always get back in through them. The gift shop, for instance, had a very strict routing so that no one could use it to get into the Cathedral without paying. The shops in York were much more welcoming.

Before 3.45 I set up camp in the Quire on a seat from where I could see the top of Jessica's head, but she would not see enough of me to be embarrassed. Roger now came and joined me. He had come on a later train and spent a few hours at the Railway Museum. Before we had been sitting there for a couple of minutes a steward (I couldn't possibly call him a welcomer) came and turned us all out of the Quire, saying the Quire, if not the Minster, was now closed. "But we're staying for Evensong!" Roger protested. Yes, they would be opening up again at 5 for Evensong, but were closed now. It was neither the first nor the last time I have been ordered out of a Cathedral, but for some reason we seemed to manage to stay in the building this time, but strictly the other side of a stout red rope. Indeed ropes had been put in place here, there and everywhere.

Roger went off to the loo and we agreed to meet at Philippi. I sat on a nice wooden bench just the west side of a rope. I saw that the iron gate at the west end of the north aisle had been shut too. At least no one bothered me where I was. I got bored and started swinging the rope near me. Each end was attached to a metal hook in a stone pillar. I swung the rope round and round. What fun! Then suddenly – ping! I heard metal. The rope lay on the ground and the hook near my head had disappeared. Goodness knows how many centuries it had been holding that rope up! Well, probably only since the 1950s when the current wave of tourism began. Amazingly none of the bouncers caught me in the act. They were in dereliction of duty! Eventually I saw a couple of people, who were obviously in the know, open the Quire door and go in, closing it behind them. Oh well, I thought, if they can go in, so can I. I peeped through and saw that the door the other side was open and one or two other people (not tourists, and therefore to be trusted) were gathering. I opened the door and went in, and got no more rebuff than a suspicious glare.

By now the choir were dispersing for their last comfort break, and I made my way to my chosen spot. There were plenty of people in the service, sitting in the spare choir stalls and on chairs higher up, and some of them may have been regulars. Undoubtedly a lot were parents and hangers-on of the choir, and some may even have been tourists, but they'd have had to be brave to withstand the earlier rejection. When you are officially told that a place is "closed" you tend to crawl off with your tail between your legs.

Roger came and sat with me. It was a lovely service. Jessica's solo was in the Parry anthem towards the end.

There was a long bass solo piece, then Jessica with a long soprano piece at the other end, and a lot by the whole choir together. Jessica sang beautifully, and a lot of people were telling her so when I went up to fetch her. It seemed Andrew was pleased with her too. As we had left the Quire we came upon a sidesman holding a basket. I left him holding it. They had had £9 off me, and I thought that was quite enough in the circumstances.

York Minster illustrates a perennial problem of Cathedrals: how to preserve a valuable and sacred building from the depredations of tourists for whom the place and its heritage means very little. A great deal of manpower is needed, some paid and some voluntary, and they are not required to even be Christians, let alone have a feeling of loving care and welcome for visitors. The bigger the Cathedral, the greater the problem. It is much easier for places like Southwell or Leicester which are less on the tourist map. Many people who visit York Minster will not have been motivated by their own interest but because it is included in an itinerary. Whether they feel inspired or repelled depends very much on the attitude of the so-called welcomers. Suffice it to say that I left without any great wish to return (unless Jessica was singing, of course).

On Ascension Day we had a special Eucharist in the evening. Clare preached, and once she told us all to look up. We looked up, and were directed to a cloud of incense floating above the nave with the sun catching it. Clare said every tiny speck was part of God blessing us through the incense. At this point someone said "Stupid woman!" but I don't think anyone heard me. As everything was happening in the Quire tonight the incense was pretty concentrated, and I did not regard it as a blessing from God, any more than I regard cigarette smoke as a blessing from God. But it served to remind me what a blessing we enjoy in clean air!

The following Sunday, at Red Wine and Tomato Juice, Father Steven asked what topics we would like to discuss at future meetings. There was a silence, then I said "What about whether we should burn incense in the Cathedral or not?" There were a number of noises which I couldn't interpret but I gathered they were in at least slight agreement with me. Clare laughed, and said she had never been in a church that used incense before, but that we should be using it less in future because they had decided to confine it to special Sundays. I told her that my only objection was exposing children to carcinogens, and that I had been planning to write to her about it. I had written to the Dean a long time ago, and he had brushed me off by saying that the Cathedral was very well ventilated and if he thought there was the slightest risk to their health he would not have allowed his own children to sing in the choir. Clare seemed genuinely surprised about the carcinogens and asked me if I had thought of writing to the Dean. I said I had done so with no satisfactory result. I asked her if I could still write to her, and she was keen for me to do so. One lady, as we left, told me that her grandson had asthma and found the incense very upsetting and often had to go out, though I think this was at another church.

A week or two later Clare and Katherine Govier were standing at the west door saying good night to the Evensong congregation. Clare asked me if I had noticed that they were not having so much incense now and would not be having it for a long time because we were now in Ordinary Time, and if I had noticed that, at her behest, we now used two pods of incense instead of three. She will do her best, she said, but we cannot hope to stop using incense as the Dean wants it. I said in that case I should pray for the Dean. Clare and Mrs Govier fell about laughing. I am still at a loss to see what was so funny about it.

During summer half term Jessica attended a three-day, two-night singing course at Whitby, as we had seen advertised at Sing4Joy in February. It was led by Andrew Reid, and it began on the late morning of the Tuesday. It didn't seem that we could easily get there in time on the day, so we went down on the Monday in order to give ourselves breathing space and see just a little of Whitby. We travelled to Middlesbrough by train, then by bus over a very foggy moorland to Whitby. We found a busy seaside town full of razzamatazz but still presided over by the ancient abbey. Our first port of call was the public loo which cost us 40p each – the most expensive penny I had ever spent, including at mainline railway stations.

The company that owned the accommodation we had booked were a little cagey. They did not tell you the address of the place where you were to stay, let alone how to get to it. The system was that, shortly before you were due to arrive, they would text you to give you the necessary information. They didn't, and Jessica, who is more *au fait* with such matters, phoned them for me, and was given an address and directions. Our mini-suite, as they called it, was in Silver Street. Like Lincoln, Whitby had some very steep streets, and Silver Street was one of them. It was not only steep but narrow. We had Jessica's big suitcase, and it seemed a good idea to get a taxi. The taxi driver had naturally been up Silver Street before and knew it could be done, but we couldn't help feeling we were about to be wedged between buildings and stuck forever. When we got out, in the region of the house number we had been given, we had some difficulty finding the address we wanted. We knew it must be very close, but we couldn't see it. It was certainly nothing like a guest house in appearance. Eventually we found the number on a narrow door, and entry was by keypad. We had been given the keypad number, but it didn't work. We were beginning to feel we didn't like Whitby when some kind people stopped and asked if we were having a problem. One of them boldly approached the keypad.

"What's the number?" he asked. It isn't usual to give your security numbers to total strangers, but we needed their help. As the number still didn't work the nice people took us into a little office across the way which was the headquarters of the letting company. They were very nice (as they jolly ought to be) and helped us to get into our mini-suite.

Inside we were faced with a narrow, carpeted staircase that had no handrails. Getting up, even without luggage (Jessica was carrying ours) was quite scary. At the top was a door, leading to what turned out to be a delightful room. Its claim to call itself a suite lay in that it had a tiny equipped kitchenette in the wee corridor between the bedroom and the shower room, with kettle, toaster, microwave cooker and fridge-freezer. The only thing lacking was a sink, but we supposed the handbasin would serve. In fact the handbasin was so small we could not fill the kettle under the tap, and we had to use a cup to fill it. Washing up properly was quite impossible. But we were both very pleased with what we had. We went out and did some shopping for supper and breakfast in a late-opening Co-op, then we looked for a café. We couldn't find one that wasn't full, and we ended up eating fish and chips on the hoof. As I staggered back up the stairs, vainly trying to hold onto the wall, I thought of the poor room-maid who would have to climb the stairs each day with a vacuum cleaner and a caddy of cleaning materials with no handrail to steady her. No expense seemed to have been spared in the furnishing of the mini-suite, so I wondered if the owner was simply bloody-minded.

About 4 am a million-decibel voice in the street below us yelled "Happy Birthday!" I bore the birthday boy no malice, but I wished his friend no happy returns at all.

Next day, after eating up our Co-op breakfast bits, we set off by taxi for Sneaton Castle where the course was to be held. Sneaton Castle was the mother-house of the Order of the Holy Paraclete, and the priory had guest accommodation and a conference suite. We followed the signs and found ourselves inside the hallway of a modern stone building. One family was already there, and told us that we were having to wait till Andrew, who was giving his staff a briefing, allowed us in. The briefing must have been running late, because we stood there for twenty minutes or more, squeezing up as more and more families arrived. On a wall opposite me I was delighted to see a Helen Bradley painting from her collection *And Miss Carter Wore Pink*. This comforted me, as it told me the Sisters had good taste and a sense of humour.

When we were finally allowed in I checked that there was nothing else for me to sign and said goodbye to Jessica. Someone made a brief announcement, reminding us that we were to collect our children from St Hilda's church on Thursday afternoon. There were two St. Hilda's churches in Whitby, one RC and one C of E. We, he said, should make for the C of E! Useful to know that. I now needed a taxi to take me back into Whitby, and I began to phone for one but it occurred to me that I had been born into the hitchhiking generation and there might be a quicker way of proceeding. I looked back to see if any other parent was coming to the carpark. Yes, there was a nice looking father! I asked him if he was going in to Whitby. Yes, he was. Would I like a lift? Thanks, I would love one! As we drove off I said lamely that I didn't normally ask strangers for lifts, but I was getting to the age where I could get away with outrageous behaviour! It transpired that he knew Canon Clare, and asked me to give her his good wishes. In Whitby, when he dropped me off, I pressed upon him my taxi money to give to his favourite charity, which he was happy to do. He was from Ripon, and his first name was Scott, but I never knew his surname. Hello Scott! If you are doing, thank you for reading this!

I conveniently caught the hourly X93 bus to Middlesbrough where I expected to get a train. I had not got a ticket yet, as Jessica and I had travelled with a Family Railcard but on my own I had to use my Senior Railcard. It occurred to me that now I had all the time in the world I might as well go all the way on the bus with my free pass! It would take ages, but that was no problem as I had a good book to read – *Hidden Lives* by Margaret Forster. So at Middlesbrough I visited the facilities, bought a Cornish pasty and got the Newcastle bus. I was on it for two hours and twenty minutes, but they passed quickly enough. In Newcastle, after taking full advantage of what M&S offered, I caught a bus home. Now I had a 36-hour holiday!

I decided to go back by bus on Thursday. I could not start before 9am, as I could not use my bus pass till then. I got to Eldon Square bus station in good time to catch the 10.30 bus to Middlesbrough. This service went via the coast and Peterlee. It was a much nicer day, but I still couldn't see any decent views because the bus windows were dirty outside and steamy inside. In Middlesbrough I had half an hour to wait for the X93 to Whitby. Sarah King, of RSCM, had sent parents a useful little map of how to get to the correct St Hilda's. When I got to Whitby it was almost 2 o'clock and I was ready for lunch, but every café was full and some had queues. I walked uphill towards St Hilda's hoping to see somewhere I could eat, and diverted from the map route to what I knew was a main shopping street, and just when I was nearly at the end of it and the shops petered out I found a restaurant called Botham's. I went up to their first floor tearoom where I found another queue, but this only had three people in it. I hoped to have their roast-dinner-of-the-day, but that ended at 2 and it was now 2.20, so I settled for egg and chips. The eggs were very good and I wish I could say the same for the chips. The whole outfit could best be described as faded elegance. It gave a pre-war feel, and I couldn't be certain which war. Indeed I could imagine its clients discussing the Siege of Mafeking. I'd go again but I wouldn't have the chips.

I had lost the map trail now, and I only knew St Hilda's was not far away. Asking a passer-by where a church is can be frustrating, because so many of them know where churches are but don't know one from another. I eventually found a little cake shop whose proprietor was very helpful, and soon I could see the church. The whole area looked deserted and asleep, but I found a door open into the church and went in. It was now about 3pm.

The choir were rehearsing. At that point there were only three parents there, sitting at the back as I did myself. Just before 4 when the service was to start I moved forward where I could see Jessica but more importantly she would be able to see me and know that I was there. We had a very nice service on the theme of Redemption, from Genesis to Romans. There were five congregational hymns and umpteen choir anthems. Sadly the readings were, in most cases, incompetent. Jessica told me later that they had only been given out at the last minute with no time to practise, though I doubt that. We had been told that RSCM responsibility for the children ended at 5, but at 5.15 the service was still going on.

Afterwards, when the children were gathered with their suitcases at the back of the church, Andrew made a speech to thank them and everybody else, and gave them all a certificate. This time his daughter Sarah was there, to Jessica's delight, and his wife Louise who had been giving individual singing lessons. As everyone left Andrew stood at the door and solemnly shook hands with each of them. It felt obvious, from the children's enthusiasm, that the course had been a great success.

Now we had twenty minutes to catch our bus. It was all downhill to town and the suitcase had wheels, and we did pretty well and had time to spend 40p. I didn't think we should catch the bus, but we did. We were in

Middlesbrough by 19.06. At this point we reverted to train travel as it was getting late and we had return train tickets. We taxied to the station which was rather a disappointment. There were a couple of automatic vending machines, but otherwise everything was locked up. A poster asked us to "Keep York Station Tidy", which suggests Middlesbrough has no sense of identity! After fumbling for the right change we got some pop and crisps out of the machines. Jessica didn't want chocolate but I got a Kitkat. You never know when you, or someone you meet, might need a Kitkat. Our train arrived in good time and took us to Newcastle. There was still a bus, but I was tired and preferred to get a taxi home. Jessica had phoned Roger from the train and he had cooked her supper.

The well-planned return trip having been so easy, I said she could go again next year if she wanted to. She only has one more year of eligibility. She seemed to have had a very good time. Apparently Andrew was very appreciative of her and often said "Thank you, Jessica!" and told the choir that she would be having a choir of her own one day. At one of their services he had asked her to be cantor, and was very complimentary about how she did it. Yet again I felt it had been well worth the chaperoning.

In June the Church of England celebrated the 90th birthday of their Supreme Governor. Other churches, whose Supreme Governor she was not, also took pleasure in marking our Queen's special milestone which, if not a very unusual age for a person to achieve nowadays, is a first for a British monarch. Although we were still in Ordinary Time the Cathedral burnt incense, though whether for God or the Queen might be wondered. Jessica had a couple of solos, one of which was Parry's *I was glad* which is a favourite of hers and also of mine. Father Steven preached and told us a great deal about the Queen's religious activities. We sang the

National Anthem which to my dismay had been sanitised. Instead of singing

Oh let the nations see that men should brothers be …

we had to sing

Oh let the nations see that we in unity …

I sang the proper words. Later Jessica told me that the choir had also sung the proper words because that was what they had!

The Lord Lieutenant, Lord Mayor and Lady Mayoress were there, but apart from the Mace Bearer they had no entourage. Either the Corporation were worshipping elsewhere or they didn't want to come. After the service there was cake and "sparkling wine" in addition to the usual coffee and biscuits. The Dean proposed a toast to Her Majesty. The choristers, who were now with us to hear the Dean's speech, did not get any cake because some miser had told them the adults must be served first and the children could only have some if there was any left. Naturally there wasn't. This was by no means the first time such a miserable attitude had been taken, and it always annoyed me. The choristers give us so much beautiful music, and they deserve any treats that are going. But then the people on the other side of the counter are volunteers, and must not be offended by criticism in case they stop volunteering.

The last Eucharist of the choir term was on July 7th. Towards the end of the service Clare called Kris to come forward. She told us that when Michael left they were in a quandary. Kris was so new on the staff, and it fell to him to pick up the reins with very short notice. Could he do it? Well, he had done brilliantly! The Dean and Chapter would have been very pleased, she said, if he had simply managed to keep things ticking over till a replacement came, but he had done far, far more. She gave him a small gift, and we all clapped with enthusiasm. Whatever stresses Kris might have been under, from the congregation's point of view he seemed to have taken over seamlessly. He would still be Acting Director of Music till Ian Roberts came in August, but his work with the younger choristers was over till next term. No doubt he was relieved. He had been kind and encouraging to them, and they liked and respected him. He had indeed done very well.

The choir end-of-term concert took place about 12 o'clock when the nave was clear. This was a good time because any interested members of the congregation could stay and hear it. It was a jollier concert than last year, with generally shorter and brighter pieces. The choir sang three items together. Alison Russo, back for a visit, sang with the choir. Jessica sang *Tit Willow* with Kris accompanying her. When the concert was over we repaired to the Refectory for a BYO lunch. It was a pleasant way of winding up the choir year.

At Evensong we again found envelopes on our seats with a letter from the Dean. It was to say that he and Chapter had decided to have a trial run of an earlier Sunday Evensong. From September to Lent we should meet at 4pm, and see how things went. The matter would be reviewed in February. He stressed that this was not for the convenience of singers or the clergy, but in the hope of attracting more of the general public to come in for Evensong. More people would be around in the town at 4pm than at 6pm. Well, yes. Nevertheless I think the children and parents considered this a good move, and we looked forward to an easier winter and a favourable review in February.

This summer Jessica was off to Rochester for the RSCM summer course. On Sunday, August 4th, the day before the course began, she and I got up at 5 to be ready for our 6am taxi to Newcastle Station. I had rather dreaded this trip, as I had formerly vowed never to travel via London again, but in spite of poring over atlases and railway time tables there seemed to be no other way to get to Rochester, so I had to bite the bullet. Happily our Rochester train left from St Pancras, so it was only a short walk from neighbouring Kings Cross with no need for the Tube or a taxi. We had a pleasant trip down, and I found my average time for solving a Starhunt (clueless) crossword was fifteen minutes. I was stressed by the roof at St Pancras, where the appliance of science had taken no account of aesthetics. It was very ugly and difficult to ignore. Then when we were finally on the Rochester train it was very fast and felt like a horizontal lift, giving me a sensation that I always call "the bends" thought probably wrongly. It was great to get off at Rochester, where a very kind taxi driver told us the Cathedral was only walking distance. We certainly needed a walk.

Rochester just has one main shopping street, with lots of touristy boutiques. I never did find out where the populace bought their baked beans. First we made our way to the Gordon House Hotel where we had booked a room. It had everything we wanted except, oddly, drinking water. A notice on our dressing table told us not to drink the water from the taps but to help ourselves to the (one each) bottled water provided. More bottled water could be bought (yes, bought) from the bar. We went out to look at the Cathedral which was across the road, and enjoyed a late lunch in their nice teashop. What impressed us most about Rochester was that it was far hotter than Morpeth. We wished we had brought hats, and Jessica wished she had some shorts – a garment not often needed in the north. We decided to buy her some if we could, but it really wasn't that sort of place. Oh Marks & Spencer – where were you? I told Jessica that if she was too hot during the week she might cut a pair of jeans down, but the idea horrified her. One delight was the famous bookshop, Baggins Book Bazaar, a small double-fronted three-storey shop crammed with books. We both love bookshops so we had a happy time browsing in there, and we each bought a book.

Lastly we set off to look for food. We found a very good Indian restaurant, The Two Cities, and stoked our boilers enough to last us till breakfast. We spent the rest of the evening reading, and phoned Roger who had been to Craster Church fète and brought a Craster kipper home for his tea.

We woke early next morning and had an early breakfast, then as soon as the shops were open we renewed our search for shorts, but with no luck. We had three hours before Jessica had to be at the school. Where she had to go was called St Margaret's, but everyone we asked seemed to send us off on another wild goose chase. In the end we gave up and went to the Cathedral café for elevenses. We sat till about 10.30 then went back to the hotel to collect Jessica's suitcase and search in earnest. This time we met another chorister (recognisable by her cassock bag). A man who Jessica thought she had seen around the Cathedral asked us if we were lost. Yes, we were! He invited us to follow him. After a few yards he met another man who he hailed as Steven, and it seemed that Steven was closely connected with St Margaret's and was on his way there. "Can you take these guys?" the first man asked him. I said it was the first time in my life that I had not minded being called a guy, because we were so grateful to be rescued! Steven knew the code number to some anonymous black gates and took us through them to the manicured grounds of a big house. When we got into the building we were welcomed by the course director himself, Christopher Ouvry-Johns who is Director of Music at Leicester Cathedral. I told him I was a Leicester girl and that their Cathedral had improved a great deal since my day, but it was now the friendliest cathedral we had been into. He said yes, it had impressed him and his parents when they went there on a pre-interview recce, and visitors frequently made the same comment. I stayed till the house-mother, one Mandy Walker, arrived, and I was asked to fill in yet another indemnity form for their visit to Bromley later in the week. Other girls started to arrive with parents so I kissed Jessica and left. I know she often finds me embarrassing now, and I guessed she would be glad to fly alone.

My main memory of my journey home was having overheated feet, and I looked forward to being able to take my shoes and socks off in the train. As soon as I got to Newcastle I went to M&S and bought Jessica a nice pair of denim shorts. If I posted them tomorrow she might get them in time for them to be some use to her. In the late evening she rang us and sounded to be in hysterics. At first I couldn't tell whether she was laughing or crying, and she said she wasn't sure herself, but as she talked it was obvious that she was crying a lot. I was quite worried. Could I talk to a housemother? Jessica didn't know where there was one. The trouble, it seemed, was that they were not allowed to have the Wi-Fi code because the RSCM had decreed they should not. It seemed incredible to me that such a deprivation should be so serious. It sounded like a good thing to me! I promised that tomorrow I would email Sarah at Salisbury to ask why. Maybe it had been a misunder-standing. We advised her to get to bed to sleep as soon as possible. After an hour or so she phoned again. She seemed calmer, but only just. She told us she had had five glasses of lemonade with her supper. Aha! That no doubt accounted for her hysteria. I could not contact the housemother apart from via the office, so I emailed Sarah and asked her to ask Mandy to only give Jessica water to drink, and tea or coffee if it was offered. We have to fill in forms to say whether we approve of paracetamol or ibuprofen, but nobody asks our approval to give children food and drinks with unknown additives in. I don't suppose anyone had cared to look at the label on the lemonade to find out what was in it. Certainly not lemons, we may be sure!

The following Saturday I was up early and back in Rochester by midday. I had booked into the same hotel again, but it was too early to check in. I had a lovely lunch in the Cathedral café again. I looked in local shops for some nice approved drinks for Jessica – wholesome fruit drinks with respectable ingredients. She had been furious at my banning chemical drinks, and assured me I had ruined her life. Now tonight there was a barbecue, and she would not be able to drink anything! By 2 o'clock I was sitting in the Quire waiting for the girls to come in. When they came I heard a pleased voice say "There's Grandma!" and she came to see me with no apparent embarrassment. Most of the girls (only about a dozen) smiled at me in a friendly manner. A lady who I recognised as Mandy Walker was with them, and at a suitable moment I introduced myself and asked if I could give her the drinks to take back for Jess to have at the barbecue, and she was most kind and gracious. I sat through a very nice service with beautiful singing. After it was over I did not see Jessica again that day.

I went for another browse in Baggins Bookshop and looked for a book to save the battery on my Kindle. I was looking for something short that I could read overnight and push through a charity shop letterbox before I left Rochester. However I was taken by a book called *This is not about Me* by Janice Galloway, a Scottish novelist who I hadn't heard of. This was officially an autobiographical novel, and it was riveting. I booked in at the Gordon House, and was given a different but equally satisfactory room. When I had sorted myself out I went across to The Two Cities for another delicious meal – vegetable curry with lemon rice and mango chutney, with a big glass of orange juice. I was too full for pudding. Back in my room I read for a while, then turned in for an early night. Through my open window I could hear lots of trains, but I like train noises.

Next day after an early breakfast I went across to the Cathedral to listen to the 9am rehearsal. Jessica greeted me again and I got more smiles from her friends. Just before the 10am service began Jessica's cousin arrived with her husband and baby daughter. They live in London and had been glad of an opportunity to hear Jessica sing. I had already asked Mandy if Jessica could go and speak to her cousins briefly after the service, and Mandy agreed. Jessica was allowed to come to the café with us for ten minutes, and Mandy kindly stayed long enough to have a cup of coffee with us while Jessica played with the baby on the grass. I gather it was not their lunch they were hurrying back for but last minute tidying and packing, then lunch. After their 3.30 Evensong there was a goodbye mingle in the cathedral. We all trooped back to Margaret House and waited in the common room while speeches were made, certificates presented and last goodbyes said. See you next year!

We accompanied the cousins to the station where they, and many of the choristers, were getting the London train. We, however, were not. During my short holiday at home I had decided to make the most of being in the south east by visiting Canterbury Cathedral and St Paul's Cathedral. I had told Jessica about Canterbury and she was thrilled, but not yet about St. Paul's. I had been pleased to notice that Rochester station, like Newcastle, has a piano for the public to play.

We made for the hotel I had booked, the Cathedral Gate which was old and atmospheric and just by the Cathedral. Suffice it to say I would not go again. We went out to look for food and found a burger restaurant that suited Jessica well. After a poor night and disappointing breakfast we made our way to the Cathedral on Monday morning, leaving our luggage at the hotel to collect later. At the point of entry to the Cathedral close we came upon a kiosk where a pleasant clerk sold us tickets. His being pleasant made all the difference. I had a free entry voucher for Jessica which I had printed from a website, and my own concession rate entry was £10.50. Old age has its compensations. I paid it more in sorrow than in anger.

Inside the Cathedral we were graciously greeted by an elderly lady who asked us what language we spoke. She seemed very excited when I told her we were English! It seems they don't get so many English people visiting. She gave us a leaflet in our language. Jessica remembered that there were audio guides, and she had one. She found it fascinating. I just went round with her, enjoying the ambience. I left her briefly to go to the Ladies which was outside, but she was quite happy to be left. On the hour was the usual prayer from the pulpit, but it sounded more sincere and inspiring than they often do. Whenever I go into a Cathedral I light a candle for a friend's grandson who is having a troubled life, so that I can tell him I have done. Today I added another. Ian Roberts, our new Director of Music, was taking up his appointment at Newcastle that very morning. I lit a candle for him, with the prayer that he and his family would be happy with us.

After we had finished in the Cathedral we went for a hot drink in a little tea garden across the close. It was served by a permanent kiosk that did a limited range of just about all you could wish for in the way of light snacks. We had hot chocolate and a cookie. Jessica left me briefly to pop into the adjacent gift shop, and was rather a long time. When she got back she was quite upset. She had had a look round the shop, then retraced her steps to return but was told there was no exit by that door. She would have to go out by the other door which led to the street. If you went out before you were ready to leave you had to show your tickets again at the entry kiosk. Jessica explained her plight, and that she wanted to join her grandma who was in the tea garden, and they asked to see her ticket but she said Grandma had got it.

They took pity on her and allowed her to wait by the entrance till someone else came in, then slip out when the door opened. This ruffled her a lot, and I never knew what was happening. She looks such a big, confident girl now and people would not readily realise that she is a child still. I cheered her with the good news that we were now going back to London to visit St Paul's, and that I already had the tickets. She was thrilled to bits. We spent a little time in the gift shop looking at their rather super merchandise and buying the odd souvenir, then off we went, this time by the proper exit. We collected our luggage, then a called a taxi.

We had a nice trip to London with plenty of room to spread out. At St Pancras, as we could not take our luggage into St Paul's with us, we looked for the Excess Baggage Co. where we could leave it for a while. They asked us if we had anything electrical in our luggage, because if we did we should have to unpack it and have it scanned separately. Oh yes, it all had to be scanned! I forgot about our electric toothbrushes, but nothing bleeped. We could leave our cases there for three hours for £12. Well, it was worth it in the circumstances.

At St Paul's we had our hand-baggage scanned by a very nice security guard, then we went to show our tickets at the fast-track desk where there was no queue. The clerk looked at them and gave us a voucher for a guide book I had paid for but forgotten about. We had to take the voucher across to another desk where we were given a book. Everyone was very pleasant, and nobody treated us like vermin which is not unknown in cathedrals. We got an audio guide for Jessica which was included, and sat on the back row of the nave while she listened to the preamble. As the voice guided her she got up and moved off and I went with her. I would have been quite happy to sit and read my book, but she wanted me to go too.

My general impression as I looked at the whole Cathedral was that it was rather tawdry. It was far too decorated. I had no doubt that only the finest quality materials had been used, but tawdry was the word that kept coming to me. I followed Jessica round, but I wasn't greatly moved by what I saw. Eventually we went down into the Crypt and I liked that much better. Apart from memorials added long after it was built, the walls were white and fairly plain. Rows of seats in different parts suggested it was well used for services at times. The massive tombs of Lord Nelson and the Duke of Wellington were depressing in their huge size and waste of money. We went back up to the nave and I sat and read while Jessica went off to explore the higher reaches. She came back breathless and excited. She had walked round the Whispering Gallery and round the outside of the dome, and although it had been a bit scary at times she had loved it. We had to collect our luggage by 4.40 or pay double, so I was anxious not to be late leaving. We had a quick look in the gift shop and bought a snow-globe like Mary Poppins had in the film where she sings *Feed the Birds*. Jessica was sad to leave but, as I said, she would probably see it again many times in her life. I would probably never see it again, but I wasn't a bit bothered. Back to the station where, when we had retrieved our luggage, we had time to look at Platform 9¾ and then have an excellent meal at Giraffe before getting our train home. Phew.

2016-2017

On Saturday, Sept 10th, the NCS visited Liverpool Cathedral. We got up at 5am and set off by taxi and train for Lime Street station. Near us on our train were three young men who were doing what they had doubtless been brought up to think was the proper thing to do on a pleasure trip – drink lager. They had several carriers full of bottles, and they drank steadily. They had been quite sober at Newcastle, but by the time they got off at Manchester they were rather noisy and excitable. I wondered how much more they would drink over the day, and hoped they would not be on our return train. At Liverpool we hurried to the taxi rank, knowing we should be late but having asked for David's understanding. I occasionally suffer from sensory overload, and I had quite expected Liverpool Cathedral might affect me badly, so I asked the taxi driver to drive as close as he could to the door. All I had to do then was keep my head down and run, or in this case walk, holding Jessica's hand, trying not to see the massive edifice above me. Soon I was safely through the door, but the sight I saw inside the Cathedral was almost as daunting. The lofty roof was only visible if you threw your head back at an uncomfortable angle, and when you did there was not much worth seeing because the architect had aspired to vastness rather than beauty. I tried to pull myself together. I had got to endure this place for several hours, so I had better try to like it!

A big desk marked WELCOME (which really means PAY UP) was the first thing we encountered. It was saved from being off-putting by having two very cheerful ladies on duty. Jessica explained that she was there with the RSCM and I was her chaperone, and they waved us through. We knew how to get to the Song School from the directions and key code David had given us, and the nice ladies confirmed that. "Keep going as far as you can!" they said. Far away, at the end of a gloomy side aisle, David was waiting for us, and Karen (the pastoral assistant for the day) appeared at his side. They led Jessica off into the bowels of the earth. I had already arranged with her that at lunchtime she should look for me in the Mezzanine café, and that was where I decided to start the day with a cup of coffee.

I only knew of this place from the web. It sounded a good place to sit and snack. I found it was accessed from the shop, and when I got half way up the stairs I realised it was not in my comfort zone. It was like a wide shelf hanging in space, surrounded by Gothic red sandstone vaulting and backed by a huge stained glass window, and it gave me vertigo. I knew I could never walk across to the counter, so I scuttled back down the stairs. Happily there was also the Welsford restaurant at floor level and much more normal. I sat there with a cup of cocoa and a caramel slice and wrote a note to Jessica saying we would meet in the restaurant instead. This had to be done by primitive means as although I had a phone for calling taxis, Jessica still did not have one. I took the note down to the song school, which was quite a business in itself. I managed to let myself through a locked iron gate at the top of a flight of stairs, using the code that David had thoughtfully given us, then went down two flights of stone stairs to another iron gate with a similar code. I followed the sound of merry voices and gave the note to Karen who promised to pass it to Jessica. Going back up presented problems. I got through the lower gate by just turning the knob, but not the upper one. I went back down and asked Karen how I could get out, and she said I had to do the same things in reverse. Something worked the second time.

Now I went to the shop and browsed. It was a decent looking shop, but didn't have a lot that interested me. By now there were lots of people in the building and I felt less stressed, so I walked around exploring a bit. I couldn't help thinking that if the architect (Giles Gilbert Scott) had lowered the roof by about fifteen feet it would have been just as good and a lot cheaper. And we could have seen it without binoculars. One thing that really did please me was the toilets. They were in all respects excellent.

Before the lunchtime rush began I set up camp in the Welsford restaurant. I thought I had better have my lunch directly in order to be able to keep a table. I chose Blind Scouse, a vegetarian version of the famous Liverpudlian lamb stew with bread. The meal that came was in a tiny black pot and heaped up with lumps of swede, carrot and potato, with juice dripping down the side, and a very small ciabatta. I had to eat it very carefully, picking off the top lump each time delicately with a fork so as not to precipitate a volcano. As I got to the bottom the juice revealed itself to be of mainly Mediterranean vegetables, some of which Liverpool would not have known about before the C20th. Poor Jessica did not do so well. Her 45 minute lunch break was late starting, and she came at 12.55 leaving not a lot of time. She ordered a jacket potato with cheese. At 1.10 it had not come and we got anxious. She had to be back and ready to sing at 1.30. I asked a passing waitress if she could hurry things up a bit, and it finally came about 1.17. Jess had to gobble it, and I gather it was not very well cooked. She left me just before 1.30. The Welsford is obviously geared up to feed the leisurely tourist who has all day.

One interesting feature of the Cathedral, which Giles Gilbert Scott would not have foreseen, was a bank of four huge clear plastic boxes with slots in the top. This was where people could put donations of food, toiletries, and household items to be distributed among the poor. They were about four and a half feet high, and they were locked (to prevent the poor helping themselves. The poor are not allowed to help themselves). They were for an organisation called Hope which I suppose is Liverpool's answer to Newcastle's People's Kitchen. When we arrived there was just one tin of soup in one, but by the time we left at 4.30 they were all at least half full (and half full was a lot of stuff). It was a very good idea.

I sat on a nice padded seat in the nave and read my Kindle, listened to the full rehearsal and finally took part in Evensong at 3 o'clock. Andrew Reid conducted it, and it was very enjoyable. Afterwards I went down to the dungeon to collect Jessica and sign her out of their care, then after protracted goodbyes we looked at the shop to see if there was anything she fancied. We still had quite a while before we needed to leave, and she didn't want to go back to the café which was still in business. She wanted to go up the tower! There were lifts and tower tours, and a guide told her to buy a ticket and give it to him or his colleague at the bottom of the tower. She did, but was told in the shop that she was too young. She had to be 16. Drat! She told the guide she couldn't join the tour, and why. He was surprised, and after a minute he called her back and said she could go up for nothing! I thanked him and said I would put the appropriate amount (I think £5) in the donations box, and I did. I sat in the nave and read some more. She was not gone very long, and was very pleased with her adventure when she got back. I gather there was sufficient protection at the top for most people who were careful, but none whatsoever for intending suicides. Fortunately Jessica seems to like heights.

It was time for us to go now. I hurried across the little green at the front to the pavement before I dared to look back, and when I did I was still unimpressed by what I saw. It's a pile. It took 74 years to build, and Scott did not live to see it finished. The words of the song came back to me:

*If you want a cathedral we've got one to
spare, in my Liverpool home.*

I wonder which was the spare one? We had a good journey home. The lager louts of the morning trip were on the train, but much further along and did not bother us. I passed them once, and they were quiet. I suppose they were more than half asleep. Now the bottles had been replaced by cans which were all over the table.

Ian Roberts duly arrived and seemed to settle in easily. Happily he and Kris got on well together. New brooms sweep clean, and one of Ian's first decisions was that the younger choristers should not go to Sunday school but should sit and take part in the service. I don't know if he asked their opinion, and I don't know what it would have been, but all the choristers got out of Sunday school, that they did not get out of church, was a drink of squash and a biscuit. Certainly they were all old enough to hear the Bible read and to listen to a sermon. Sunday school suffered as a result because it lost the greater part of its pupils, but the choir does not exist to provide Sunday school fodder. Another innovation was to sometimes have the choir sitting on chairs on the crossing dais, behind the altar, and singing from there till the communion. Other times he had them sitting at the back. Variety is the spice of life. The probationers, who he considered not yet ready to sing in services, sat demurely in their little cassocks at the side, so they felt part of the family while they were still learning the ropes.

As soon as Ian came we wrote to him and asked him if he would give Jessica organ lessons. He replied promptly that he had two small sons and he had promised his wife that he would always do his best to be home in the evenings to play with them and help put them to bed. However, he said, Mr Thomsett was a very good organist and was thinking about taking pupils, and he commended him to us. But one way or another, he said, he would make sure Jessica had organ lessons. Well, it would not have seemed quite right to ask Kris in the first place, even though it would have advanced things by six months, but now that we were being invited to ask him Jessica was quite pleased. Kris thought Sunday afternoons would be the best time, and that suited us well too. Further chaperoning duties necessitated me loading more books onto my Kindle. At that time I was reading *It Takes a Village* by Hillary Clinton. The Cathedral was quite definitely part of Jessica's village.

Now, if someone asked you to shout out the first hundred words that came into your mind when they said "Cathedral", sooner or later you would probably say "Bible". There were indeed Bibles in the Cathedral – at least two: one on the lectern and one on a reading stand in the north quire aisle for anyone who fancied looking at it. I was privileged as a Sunday school teacher to know that there were, at the back of an Education Suite cupboard, a small set of Bibles that had been given to the Cathedral by a former Provost. But that was about it. The Cathedral was very light on Bibles. People could drift into the Cathedral any time during the week and sit and think and pray and meditate – but they couldn't read the Bible because there weren't any. I felt this was a pity.

One weeknight Evensong Father Richard went up to the lectern to read the lesson. He paused. "I'll be with you in a minute," he said. "There is no Bible for me to read from." He disappeared to the vestry. After a few minutes of embarrassed silence (and whispers of "What did he say?") Kate Sussams, the Operations Manager, came back with a lectern Bible. She would not normally have been around at that time, so I suppose we were without a verger. Father Richard continued, apparently unruffled. That could never have happened in a Methodist church! We Methodists might conceivably lose a lectern Bible, but we would have plenty of others.

Very soon after this, at another weeknight Evensong, a visitor asked me where he could find a Bible. I told him apologetically that we were not well provided with Bibles, but that there was one in the north quire aisle. No, he said, he wanted one so he could follow the readings! I slipped out and asked Alan if there were any Bibles a worshipper could use. He looked puzzled, and went into the Vestry. I heard him discussing it with Canon Clare. I heard her say, rather crossly (well, it was about time for the service to begin) "I'll get one from the chapel." I supposed she meant St George's where there were some odd books about at the back. She hurried off, then brought the visitor a Bible and he was very pleased. After the service I thanked Clare for her trouble and said I thought there ought to be Bibles available in church so that anyone who came in might sit and read one. She looked sceptical. "Yes, but they might go walkabout," she said. I asked if that would matter. She looked surprised, then said no, she supposed it wouldn't. She would get some. Yes, she would get some. I said she could put me down for three copies. She seemed to agree, in principle at least, that there ought to be Bibles available in a Cathedral! A few weeks later a dozen or so Bibles appeared on the Quire bookrests, and were left out for general use.

But these few Bibles were only in the Quire, and the casual daytime visitor rarely went up there. I felt we ought to leave little copies of a gospel available at the back. I asked Clare if I might do that, and she gave her permission. I chose Luke's gospel because he was writing for people like me. I put a sticker inside each one (thank you, Ellie, for printing some stickers for me!) inviting anyone who picked it up to feel free to take it away if they found it helpful. I left three or four at a time on the bookrests of the back few pews, where daytime visitors most often sat, and topped them up as necessary. I hope at least one of them might have changed somebody's life.

Early in October I supplemented the day-job with organ chaperoning. We met Kris by the organ loft at 12.30. I gave him an envelope with £12.50 for half an hour, though we soon realised between us that an hour was a more suitable time length. We were negotiating with the Young Organ Scholar Trust who we hoped were going to pay for her lessons, but that had not been finalised. I looked for a padded seat and the only one I could find was under the organ. I set up camp there and began to read, but suddenly there was a loud boom from the pipes above me and I was terrified. I decamped a few feet to the front pews, talking the pew cushion with me.

I noticed, during our late lunchtime lessons, that many visitors wandered in and out. There were no welcomers or anyone on duty except the verger somewhere out of sight. Sometimes visitors looked as if they would be glad to talk to someone, and sometimes I chatted to people myself though I'm not good at that. I felt a welcomer presence would be good, but the people who normally volunteered for that job were no doubt at home having their Sunday Dinner and Afternoon Nap. Often I wished I could make someone a cup of tea, but at that point I did not feel at liberty to go into the Vestry, nor would I have known where to find the necessary stuff or felt authorised to use it. That was far in the future. I did once tell a homeless refugee that if he waited I would go and get him a cup of hot chocolate (from a secret store of my own in the Education Suite) but by the time I got back he had disappeared. He obviously didn't understand what I said.

At the end of October the NCS had a day at Selby Abbey. This was an easy journey for us, and we just had to change trains at York for Selby. The Abbey was within walking distance of the station, and we knew where to find it. At the Abbey we found the choir room, a nice place called the St Nicholas Centre, consisted of a large, clean room with a carpet and chairs, and other rooms above where rehearsals were held. I said goodbye to Jessica and made a bee-line for the loos. To my surprise they consisted of six unisex cubicles in an open area. Obviously once a part of it had been a Gents and they had knocked a wall out, and an enlightened power had decreed that they should be for everyone, all pals together. The cubicles were private enough, and as you washed your hands you would be able to ask a fellow ablutioner "Do you come here often?" I wasn't entirely happy about it, but it was all very cosy, and I was thankful for it anyway. There was also a nice little shop-café where you could browse among merchandise and have a limited but graciously served snack. I didn't have anything at that point.

My first object was to find M&S and get Jessica some lunch to take back to her. I walked up and down the main street, but with no luck. Where could it be? Had I passed it without noticing? I asked a passer-by where M&S was. Oh, there wasn't one! There used to be, but it closed. Well, I'm afraid that reduced Selby to a village for me! I searched for a substitute and found a few, and managed to get Jessica a selection of stuff that I hoped would do. I went back to the Abbey. Did she want me to stay with her over lunch time or not? No, she was quite happy. That was good. As I continued exploring the town I found a modern shopping precinct with a Morrison's who had an excellent café – as good as the one in Morpeth! Later I found a small department store with a café where I sat and read over a glass of apple juice (*Colour Bar: the Triumph of Seretse Khama* by Susan Williams).

Back at the Abbey I had a cup of coffee in their tiny café. It was nicely served on a tray. I sat at a little tin table and read. The café only served tea and coffee, in nice cups and saucers, with little packets of biscuits, unless the lady on duty had been in the mood to bake (I was told) and had brought a cake. Today's lady had certainly been in the mood and there was a small selection of nice cake, but I was full. About 3 o'clock I moved to the nave to listen to the choir rehearsing in the Chancel. After that I would have liked another cup of coffee, but by now the café was full of arriving parents. It is a beautiful church with a generally warm, friendly feeling. The Abbey's chosen charity for the time being was Toilet Twinning, and the children had made a very attractive floral decoration entirely from pastel-coloured loo paper! There was a Children's Corner, much smaller than ours and not in a corner. It was at the bottom of a nave pillar and had a small piece of carpet, a decent little plastic chest of drawers with art and drawing materials in, and a small plastic kiddy-table with three chairs. That was all, and if one little family was using it there would be no room for anyone else. But they had tried, and it was better than many cathedrals have.

About 4.25 I put my Kindle away and waited for the service to begin. It was quite nice, with two hymns: one I knew and one I didn't. Jessica had told me she had a duet but it was rather short and I hardly noticed it. It was part of the *Magnificat* to a Byrd setting. Afterwards everyone was busy saying goodbye to David Rothwell whose last girls' service it was before he retired from NCS. Such occasions are very emotional. I had not been terribly impressed with Selby as a town, but I loved the Abbey.

We walked to the station and caught the York train. We were told in York that the Newcastle train was running to time, and as soon as it came in we jumped on without further ado. We settled ourselves at a nice table seat. Jessica finally began to eat her Selby lunch which she assured me she had been too busy to eat at lunchtime. We rolled into a station, and were calmly looking out at the passengers on the platform when we heard Leeds mentioned over the intercom. *Leeds*? Why would a train from York to Newcastle go by Leeds? We both realised to our horror that we had got on the wrong train. Oh dear! We scrambled off, hoping we would have time. To me there was no problem – we simply had to get a train back to York. If it cost me extra, well it was my own fault. Jessica, however, panicked and went rushing down the platform to pour out her woes to a lady guard. The lady guard was kind but busy, and said she would have to finish seeing a train off first, then she would see to Jessica. I caught up just as Jessica was being told to go to an enquiry desk where our tickets might be changed (if we were lucky). First we had to change platforms, and I detest Leeds station so I wasn't very pleased about being on it anyway. I said no, we wouldn't bother with enquiry desks, we had nothing to enquire. We simply wanted the next train to York. As I was looking for one Jessica very intelligently spotted a sign to a Newcastle train which was even better. Yes, it was, but I hadn't thought that far because I was busy trying to control my general vertigo and sensory overload. She found us a Newcastle train and soon we were comfortably seated again, and she resumed her packed lunch. When the nice ticket collector came round I explained that we were not on the train we had paid for, and why, and he very kindly said it was OK. At York his shift ended and he changed with another collector, but he explained about us so we didn't have to tell our story all over again. The train took us all the way to Morpeth. All's well that ends well. It had been a pretty good day.

In November a small service was held in the St Andrew's Way section of the Eldon Square mall to celebrate the 40th anniversary of the Eldon Square Chaplaincy. I knew nothing about it but I went along to support the choir. A small area was roped off with six rows of eight chairs, and when I got there a few people were sitting waiting. I went in and joined them. I got an effusive welcome from Canon Glyn Evans who for some reason was literally bouncing with excitement. I'm sure he didn't know me from Adam, but he was doubtless pleased to see someone he thought must be a casual dropper-in, and hoped there would be more of me. The choir arrived, and he organised them all. He was obviously in charge. The man I found myself sitting next to was clearly an insider, so I said to him, "I've been coming here for 35 years and I never knew there was a chaplaincy. Is that my fault or someone else's?" He clearly though it was my fault, but explained that the Chaplaincy was not so much for the shopping public as for the staff of the mall and shops. I couldn't help wondering if they knew about it. We said prayers and responses from a sheet, sang a hymn or maybe two, and the choir sang. It was strange. The passing public sometimes stopped for a minute, as people stop to briefly watch buskers, then drifted on. I found the whole thing embarrassing.

Next day was Armistice Day, and we went to the Cathedral where Clare was doing an outdoor Act of Remembrance. She had specially asked for support because she didn't want to be there on her own! There was a big civic service in the city centre, but Clare thought there ought to be one at the Cathedral too. I will not be so ignoble as to wonder if Clare had not been invited to take part in the civic service. When I got to the Cathedral the bell was tolling. It seemed that it must have been detailed to toll till 11, and Clare needed to start the Silence at 11 so she had to yell her way through the preliminaries against the noise of the bell tolling above. A chap was going round with a tray of little wooden crosses with poppies which the few people gathered were buying and sticking in the grass under Queen Victoria. I can't imagine what her late Majesty thought.

I naturally wanted to have lunch in the Lantern Café before attending the lunchtime organ recital. There were very few customers. I asked for coffee and the hot meal of the day which was quiche and chips with a salad garnish. I was graciously served by a new lady who had not yet learnt to be offhand with the customers. I had taken some sachets with me, knowing that I would need them and not wanting to be fleeced of 15p a time. The Lantern do not serve salad cream at all, even for 15p, so I was glad I had a sachet with me and I poured it onto my garnish. After a few minutes one of the regular staff, who I will call Dolly, came over to my table. She bent to speak to me in a confidential manner. What could she want? She said, quietly and apologetically, that I was not allowed to eat that (pointing to my salad cream which was now all over my lettuce). I was astonished – was this some crazy new Health & Hygiene regulation? No, it was not allowed, she said. There was a notice on the wall. I guessed at once which notice she was referring to. Who had put the notice there, I asked? Oh, it had been there a long time, said Dolly. I asked who was responsible for it being there at all. Sheila Cavanagh, she said. Then I would like to speak to Sheila Cavanagh if she was there, I said (once a school-ma'am, always a school-ma'am). Yes, she was there. Dolly would ask her to come over. Sheila was the Manageress. I had often seen her, but never to speak to. She came across and was very polite but explained that the notice clearly said people were not allowed to eat their own food in the café. I was gobsmacked. I said I could quite understand that people should not bring their own sandwiches, fish'n'chips or take-away curry to eat in the café, but I had bought their coffee and a main meal and I liked salad cream which they did not serve. I think she could see her objection was ridiculous. I asked her who she was responsible to, and she looked puzzled. Who was her line manager? She said it was Kate Sussams. OK, I said, I would write to Kate Sussams (who rejoiced in the title of Operations Manager). Sheila said she hoped I wasn't offended, and I said not at all. I finished my salad, forgiving it for the trouble it had got me into, and then ordered chocolate pudding and custard and more coffee. I did write to the Operations Manager, but my letter must have got lost in the post because she never replied.

Two particularly enjoyable occasions were provided by Quiet Days at Shepherds Dene, organised by Father Steven. This was not much to do with chaperoning, but it was a spin-off. The first had been at the beginning of Lent this year, and the second to prepare us for Advent. Aspies love quiet days. In both cases they were intended to be religious almost to the point of being monastic, and the participants were supposed to spend some time with a leader and some time just being quiet and thinking, reading, praying or whatever. It was socially undemanding, except for the courtesies required of us all to co-exist comfortably. Father Steven gave me a lift, and I got myself to the Cathedral in good time for him. Shepherds Dene is a beautiful house not far from Riding Mill, and I had often heard of it. Among other things I had heard that the food was very good! James Lancelot was to be our leader for the first one, taking the theme of *Opus Dei*. There were altogether 12 of us. We began the day by having a free run of hot drinks and delicious home-made cookies in the dining room. Every likely need had been catered for, and there were gluten-free cookies and decaf coffee for fussy people. The equipment was left there and topped up occasionally in case anyone wanted a fill-up during the morning. We had three sessions during the day that consisted of a talk from James followed by a DIY period to make up 45 minutes. We could get lost in any of the public rooms or the beautiful garden, and it was pretty easy to get well away from each other and not disturb each other's meditations. Under the main staircase was a table and shelf bearing fund-raising merchandise, mainly books of a devotional nature and nothing that tempted me, but there was some nice chocolate that I bought for a fairing for Jessica. It was a comfortable, homely place.

Lunch was excellent. We sat at a long refectory table. We were each served with a big jacket potato and we could help ourselves to baked beans, grated cheese and coleslaw with lovely green salad and a tasty salad dressing. It was very good. I can't remember what we had for pudding, but it would have been lovely. Steven told us we might chat over lunch. This had exercised him somewhat, as he wondered if we should continue the silence while we ate, but he had (wisely) decided the fellowship of conversation would be relaxing and spiritually beneficial. Yes. I would not much have minded eating in silence if I had been required to, but I think twelve people chomping coleslaw would not be very silent anyway and might cause embarrassed levity. After the third session and a communion service we had tea before we left, and there was a selection of four kinds of cake, two of which were gluten-free, dairy-free or egg-free. On the way home we discussed how much we had enjoyed the lunch (appreciation of hospitality is a grace). I remarked that my jacket potato had lasted all the time I wanted it to, like the widow's cruse. "I've never heard that expression before," said a fellow passenger. "Nor have I," said Steven. I said Steven must know it because it was in the Bible. No, he could not place it. "Elijah," I prompted, and fumbled in the back of my head for the story. "Oh, the jar of oil!" he said at last. Maybe modern translations of the Bible don't use the word cruse. Oh dear – is nothing sacred? We got back to the Cathedral in time for me to join Evensong and hear the choir sing.

At the beginning of Advent Steven took us to Shepherds Dene again for another Quiet Day. My spiritual reading was my Kindle, which might look a bit suspicious, but I had downloaded Tom Wright's worthy book *Advent for Everyone*, and if it got too boring I could read *Barnaby Rudge*. The main thing was to be quiet, and this was the main attraction of the day for me. After our welcoming cup of coffee and home-made shortbread I had a look at the bookstall. There was nothing that appealed, but I bought a book I thought Jessica might like. I found myself reading it quite a bit, though it wasn't as good as either Wright or Dickens. Our leader this time was Revd Lesley Chapman, Priest-in-Charge at Riding Mill and Spiritual

Advisor to the Bishop. I didn't know Bishops had spiritual advisors. I learn something new every day. Lesley talked a bit about waiting, and read us some poems. Eventually she told us to go off and be quiet somewhere till the lunch gong rang. We could read, think, pray, even sleep if we wished. One lady, a newly ordained priest who I didn't know, knitted, but I suppose it was holy knitting. I didn't ask. I even saw one or two people reading a newspaper, but I think it was probably *The Link,* a very holy paper whose crossword competitions I have sometimes won.

This time lunch began with soup, which I love. We were given a tureen at each end of the table, and there were plates with small bread rolls, more than enough for one each but not enough for two each, so no one had a second roll out of politeness. There were pats of butter and little sticks of about an ounce of cheese, also too few for two each. Never mind. But oh dear – I suddenly realised that there were no knives and forks by our places. This soup was our main course! Most of us passed our bowls up for seconds. Pudding, when it came, was served on large plates, each with a small ramekin on it, and when it was passed down to eye level we saw to our dismay that there was nothing on the plate but the ramekin. What a waste of labour, washing up all those big clean plates! The ramekins contained a very thick lemon curd yogurt with three submerged fresh raspberries that looked either pretty or alarming, according as your imagination ran. What it lacked in volume it made up for in yumminess. We polished that off with coffee. Later I had another cup in a quiet period, but no more shortbread appeared.

In the afternoon session we talked more about being ready for Christmas, and Lesley read us some more poems. She told us a rather long story about how one Christmas, when she had to provide a dinner for her extended family of eleven, the turkey was stolen from the car on Christmas Eve. This was apparently a major catastrophe for Lesley's family who had to make do with a small frozen chicken and lots of love. I forget the moral, but I can think of several. But another story she told had more significance. She related how, one Christmas when she was welcoming people into church, a young woman visitor came in with a little girl. Would the little girl like to join the other children for Sunday school? The mummy wasn't sure. Lesley said that if the mummy would like to go with her that was fine! After the service she met the mummy again and asked her if she had enjoyed Sunday School. Yes, the mummy said, she had! They had been told the story of how Jesus was born, and she had never heard that story before! We take so much for granted.

On December 3rd we had our Patronal Festival. This year it seemed the refreshments were simply wine, juice and mince pies, and nothing for the choir. The choristers were supposed to take packed lunches. And St Nicholas was supposed to be a generous old bishop! I shan't go to his party again if he is going to economise on the choir. After I left Jessica I went to get her some food from Gregg's, and gave it to Emily to pass on to her. It was quite a nice service with the Bishop presiding and Mark Tanner, the new Bishop of Berwick, preaching. I suppose he was the replacement for Bishop Frank who had retired, but Bishop Christine knew there had once been a bishopric at Berwick and got permission to revive it. Inevitably we had incense and the censer stopped just in front of us and swung like billy-o while the choir moved to their places and the procession filled up the space. After the service the choir were invited to get lost till 2pm when they were required at the Central Station to sing. Roger went with them to shake a bucket. The CCA never liked to miss an opportunity.

Next day, as I sat on a front pew chaperoning Jessica's organ lesson, I heard puffing and gasping behind me. It was Gordon, lugging a very heavy wrought iron stand, about five or six feet high, through the crossing. It was the stand for the statue of St Nicholas and the Pickled Boys that normally stands in a discreet corner near the organ. It was too big and splayed to be carried on a trolley or sack barrow. "This will do me in one of these days!" he gasped, and indeed it would not have surprised me a bit if it had done him in there and then. Why had the statue been moved anyway, I asked? Oh, someone had thought it would be a good idea to have it at the west end of the church for St Nicholas Day. I suppose that person had not offered to help move it. Gordon told me some of the things he had had to do over that weekend, including moving umpteen chairs around for various events. He and Alan were now the only verging staff, and they mainly took turns on duty and had no help.

One cold Monday night in February Canon Clare led Evensong as she often did, and as there were no other clergy present she read both the lessons. The first one was from Deuteronomy and was all about Jewish food laws, and the second was from an epistle: Paul pontificating on how women should learn in silence and not take any active role in the church. She read it very well, but rather defiantly, with many arch glances at the congregation. Kris, who as composer of the evening's anthem was there to listen, seemed to find it very funny and grinned broadly. Later in the prayers Clare thanked God that the Bible has the first word but not always the last, and that we move on as the Holy Spirit leads us. Hmm.

The next NCS day was at Durham on Feb 18th. For once we were able to go all the way by bus, which was a financial relief to me. At Durham Cathedral I signed Jessica over to the nice RSCM pastoral ladies, confirming that she was allowed to go off with friends in her lunch hour, then I went down to town to seek my fortune. It had been my intention to have lunch at Vennel's, an old café up an alley that used to do a good range of English "meat'n'veg" food. I had to go up a lot of stairs to the second floor to find a table, then I was told it was counter service. The chalkboard menu on the wall offered a rather veg-less diet of paninis and jacket potatoes, and I changed my mind. I didn't want to go all the way down to the counter and all the way back upstairs. There is a lot of upstairs in Durham. Many premises are narrow and three or four storeys tall, land being so scarce. I decided to go to the Café Continental, a favourite eatery of ours at the far end of Elvet Bridge. Alas, it had closed forever. Was it something I said? At the town end of the bridge was a small Italian restaurant, and as my hunger was getting the better of me I went in there though I could see they were no more into vegetables than they needed to be. I had some excellent ravioli, but it was a rather small helping. I didn't realise till too late that they had charged me £1 too much. I mooched round the shops for a while and visited the excellent new library which had a drinks machine (which I did not patronise) and very good toilets. I sat and read *Toast and Marmalade* by Emma Bridgewater – an enjoyable light read. In the Market Place I heard young female voices calling "Christine! Christine!" but I took no notice because every Tom, Dick and Harry is called Christine and nobody in Durham knows me. However it persisted, and turned out to be Jessica, Laura and Clarissa who were about to return from their lunch break. They had apparently bought themselves takeaway food and then gone into Claire's Accessories to buy each other friendship necklaces as souvenirs, and one of them (not Jessica I'm happy to say) had spilt her takeaway drink on their floor and was in the doghouse with the management.

Back at the Cathedral I went to the Undercroft for a cup of coffee and was tempted beyond my strength to have a second lunch of root vegetables, mash and gravy. I sat reading as long as I could. On the next table sat two elderly ladies (maybe not as elderly as me, and certainly not as elderly as I intend to be). They looked as if they were killing time. They had finished their coffee and cake, but seemed in no hurry to go. I sat on, and so did they, till it was almost 4.30 and time for the full choir rehearsal. I went to choose a seat in the nave where I could listen. I was settling comfortably on the second row back when a gentleman in a black frock came and asked me and a few other people if we would like to move into the Quire where the congregation normally sat for Evensong. We meekly followed him. In the Quire it mattered where we sat. We must not sit *here* because it was for the choir, and we must not sit *here* because a party of pilgrims from Mirfield were coming. Trying to do as I was told I ended sitting almost opposite to poor Jessica, but happily the Conductor, Martin Rawles, generally stood between her and me when they were singing.

It was a lovely service. Next to me sat the two old ladies from the café. So that's what they were doing! I said to my neighbour, "You were obviously in the café for the same reason as me!" Yes, she said, they had had lunch and endless coffee to entitle them to go on sitting there. Just before we began there was a terrible barking cough along the row. It went on. I got out a Werther candy and passed it to the other elderly lady. No, she said, it wasn't her. I said would she pass it along till it came to the cougher! At the end I went along to find the cougher with another sweet and it was a little girl of school age, sitting on her father's knee looking very miserable. I gave her the sweet which she seemed glad of, and said I thought she ought to have a fortnight off school. "Oh no!" said her father. Her mother said, "She's got a week off this week". I said that didn't count. (Well, it was half term. Good heavens, if parents had time off work for illness they wouldn't expect it to come off their annual leave!) I went to the Chapter House to collect Jessica, and after the usual lengthy farewells we set off home.

In mid-March an email came round to parents from Ian, asking us to respond to a SurveyMonkey questionnaire. It asked only one question and invited only one comment. The question was whether we, the parents, would prefer choir nights to be Monday and Wednesday or Monday and Friday. I replied that Monday and Friday suited me better as Marks and Spencer were open till 8 on Fridays and we could wait there in warmth and comfort for our bus. My comment, perhaps a little less selfish, was that I felt children were slightly less tired on a Friday night because of the euphoria of not having to go to school for two days. Alas, I was not in a majority, and Ian chose Monday and Wednesday, but more often than not we found M&S still open to provide us with hospitality till our bus arrived.

In mid-March the choir were invited to sing the *Chorale* from Bach's *St Matthew Passion* at The Sage with the Bach Choir. It was in the evening, but the whole afternoon was taken up with rehearsal. We arrived in good time and looked for somewhere to eat, but there was absolutely nowhere to sit. The Brasserie was not open, and the café was very busy and the service was slow. Every chair had either a bottom on it or, in a few cases, a coat or violin with which I was not prepared to argue. Jess had her packed tea for later and assured me she did not want to eat then anyway, so we went off to seek our fortune. On the floor below were 26 small rooms for practice, meetings or whatever. They all seemed to have a piano, carpet, nice chairs and a large blue curtain which as far as I could see hid nothing but an area of wall and was probably for sound muffling purposes. Room C22, where our choir was to be based, was open and we went in, having been joined by Megan Kelly and her dad Mike. Then Kris arrived, so I was surplus to requirements.

Back in the foyer café more places were becoming vacant and I bought a cup of coffee and sat at a little table to drink it. I surreptitiously ate a round of my own ham sandwiches. I read for a while, then about 3.15 I moved down to a nice area below where there was some fairly comfy bench seating and a water dispenser with cups, possibly the only freebie in The Sage apart from hygiene consumables. Ah yes, I must mention the loos, in case you have not been to The Sage. They are excellent, but black. It's very oppressive to be surrounded by black, but I expect it has a psychological effect on would-be vandals. It certainly had one on me. I wanted out.

Eventually the choir came back from rehearsing, about ten minutes late, and could not get into C22 because it was locked. The big girls sat on the floor and sang and giggled, the little girls hung around their parents, and Kris went off two or three times to try to find someone with a key, but with little success. It looked as if we were to be locked out forever. One daddy who was fairly new to the choir was very worried because his parking time was running out. Kris got quite irate about the situation and when he went off for the last time I wondered if he was going to lose his temper with someone. I shall never know, but he eventually came back with two unamused looking chaps who opened the door. Well, one of them did. Maybe the other was his apprentice. The Sage must be a terrible place if the key-holders have to go round in pairs! The choir were to have the use of another room in the evening, and in the meantime there would be nowhere to leave their cassocks etc. Megan had very kindly agreed to take Jessica's to their car and look after it. Mike offered us a lift back to civilisation on the north side of the river and we gratefully accepted. Jessica and I wanted to go to Windows music shop where she hoped to buy a copy of the score of Bach's *St Matthew Passion* which they were singing tonight, as they only had old photocopied sheets. That was £14, even more expensive than Sage coffee.

Mike had a free ticket for the concert because, having now got a new DBS he wanted to break in, he had offered to be a parent-assistant. I had not, and I had paid £12 for my ticket. Jessica went off to join the choir and I sat and read with a glass of orange juice in an upstairs bar area. About 6.45 I made my way to Hall One. I had booked a seat in the stalls, on the second row back at the end because I get vertigo higher up, but I'm afraid I got vertigo in the stalls too. It is such a visually overwhelming place. I was comfy, but unnerved by the perpetual bouncing of my seat as if someone sitting behind me was shaking me, but there was no one for several rows. The floor is very highly sprung (probably highly strung too for all I know) and can easily be made to bounce. It stopped as the auditorium filled.

I found the whole performance rather tedious, but of course it was nice to hear our girls' choir. They sat along the back of the massed choir, and although they must have been getting tired they behaved with dignity and sang well. They all had their names printed on the back page of the £3 programme, which I was pleased about. This often gets forgotten. I was astonished how many choristers we'd got – at least 22. We never see that many singing at services. After the interval their part was over, and they could go home. Kris was a bit frazzled because some of the girls had gone off without telling him, but he was generally able to phone them or their parents to see where they were. I think he must have been pretty tired too, at the end of it all. Jessica told me that when they were introduced to the Bach Choir at rehearsal the Bach Choir very kindly clapped, and at the end they gave them another clap for doing well. What a nice Bach Choir!

The next NCS trip was to Halifax Minster in March. We had a pleasant journey, changing at Leeds to a train on an adjacent platform without having to go up escalators. At Halifax we could see the Minster as we came out of the station, and it was only a couple of minutes' walk.

We had to check that it was indeed the Minster, and most local people we asked had no idea. To many people churches are just features of the landscape, largely ignored. Maybe that is what some churches have come to deserve.

We were kindly greeted by a welcomer who discreetly told us where the toilet was and where the RSCM were assembling. There was no café as such, but (as I saw later) there were three little tables with clean white lacy cloths on and each had a notice "We welcome you to tea or coffee and a biscuit. If you would like to leave a donation we should be very grateful." There was a long servery where you could help yourself to a mug and make a drink, and some biscuit tins at one end promised biscuits. I suppose when they are open they normally have a welcomer, but even so it is very trusting of them and gives a very good impression. I handed Jessica over to the pastoral carers and left.

It was probably my first visit to Halifax, and I had no idea what joys it might offer. I crossed a very fast and busy road by a controlled crossing, and found myself on the edge of the town. A signpost pointed, among other things, to the library and I set off to look for it. It was not far. What I could see of Halifax looked attractive. They have some very elegant Victorian architecture, and an intelligent and sensitive City Council who have not allowed modern high-rise rubbish. Wherever you are you have an impressive view of the moors above Calderdale. I started off with a snack and a read in M&S, then I found the modern but very nice Library and sat and read in there for about an hour. I walked round a pedestrian shopping area which is called The Woolshops.

I began to feel peckish again, but it is not good to be peckish in a city on a Saturday lunchtime. Every eatery was crammed. Next to the Minster was a pub called the Ring o' Bells that did food all day. I suddenly fancied fish and chips. I stuck my nose inside, but I didn't think the canned "music" was likely to be endurable for long, although it was not loud. I walked round for a bit, then decided to give the pub another chance. This time it was quiet. I found a little table in a corner and looked at the menu. There was this-and-chips and that-and-chips, but no fish-and-chips! The nearest was scampi-and-chips with mushy peas and tartare sauce. I settled for that, with a big glass of orange juice. As I looked around I was reminded of a song The Spinners used to sing:

> They're pulling them down, the old pubs,
> And plastic's all the go.

This was undoubtedly an old pub, and as I looked around I couldn't see any plastic anywhere, except a little frame to the top of a juke-box (or was it a fruit machine?). Everything was stone, wood, leather or brass. In front of the old iron stove in the fireplace was a small rug. It was a time capsule. But my food, when it came, was very wholesome-looking and tasty.

Eventually, when I knew it was time for the break before the final rehearsal, I went back to the Minster and had a mug of their excellent coffee. I visited their loo which was built into an old entry to a former south doorway. It was a fascinating mixture of modern and mediaeval, with mod cons set in ancient oak. The choir sang their way through the service, then came to the back for another break. A visiting parent came and sat behind me and started talking. He had never sung in there before, he said. He had sung in most Cathedrals of England, and lots of others, but never this one. I tried to pretend to be neurotypical and return the conversation, but I think he only wanted to talk about himself. He had met the Queen face to face, he said! I did not ask how, as I felt sure he would tell me. He related their conversation, which I only half believed. He had been offered the post of Governor of the Falklands, he said, but he had turned it down. I did not make impressed noises, nor did I ask why. After delighting me long enough with his other adventures he said, "I wish I'd accepted the Falklands now." I laughed Aspergically and said that the only Governor of the Falklands I had ever heard of was Rex Hunt. Governor of the Falklands was an office that most people never heard of till there was an invasion! I don't think he was pleased.

As usual there was a very protracted period of saying goodbye after Evensong, but we had plenty of time. Our train from York to Newcastle was full, many of the passengers being either drunk or anxious to give the impression that they were, and it was a somewhat stressful journey, but we got home safely. I was pleased to have added Halifax to our experience.

Easter was late this year, in mid-April. When Roger and I went into church after our hearty Vermont breakfast we were warmly greeted by Bishop Mark who was taking the service. I noticed someone was using a long pole to remove the little purple bags that are always put over any crosses for Good Friday. As I held out my hand to shake Bishop Mark's I said "Popish nonsense – good morning!" I asked him why they did it. I had asked before, and been told, but never in such terms as I understood. Bishop Mark explained, then said apologetically that it was not part of the tradition he was used to. I was afraid the man with the pole, who must have been one of the churchwardens, would hurt himself or pull his shoulder. I had thought they had abandoned that questionable custom. Gordon had told Roger that he no longer covered the crucifix over the rood screen because the screen wobbled making it too risky to lean a ladder against.

Bishop Mark both presided and preached, and did very well. He began by saying how nice it was to have children there, and they might make a noise but it was all part of the sound of God's creation. We should think of it as a kind of birdsong. Lovely! Early on in his sermon he suddenly said, "And the verger is creeping up behind me

..." Yes, Gordon had gone up the pulpit steps and interrupted him. Mark listened to him, then said to us all, "Has anyone left a rucksack at the back of the church?" No, it seemed nobody had, or nobody wanted to draw attention to themselves by saying so. Mark said Gordon had better do what they did with such things (I suppose take it outside and blow it up), but then came a shout that someone had claimed it. The trouble was, of course, that people were nervous about terrorism. I think they should simply have commended the suspicious rucksack to God and carried on. "Now, where was I?" asked Mark, and continued very competently. The Dean marked Easter by giving all the choristers a chocolate rabbit.

At the end of April the Cathedral held its AGM after Eucharist. First we had a lengthy presentation of financial matters from someone I didn't know, and it sounded a bit dire, but never mind. Then the Dean rushed us through the rest of the agenda which basically involved accepting a large number of reports that we had been given copies of. Any questions? There were a few, but as there was no roving mike I didn't hear much. Someone said the music was fantastic and Ian looked all pink and pleased. Another person said they wished the children's play area could be moved from the St Margaret Chapel to the opposite corner (where it used to be during morning service, and where it is gloomy and surrounded by funeral memorials and is generally used as a bit of a dump). Someone else asked a different question entirely, which might have diverted us, but Helen Robertson jumped up and said she couldn't let the children's chapel matter get by because it was very important. The children and parents loved it and used it on weekdays if they dropped in, and people had left kind comments in the Visitors Book and even on Tripadvisor! It made families feel welcome. When she sat down I called out that I seconded her. I do feel it's a pity that such a lovely facility should be resented by anyone, even if they have no interest in children.

The Dean also told us that the Lantern Café, now alas no more, has been outsourced and would re-open on Tuesday as the Dog Leap Café. It would henceforth be managed by a chap called Dean, which will cause some confusion! Just behind the Cathedral is a flight of stone steps going down to the Quayside and it is known as the Dog Leap Stairs. It still seems an odd name for a café. It was part of the contract that Dean should retain the present staff, though I would not weep if he didn't. I have seen the new menu and it looks pricey! This was not, of course, a chaperoning matter, but I have developed a keen interest in the Cathedral and its affairs. My protégée was at that moment lunching in McDonald's, unchaperoned.

On May Bank Holiday Monday the NCS were meeting at York Minster. I had been looking forward to using the entrance ticket I bought last year, which expired that day. I felt very proud of myself for having got one up on wicked Anglican commercialism. And indeed the ticket was used, but not by me. For the first time in my years of chaperoning I had to take sick leave. I did not feel at all well when I got up, and I had to ask Roger to take Jessica to York. He was happy to do so. He took great care of the ticket, and felt smug as he handed it over at the welcome desk. I gather they both had a good day.

On May 4th ("May the fourth be with you") I had to go to the Cathedral to return Jessica's cassock which she had borrowed for Monday. As my tummy bug had gone away I decided to case out the new Dog Leap Café. It looked busy when I went in, but I saw some empty tables at the back. Ian and Kris were having lunch at a table near the counter. They smiled and said hello to me, which not all Cathedral staff have done in the past. I went to the counter to order lunch as had been usual, but I was told to sit down and they would come to me. I saw that although the old tables and chairs were still there, more had been added, of various types. It looked as if they were hoping for more trade than they had been accustomed to. Best of all, on each table was a jar of sugar (covered), a jar of Colman's mustard, and bottles of Heinz tomato ketchup, HP sauce and vinegar. Wow! Under the old system you had to pay 15p a sachet for any sauce or vinegar, and they did not do mustard at all. Imagine sausage without mustard! "It's better already!" I said to the waitress, waving my hand at the sauces. She tactfully pretended not to hear me. The previous manageress is still her colleague. Dean (Dean Eccles, not *the* Dean, you understand) was tall and youngish and pleasant. He seemed to keep a cheerful workforce, or they may just have been excited by the proximity of a male of the species. They had been a pretty dour bunch when they were all women. I ordered a roast salmon salad and a bottle of apple juice. The salad came in a large soup plate and looked generous. It consisted of couscous mixed with fresh herbs, and covered in marinated salmon, cooked cherry tomatoes and rings of roast leek – all cold. It was very good and I felt nice and full when I had finished it. I began to feel like coffee, and maybe a pudding just this once. Nobody came, so in the end I went to the counter and asked if I could have coffee and lemon posset. They looked shocked at my temerity. They would come to my table and take my order, and they did. But if I hadn't been bold and assertive they'd have lost a sale, wouldn't they? What kind of coffee would I like, asked the waitress? I confessed that I only knew one kind (Nescafe). She agreed to bring me a standard filter coffee. I thought filtering was a process, not a type of coffee, but then I am very ignorant. What she brought me was good. The lemon posset, which I expected to be light and fluffy, was the consistency of clotted cream and a generous helping. With it came a home-made shortbread biscuit the size of a saucer, liberally dusted with icing sugar – yum!

Ian and Kris sat over their lunch for a long time, talking about work in rather loud voices. It was obvious they get on really well together as working partners, which is such a good thing for both the Cathedral and Jessica. I had wondered if Kris, having got used to being Number One in the department, would be off looking for a better job, but apparently he is happy where he is. He has settled back very graciously to being Number Two.

At May half term Jessica went to Whitby again. This time we decided to make the journey in the morning, and it was easier than we expected. We did not have to leave home till 6.45, and our friendly local taxi driver, David Routledge of Castle Taxis, drove us to Morpeth station. We did not have reserved seats on the train but there were plenty to spare and we travelled very comfortably to Darlington. We had time for a caramel latte on Darlington station before catching our connection to Middlesbrough. It wasn't far from Middlesbrough station to the bus station, but we had a big suitcase so we got a taxi. Our bus to Whitby left at 9.20. The driver said I could not use my concessionary bus pass till 9.30, although it is 9.00 in our neck of the woods. She very kindly calculated where we would be at 9.30 and just sold me a ticket for that distance, telling me to go back to her then and re-register with my pass. Jessica asked if she could use her Teen Card as it was an Arriva bus, but that particular Arriva bus was an exception to all the rules and she had to pay. However, the kind driver asked her how old she was and gave her a half-fare ticket. We suspected this might be a bit irregular, but as far as we were concerned it was not dishonest. We had a lovely trip with much better views than last year as the windows were clean and dry. In Whitby we had an hour to spare, which was quite a surprise to us. We spent it in Costa, before getting a last taxi to Sneaton Castle.

Unlike last year, Andrew Reid was quite ready for us all when we arrived and we were led straight into a large room they called the hall where they would do most of their practising. This year Andrew's wife Louise was there with all four of their children – Sarah, with whom Jessica was delighted to renew acquaintance, Christopher and the twins Catherine and Eleanor. I don't think the twins were staying. A lady came and introduced herself as Sarah King, and I had to take a minute to put my brain in gear before I remembered she was the Education Administrator from the RSCM at Salisbury. I had spoken to her and exchanged emails many times, but it was so nice to have a face to go with the voice. Before long all the children had arrived and been signed into the care of the RSCM, and parents were free to go. Indeed they were probably glad to see the back of us. The serious stuff started at 12.15, and they wanted to get on. The children also undoubtedly wanted to get the first session over so they could have their lunch! I was given to understand that this year there were only five girls, but I don't know how many boys. Some kind chorister parents, Mark and Penny Toomey, gave me a lift back into town.

Back in Whitby I shopped in the big Co-op for picnic stuff to eat on the bus, then I looked for somewhere I could get coffee to warm me up. Some chips wouldn't have come amiss, but wherever I could see chips there were long queues. Coffee was much easier to obtain. Now it was time for my bus, the X93 which had quite a long queue waiting for it, but happily there were far more seats than people queuing. I sat upstairs with a good view and ate my Co-op salad. It was very good – thank you Co-op. In Middlesbrough I had an embarrassing experience. I went into the Gents instead of the Ladies, and only fumbling with the turnstile slowed me down enough to realise my mistake in time. My blunder cost me 20p, but it could have been worse. It occurred to me that Barbara Castle had successfully campaigned for public toilet turnstiles to be banned back in 1963. Had this been forgotten? Further research later, in Hansard courtesy of Google, revealed that the issue was raised again in 2009 in the House of Lords. The noble lords were informed that turnstiles were still used on transport interchange toilets, but there must always be a manually operated gate as well, and someone must always be around to open it for anyone who found turnstiles compromising. That's progress! I've often seen the little gates, but rarely anyone to open them! I bought some more snacks for the next stage of my journey, and had a peaceful drive back to Newcastle. Now the sun was behind me so I had lovely views.

I had a one-day break from chaperoning, and then on the Thursday I had to retrace my steps to fetch Jessica home. This time I did not need to leave home till 9 o'clock. My Middlesbrough bus was at 10.10, and that leg of the journey was an hour and a half. I read and enjoyed views of sea and moorland punctuated by little towns. I had almost an hour to wait at Middlesbrough so I stocked up on comforts. I had coffee and a corned beef pasty at Millican's, then I bought two bottles of banana Yazoo for later.

There was a long queue for the X93 bus, and it looked as if lots of families were off to Scarborough for the day. I had never realised that Scarborough was within a few bus rides of home, though I think time there would have been pretty short. I enjoyed the ride, but not all my fellow passengers did. One was coughing a lot, and I couldn't give them a Werther candy because they were behind me and whenever I turned round to see who it was the coughing stopped. I was afraid they might think I was being critical. Another small boy was determined that he was going to be sick, and his mother gave him a carrier bag. He told her it was no good because it had holes in. She said he had better sit on the stairs and put his head between his knees. This didn't sound at all good. If her medical advice didn't work we should all have to wade downstairs through yuk. Happily he managed to contain himself till at least Whitby. On the lower deck I could hear a baby crying for most of the journey, and my heart bled for it. Some brave mum was trying to give her family a treat, but little children do not often like travelling. They prefer to stay at home.

In Whitby I drank a bottle of Yazoo, then I looked round for fish-and-chips. There's something about Whitby, and maybe all coastal resorts, that tells you you are desperate for fish-and-chips. I found a shop with a very short queue, and had a small fish with mushy peas. It was divine – really. In the big Co-op I bought some iron rations in case we needed them later, and four carrier bags – one to use and three to keep in my rucksack in case I met anyone else who felt sick on a bus.

The public loo in Whitby is very tightly run. It costs 40p for adults and 10p for children, and you pay at a desk. The clerk then presses a switch that opens a door to the cubicles. They are not glamorous, but they are well maintained and there are enough of them. When you leave you come out through a different door marked Exit, and as you approach it a sensor clicks and it opens. They are not taking any chances of people sneaking in without paying. Where you can relieve yourself if you have no money I daren't think. It is tempting to think that the clerk's wages could be saved by leaving the loos open, but at least their method ensures quality and adequate cleanliness.

I now had to find my way to St Hilda's Church. Whitby rejoices in two churches dedicated to St Hilda, a C of E and an R.C, which must cause a bit of confusion. I saved myself confusion and quite a climb by taking a taxi. It was owned by a company called The Three Vees, and Mrs V drove me up. By chance she had driven me to Sneaton Castle on Tuesday. When she knew I wanted St Hilda's she said "I was married there!" I asked her if she had been there since, but she said only once to somebody else's christening. I suggested she should go again sometime, and she said she might.

In the church I could hear a rehearsal going on somewhere out of sight, and there were one or two people floating around in the nave. I sat at the back and read till it was time to move to a more advantageous seat nearer the front so I could see what was going on. The service began at 4. It was a very enjoyable, even inspiring service. Like last year it had a theme of prophecy and fulfilment. We sang five lovely hymns and heard goodness knows how many readings and anthems. Among the anthems were two pieces from Handel's *Messiah* including the *Hallelujah Chorus* and I could hear Jessica's strong voice dominating the high notes. Sarah King played her trumpet in one piece. There was a decent-sized audience/congregation of parents who had come to collect their children, and they all seemed to join in heartily.

At the end Andrew gave out certificates to all the participants, and made a little speech of thanks and encouragement. As they left he took Jessica on one side and seemed to be specially thanking her. It is always a sad moment for emotional teenagers when they have to say goodbye to each other, never being quite sure if they will meet again, but of course most of them hoped to meet in August in Lincoln.

Now we had to trundle Jessica's big suitcase down the hill to the town, and we didn't have much time to spare before our bus at 6.03. Jessica preferred to get home rather than stop to eat, and I think sensibly. She ate some of the iron rations and drank carton juice. I suppose now the fun was over she was quite tired. Children don't usually get much sleep on residential courses! The bus was quite crowded with people coming home from Scarborough (some the same ones I had seen earlier) but many of them got off at Guisborough leaving more space. At Middlesbrough we changed to the railway, and had vending machine snacks. Our train was prompt and in excellent condition and we had an enjoyable ride to Newcastle, then a taxi home, arriving about 9. Roger had a pizza waiting for Jessica.

I had spent twelve hours travelling, and longer on Tuesday, but I had no regrets. If I drove I would have all the worry of wondering how far the next petrol station was, what that funny noise was, whether a traffic jam was going to last forever, where I could park and if I'd got the right change for the machine. Instead I had been driven in at least relative and often luxurious comfort, at no cost on buses, and had been able to soak up interesting and often beautiful scenery. And I'd heard some amazing singing! Yes, it was well worth it.

June 20th was a very special day, when Jessica took her RSCM Gold Award exam. She had planned and prepared for it almost entirely by herself, with a little help offered by Ian towards the end. It had not been without stress for us all, and we were looking forward to getting it over with. Roger and I felt fairly confident she would pass. The exam was to be in Peterlee.

It was a school day, and it was necessary for her actually to attend school for the first couple of hours, but then she had permission to leave. The school were generally very helpful about choir-related things. I was also out in the morning, and we had agreed to meet at Morpeth bus station for a certain bus. She managed it with three minutes to spare. She was bit peeved that I had brought my shopping trolley, which she felt would disgrace her, but it was necessary as in addition to other music I had to carry three music copies of *Singing the Faith* (borrowed from Morpeth Methodist Church), each one being quite heavy enough in itself. I had to ask her to lift it on to the bus but I trundled it the rest of the time. From Newcastle we went by another bus to Peterlee, where we had never been. We found a shopping precinct somewhat larger than we had expected, but not very exciting, and plenty of charity shops which are no doubt very useful in an economically stressed area. We had not yet had lunch and we looked for somewhere to eat. Jessica, who does not like breakfast and had only had a Starbucks latte in Newcastle, did not want to eat at all, but I felt she could not expect to do well in an exam on a totally empty stomach. I was very hungry myself, but then I had not got nerves. Jessica had. We found a pizzeria and a Costa, and made a note of them, but in the upper part of the mall we found an ice cream parlour, 1950s style. They looked as if they were struggling and needed support. They did a small range of non-ice cream food, and Jessica allowed herself to be persuaded to have a toastie, and ate half of it. As I ate my rather rubbery toastie I found myself crunching on a hard bit that I could not identify as either cheese or tomato. Knowing it was either a foreign body or a filling I left the rest, so it was not a very nourishing experience for either of us. Jessica lay down on her banquette and said she would like to sleep, but she didn't. The canned music was of the 1950s and '60s so it was not offensive to me, and sometimes even a bit nostalgic.

We made our way to St Cuthbert's Church which we could see on our skyline. It was quite near, and a very attractive modern building. As we approached we could hear the previous candidate singing, and it turned out to be Faith with whom Jessica took her silver exam a couple of years ago. Faith's mum let us into the hall and welcomed us. It seems it was her church, and she was running the day's domestic arrangements. She made me a very welcome cup of coffee. Jessica's accompanist, Marcus Wibberly, arrived and they had a run-through in the hall. It sounded divine, and listening to it was a great treat for me. The exam took place in the sanctuary, and I waited in the hall, sneaking into the corridor now and again to hear Jessica singing. Her examiner was Gordon Appleby, who she had once met on an NCS trip and liked. She was happy when she came out, and hopeful of her chances. Back in Newcastle we made up for lost calories in the Happiness Inn, a Chinese restaurant opposite our bus stop at Haymarket. A few weeks later Jessica found that she had passed with honours, so she was very happy. Later still she was sad to hear of the sudden death of Gordon Appleby, and she was glad that their lives had touched, if only briefly.

One Tuesday in June a special afternoon meeting was held at the Cathedral which was advertised as a "fizz and nibbles" presentation of the new work that the Dean and Chapter were hoping might be done with a Heritage Lottery Fund grant if we got one. It seemed an odd day to hold such a meeting, as most of the congregation might be assumed to be at work at 3pm. The purpose of the imagined work was to "make the church more effective for C21st worship". I had no idea what C21st worship was, and I strongly suspected, as the pews were to be removed, that it was to enable the Cathedral nave to be let for dances. I thought it was unlikely that the proposed changes would be completed in my time as a chorister chaperone, but I was interested to see what went on.

It was held in the south transept, and I found ten or so tables set up with six chairs at each. I sat at one that had one of the new experimental seat-benches behind it. It looked smart and seemed comfortable at first, but after a few minutes I found I was sliding forward. Only one other person was present at that moment, a welcomer who I had not met before. On the tables were piles of literature, biros, writing paper etc. One was a pile of colourful brochures about the project, already ongoing, to revitalise Bigg Market. I knew about that, but from what I have seen of Bigg Market there is not much that the proposed spending of money will do. It is an open area flanked by rather seedy shops and pubs, and I would avoid it after dark. A famous feature is a long-closed Victorian men's subterranean loo, and rumour has it that it is to be transformed into a bar!

A large sheet of paper was marked up as a registration sheet, on which in tabular form we had to put our name, our organisation, and our email address if we wanted to be sent more news. I felt the tubs full of biros were surplus to requirements. We were all educated people who would surely carry a pen round with us. I mean, we all carry mobile phones, so surely we would carry pens? No? I am never without a pen (if by some mischance I am, I buy one as soon as possible). I suppose the cost of the dozens of biros was included in the £2,000 a day the Cathedral costs to run.

Canon Clare welcomed us all and then said Sarah Hilton was going to take over. Sarah Hilton was the boss of Sarah Hilton Associates Ltd, and I don't know what they were doing for us. Perhaps they were co-ordinating everything. She asked if we could hear her, and we all said yes or no according to whether we could, and she fiddled about with the mic. The system made appalling noises of an echoey biscuit-tin nature, some awful and some quite painful. People were calling out "Yes!" "No!" "That's right!" and "That's awful!" and so it went on. Ms Hilton said she had a good voice and would prefer just to use it unaided, if that would be OK with us. Oh yes, said 95% of us. "No! Can't hear you!" protested 5% at the back. The fuss went on till most people were satisfied. The trouble was the layout. If we had been sitting close together on a couple of rows near to the speaker there would have been no problem. We didn't need the tables.

When we finally got down to the meeting it was 3.25 (having officially started at 3.00). It was a Power Point Presentation, though there was never much on the screen. After Ms Hilton's introduction the Dean spoke – about tradition and heritage and costs. Then we heard Neil Hammond from HLF, David Silk, the Learning Officer from the Castle, Adrian Waddell from the Business Improvement Company, Jennifer Hillyard, the Librarian from the Mining Institute, and lastly Canon John Sadler who is masterminding the whole project for the Cathedral. They all spoke briefly about how the old town, the bit including the Cathedral, the Castle and Bigg Market, was being updated to preserve it for ever. Depend upon it nobody mentioned God! At one point there was a loud noise from the nave when K–, an elderly drunk who regularly comes in to argue with God, turned up and began his usual inebriated harangue of the Almighty. Canon Clare and Kate Sussams jumped up and went over to him. They came back in a few minutes and peace was restored. I suppose they had persuaded K– to leave quietly. I felt it was unfair. K– was there to meet God, however aggressively, and we were there to ignore Him.

When the meeting had been going for about an hour Ms Hilton said we must keep an eye on the time so we could enjoy our Prosecco and nibbles at 5 o'clock, but now we would get into groups round our tables and ask questions etc. I do not do groups, and I had no wish for either Prosecco or nibbles, so at this point I snuck off. I felt I had wasted my time, and that the meeting was not for the likes of me anyway. I wondered why we had been urged to go? I suppose there has to be community involvement for brownie points, and the more people they could get there the better it would look to the HLF. And of course it is a good thing I was there or I wouldn't be able to tell you all about it.

The end of another choir year was fast approaching, and on a Saturday morning at the beginning of July a concert as held in the South Transept. Parents came, and Ian held a competition between Dec and Can. The winning team would be rewarded with slightly larger bars of chocolate. A lady called Gill Blazey who taught at Dame Allan's School had been recruited as adjudicator. Jessica was making two contributions: an organ piece (Pachelbel's *Fantasia*) and *The Cats' Duet* with Celia. At a halfway point we all went upstairs for coffee. This was a sad occasion as Celia was leaving forever. Tomorrow or Monday she would be flying off to New Zealand to join her family for the summer, then going to university. She played a cello piece. Other choristers, five from each side, gave party-pieces which we enjoyed. At the end Gill gave out the marks of which there were only three; Commended (fail), Highly commended (pass) and Outstanding (shades of Ofsted which meant she really liked it). Celia and Jess got Highly Commended for their duet (Gill wished they had spat and scratched more) and Jess got Outstanding for her organ piece. This surprised her because she knew she had made at least four mistakes, but I didn't notice and maybe Gill didn't either. She remarked that she wished she had learnt to play the organ. I think Dec were the winners, but it didn't matter in the least. The small bars of chocolate for the runners-up were Kitkats, and the bigger bars for the winning team didn't look much bigger, but having chocolate for everybody was a good idea all the same. Choristers get so hungry.

When I got home there was a large envelope addressed to me. It was Jessica's Gold Award results, sent to me because I had registered her in the first place. Yes, she had passed with honours. She was not with me, having gone on somewhere else, but I phoned her. She was on a bus. She was so happy and cried. "People are staring at you!" I said. I didn't know whether they were or not, but I knew she was on a bus and they would be. If you are ever on a bus when a fellow passenger bursts into tears, they may have had bad news or they may have been awarded an RSCM Gold Medal with honours. Perhaps best to ask them anyway. I set about ordering the medal from Norwich. It cost £25.49 including postage. Every silver lining has a cloud, but it was well worth it. We wanted to get it as quickly as possible so the Dean could present it to her before the end of term.

Next day was not the last Sunday, but it felt like it to Jessica because it was the end of an era. Celia was decommissioned and presented with her copy of *Messiah*. From being a founder member of the girls' choir as a child, her time as Head Chorister was now over. She and Jessica had got on well together, and although Jessica liked the other choristers she did not have the same rapport with any of them. Most of them were quite a bit younger, less musical and less committed. I reminded her that Mr Roberts would also be feeling bereft, and that he would need her as an ally.

The following Saturday NCS spent a day at Doncaster Minster. This was a very easy trip for us on one train from Morpeth. The only difficulty of the day came when we tried to find our way to the Minster. Nobody in Doncaster seemed to have heard of it! Did we mean St This? St That? St The Other? Sadly we didn't know which saint we were looking for. Eventually someone who was *nearly* sure directed us on quite a long walk through a market where Jessica would have liked to browse, and we came at last to the Minster where it was St George who welcomed us. It was a handsome church, restored by George Gilbert Scott (but he was probably not the George of their patronage). After I had signed Jessica over to the RSCM's tender care I spent the day exploring the city, and went back in time for Evensong where I was happy to see Jessica wearing her new gold medal for the first time. The choir was using the adjacent church house as a base for the day. The song room was weird. It had a warm carpet, but the walls looked as if they were in an advanced state of decay. The wallpaper had been removed partly, the plaster had been removed partly, and a great deal of old brick was roughly exposed. Jessica told me later that during a re-vite someone had said the wallpaper was C18th, and everything had stopped while they waited for a professional assessment. I wonder if they have had it yet? Do pop in and find out if you're passing. We rounded off our day with a bag of fresh doughnuts from a stall in the market.

Next day was the last Sunday of the choir year and we had a celebration BYO lunch. I had emailed Dean Dalliston a few days ago to ask if he would present Jessica with her medal, but I had no reply. Well, he's a busy man. After the service I caught up with him and asked him if he had received my email. He floundered, but when he finally realised what I was talking about he vacillated and said this was not a good occasion. It was obvious he didn't want to get involved with the matter, so I let it drop. After the lunch Ian held a farewell ceremony in the South Transept where he made a gracious speech thanking everybody it was possible to thank. He said Kris was a dream to work with because he was so supportive. He had asked Emily to tot up people's attendance and he gave a prize to the top boy and girl. I didn't know the boy, but not surprisingly Jessica was the girl with the best attendance. Later she thanked us both very graciously for enabling her to win the Mars Bar by seeing she got to choir regularly and on time. In her new capacity (inevitable but as yet unratified) as Head Chorister she made a small presentation to two other senior choristers who were leaving. There was still half an hour to fill in before rehearsals, so Ian said they could all go outside and play in the little courtyard at the back because it can be safely locked. Roger and I went off to town to pass the time and had hot drinks in Waterstone's.

At the final Evensong the Dean decommissioned six members of the choir, four of whom were lay clerks. They all got their copy of *Messiah*, which as the Dean said contains everything they will ever need to know about the faith they support with their singing. Canon Clare invited us all to assemble for a photo-shoot at the end, which was nice. It had been another good choir year, and the new Director of Music and his team were clearly a great success.

This year the RSCM summer school was at Lincoln again. I chaperoned her both ways, but this time only on day trips. After Evensong on the last day everyone had to disperse in silence because a recently departed worshipper was having his ashes buried in the Cathedral. The words of Jesus, "Let the dead bury their dead" came to mind, but perhaps unfairly. Anyway, goodbyes had to be whispered. It was Andrew Reid's last summer school because he was giving up the Directorship of the RSCM to take up a post with Harrison and Harrison, organ builders, in Durham, but that was good news for Jessica because she and Sarah would be able to see more of each other. Sarah hoped to join Newcastle Cathedral choir. NCS was being continued only for singers over 18, and under 18s could join the Millennium Youth Choir if they passed an audition. Adrian Lucas, who had been directing an MYC summer school at Lincoln at the same time, offered to audition Jessica at Crewe at their next meeting. It didn't sound as if it was going to be very different for practical purposes. It consists of about four events annually – three one-day events and a summer school – at a cost of £500 plus all the travel expenses. Hey-ho.

2017-2018

Kris started the new year by shaving his head at the sides, leaving a flat teacake on top. I aspergically told him he looked just like a certain far-eastern dictator, which upset him. Later I saw a photo of George Orwell, looking very similar to Kris, on a book at home, and asked Kris if he would rather be taken for George Orwell. Yes, he said, he could go with that. But I would like it to go on record that the resemblance to either of these famous gentlemen ended with the haircut. Kris is far nicer than either of them. Ian had plans for a new baby choir to which younger children of school age could come and have musical fun, with a view of hopefully integrating them into the choir in due course if they felt so inspired.

At the first Evensong of term there was no officiating priest available, so the service was taken very capably by a trainee Reader called Helen Wright. She asked to see Jessica, and asked her to be cantor. Jess had never done that, though Celia and Bella had on a few similar occasions. Both stand-ins did very well, and we didn't miss the priest. Later Helen thanked the choir and especially Jess. She said she did not start the cantoring part of her training till next week. Well, Jess had had no training at all!

I had a phone call from Joan Johnson to say she had read about Jess's gold award in the CMQ and was *amazed*. I wasn't sure why she should be amazed, but I took it in the right spirit. Joan wondered if Jess would like to have her medal presented at Durham with the Durham candidates, but perhaps our Dean had already presented it? No, I said, he had not thought it appropriate, and on Jess's behalf I would love to accept her offer. Jess was pleased when she heard about it. As for me, I love any opportunity to go to Durham Cathedral.

At the end of September Ian staged a *Last Night of the Proms* which was very successful. The choir joined with the excellent Dunstan Silver Band, and the traditions of the Albert Hall were closely followed. The children learnt some songs their grandparents knew well but that they might not otherwise have had the chance of learning. The audience were given little Union Jacks to wave at the end. The nave was full, and with the sale of tickets and refreshments quite a bit of money was raised, and of course it strengthened the wider choir community. From the chaperoning perspective it had been a challenge. Jessica worked at Alnwick on Saturdays, and if you only work one day a week it's not a good idea to keep asking for time off. I met her with a taxi when she knocked off at 4 o'clock, and we were at the Cathedral with almost an hour to spare. Some of our local taxi firms owe quite a bit to the Newcastle Cathedral Choir! Next day the choir were given a holiday to reward them for their hard work.

Sunday, October 8th was a big day for Jess because she was officially installed as Head Chorister at Evensong. It perhaps reflected the importance of such a ceremony to the Dean that it was held at Evensong when there is only a very small congregation, but tonight the chancel stalls were well filled with families of choristers – one had apparently brought 12 supporters. First four new choristers were welcomed, of whom one was Sarah Reid. Jess was very happy to have Sarah joining her in the choir. She had brought five supporters. Then the Dean installed Jess and Rachel as Head Chorister and Deputy – a yellow medal ribbon for Jess and a green one for Rachel. Jess had dreamed of being Head Chorister since she was 10, and we were so happy that her wish had come true, perhaps sooner than she would have dared to hope. All being well she will have three years in the role. Afterwards we celebrated by paying our first visit to the new multi-million pound Grey's Quarter in Eldon Square. After much inner debate Jess decided on Frankie and Benny's. The restaurants are open-sided and give the impression of dining under the stars, but of course they are all indoors really.

Later in October Jess was invited to be presented with her gold award at Durham on a Saturday evening. I fetched her from work in Alnwick in a taxi, and we were in Durham in an hour. Carol, our delightful lady driver, charged us a good deal less than we had feared. Jess ran off to find people she knew, and I went to the Undercroft café but found it full. I decamped to the University Library café on the green, and sat there till they closed. The special event was an RSCM Evensong at 5.15. When I looked for a good place to sit I found many of the front pews were reserved for one group or another, but I was happy to find one row labelled "For friends and relatives of Award Winners". Wow! You've really made it when you're a friend or relative of an award winner! I shuffled along the pew till I came to two nice comfy wooden stacking chairs. Well, comfier than a pew, anyway. I hoped Roger would find me there, but he could not see me and he was at the other side. He had come on the bus.

The service was very singing-based and to the glory of God and Bernard Gilpin of happy and blessed memory. I had never heard of him, but it was interesting to learn. You learn something new every day, in every cathedral. The presentation was done very nicely. There was one little girl getting her bronze medal, and Jess and her friend Laura Toomey from Billingham getting gold. The Dean of Durham made the presentations. It was a very nice occasion for Jess, and well worth the effort of getting to Durham. Chaperoning has many compensations, and this was certainly one of them. When we finally got home we indulged Jess by letting her order a Domino pizza for supper. It seemed to take forever to arrive, and wasn't very hot (though I'm told it was delicious). Oh dear, whatever happened to bread-and-dripping and cocoa?

On a Saturday at the end of October Jess had to go to Crewe to be auditioned for the Millennium Youth Choir. We made it the final leg of a short West Country holiday in which we had visited Bristol and Wells Cathedrals. Crewe was something of an anti-climax. We had to wait twenty minutes for our taxi which made us a bit late getting to St Stephen's Methodist Church. This was a modern brick building in the middle of a vast Victorian estate of terraced houses. We followed the noise till we found the MYC, and I handed Jess over and signed her in. They were happy for me to leave our large suitcase in a discreet corner. I set off to find the town.

Crewe was the most depressing experience I had had for a long time. I had no idea which way to walk for the town, but I tried to guess, and jotted down the name of each street so that I didn't get lost. The housing estate seemed to go on for ever, and it was totally deserted. Although it was Saturday, there were no children playing out. Where was everybody? Were they still in bed? I saw one or two corner shops, but they didn't look as if they ever opened. It was eerie. Eventually I saw an elderly Indian gentleman pushing a wheelbarrow to some allotments. At least he had found something worth getting up for. By now I think I had guessed the direction of the town, and the gardener was a bit too far away for me to speak to, but seeing him was encouraging. I soon found myself on a traffic road and started walking along it, unable to tell which was the right direction. A string of seedy shops appeared. Occasionally I saw a person sitting on a doorstep smoking or eating take-away food. They looked depressed and disillusioned. I came upon a lady with two small children and asked her if I was going the right way. No, I wasn't. I found such brief human contact reassuring. I retraced my steps, but I stopped jotting landmarks down because it occurred to me that a confident white woman, writing things down, might be construed as a spy and resented.

Eventually I came to the throbbing heart of Crewe. Even here everyone looked depressed. There was a bit of a market, lots of shops of a cheapo nature, and what looked like a brick Town Hall of the 1950s. I followed the flow till I came to a shopping centre. I had hoped to have elevenses in Marks and Spencer, but I had already given up hope of finding one. I began to wonder if there was even a toilet. I asked a lady coming out of a shop if there was one, and she said the only one was in Asda. Ah, balm in Gilead! She kindly directed me. On my way there I passed an elderly man playing lovely eastern European folk music on a cello. It was quite the most beautiful experience of my day, and I gave him all the change I had which was probably only about 25p, but he was touchingly grateful. It was nowhere near enough for a cup of coffee. I have regretted ever since that I did not give him a fiver.

In Asda I rejoiced in their comfort facilities and then bought a good selection of lunch stuff for me and Jess. I put it in separate carriers so that I could pass hers over to her without being too obtrusive. I also sat in their café with a nice cup of cocoa and read for a while. As I walked back through the centre I found a cake shop and got Jess a caramel cream iced doughnut in a nice little box. It was to encourage them as much as anything. What they were selling was probably not dietetically very good for anyone, but as comfort food it would have been invaluable. The nice shop lady told me where I could go to find a taxi. I didn't need a taxi, but I wanted to get back to St Stephen's as quickly as possible, and I would at least be supporting Crewe's economy. And it was starting to rain and I had no coat.

I hoped my presence in the church would not inconvenience anyone, and I don't think it did. I sat in a nice little meeting room adjacent to the hall, and I enjoyed listening to the singing through the wall. A man was sitting in the room working on his laptop. I wondered if it might be the minister preparing his sermon, and I said I hoped he did not mind me being there, but he said no, he was also a parent waiting! At 1 o'clock I heard the choir breaking up and I snuck in with Jess's bag of lunch. I had signed for her to be allowed to leave (in a party of three as usual per RSCM rules) but there was nowhere to go and I think most people were picnicking indoors. The odd few might have had parents with cars who knew where to go for a pleasant break. Jess was pleased to have food and tucked into it, and I went into the back of the empty (but rather cold) sanctuary and ate mine. I hoped to drink either my orange juice or my milkshake, but in both cases I was unable to open the bottle. I thought about seeking out a strong male of the species to open it for me, but I didn't in case the said male was unable to open it himself and either hurt his hand or otherwise embarrassed himself. I consoled myself with tap water.

I spent the rest of the afternoon sitting reading (and eavesdropping) in the meeting room. It was not actually cold as there was a heater on, but it was not very powerful for the space and never really felt warm. A nice man whose name I never knew came in and offered me some coffee, for which I was extremely grateful. He talked about Crewe, the recent history of the town and its hopes for the future. It may be the hub of the new HS system, and a big Bentley car factory was expanding to create more jobs, but Crewe needs a lot more than that. Small waves of immigrants had come at different times, but they too were out of work and out of hope. I had seen some of them. I suppose the cellist was one of them.

At 4pm the day was over and Jess came to look for me. Yes, she had passed her audition. I had never doubted that she would, so I did not get quite as excited as she felt was appropriate. Apparently not all of the six or so people who had been auditioned that day were successful. Adrian Lucas very kindly offered us a lift to the station, and I would have loved to accept but I had already booked a taxi which was on its way. Our home train was crowded, messy and had its fair share of drunks, but also a number who were courteous and considerate. I was never without a seat. Jess phoned ahead for a Domino pizza, and then phoned Roger to warn him not to turn it away when it arrived!

At the beginning of November an email came round telling us all that the Dean, Chris Dalliston, had been "called" to Peterborough. It was apparently quite a persistent call, confirmed by Downing Street, and he said he was only answering it reluctantly. It seemed that their present Dean, who was retiring, had been a man of God but not of Mammon, and there was a good deal of Mammon-type sorting-out to be done. Peterborough were confident that Chris was the right man to undertake it. Ah well, Peterborough had sent us the Reid family with two excellent choristers, so it was a fair swap. The Bishop asked Geoff Miller, the Archdeacon, to be Acting Dean for the time being.

Armistice Day was the last ever day of NCS, at Hull. It was meant to be for boys, but they have been in short supply lately so the girls were asked to go and boost them and have one final fling together. We set off for Morpeth station at 7.50, and had a good trip to Hull with one change at York. We liked Hull station. In one corner a professional-looking band was set up for what we supposed would be an Armistice service in a few minutes. Lots of people seemed to be waiting. We hurried on to the Minster. It was not far to walk. We were there soon after 11 and the Silence had already been observed, but we were held back by a welcomer because the duty cleric was doing the hourly prayers. We found our way to the song school where I went in to see if I needed to sign anything. For some reason I didn't.

Adrian, who knew Jess was going to be a bit late, welcomed her warmly.

Now I wanted to case out their café which was in a side aisle but had plenty of tables. Busy ladies were feeding the five thousand. I asked for some leek'n'potato soup and a cheese scone and went to sit on a big empty table for about eight. I set up my Kindle and read and ate. After a minute or two a man brought his refreshments and sat at the other end of the table. As there were still lots of empty tables this annoyed me because I guessed he meant to make boring small talk. I did not look up. "Have you come far?" he asked. Without looking up I just said "Yes," hoping he would get the message. He didn't. "How far have you come?" he persisted. I looked up, and guessed he was a sort of welcomer, and I gave up hoping he would leave me alone. I said I had come from Newcastle. Oh, he knew Newcastle well. How were the Toon? He chatted on. I gave up hope of reading quietly in my own little Aspergic world and tried very hard to make neurotypical conversation. After a while it occurred to me that there was something familiar about him. Of course, he was Bishop Frank White, and the husband of Bishop Alison White in whose Minster I was sitting. He was retired now, but no doubt she had found him useful occupation apart from washing up. I apologised for not having recognised him, but he was not wearing the clothes I had been accustomed to seeing him in. He looked more human now, though I did not say so. Of course, come to think of it, he had seen me as often as I had seen him, and I was wearing my usual clothes, but he did not recognise me at all. Of course he is much more important than I am. In the end I escaped by saying I wanted to go off and explore Hull (which I did). He suggested a lot of interesting places I should visit. He did not know, of course, that my main interest is researching coffee shops.

In the expectation of a rough journey home I had decided to upgrade our train tickets to first class. I went back to the station, but at the customer desk was told I must do it on the train at the time. "Get in the Weekend First carriage," the lady clerk advised. How many first classes were there, I asked? Well, there was only one affordable one, she said. It would cost me £45 altogether. This confirmed my long-held opinion that there is First Class and First Class (and never the twain shall meet): one for the pretentious and one for the seriously rich. Well, when you think about it, the likes of Cabinet Ministers, Richard Branson and Archbishops don't want to have to rub shoulders with the *hoi polloi* who just happen to be able to scrape £45 together. It lost its appeal, but at least it was nice to know we could protect ourselves from Saturday night drunks if necessary. I had an egg'n'chips lunch in a reassuring greasy-spoon café and went back to the Minster.

The big visitor attraction was a poppy set-piece in a side aisle. It was four life-size soldier models carrying a stretcher with a soldier on it, just shapes covered in poppies. It was certainly impressive. My first thought was that it was rather a waste of poppies. A lot of work was being done in the Minster and some of the treasures had been put in a corner and surrounded by steel mesh barriers six feet high. Peering through I noticed that on the wall in that corner, inaccessible and almost totally obscured, was a large plaque in memory of the Minster Choristers who died in WWI. I felt affronted on their behalf. The real memorial had been rubbished in favour of ostentatious artwork. But the art work had attracted visitors and brought revenue. That counts for a lot in a Minster. They have their bills to pay.

This being the last NCS gathering, the girls naturally took even longer than usual to say goodbye to each other and take selfies with each other. By now it was getting cold, and in any case the Minster would be closing, so departure became inevitable. We had a reasonable trip home, and our fellow travellers in standard class, while in some cases voluble, were home-going shoppers and not drunken revellers. I too was a bit sad the NCS had dissolved. It had been fun visiting so many different cathedrals, and MYC probably won't go to so many places.

Christmas was soon upon us, and *Carols at the Castle* was held on the Friday and Saturday, December 15th and 16th. The first night the temperature was 1°C (if not less inside the castle) and forecast to be zero the next night. There is no heating in the castle, except we may be sure the staff have their own private little electric fire in their office. Added to there being no toilets and the access being very dangerous, even without ice, it was really a diabolical liberty to expect parents to pay £12.50 to freeze for an hour. Roger went with Jess, but I stayed at home. He felt very cold. The following night, it being Saturday, I had to bring her from Alnwick again by taxi, but then I swapped with Roger who was doing the concert again. He had bought a ticket, but was wondering about spending the time in the Vermont keeping warm. He didn't want to get a chill. However he was wearing a thick coat and decided to brave it. Both concerts were very enjoyable with a little audience participation (to get their blood flowing again). Ian gave the choristers the Sunday off in recognition.

The Friday before Christmas Canon Clare devised a Walking Nativity. She had asked me several weeks before if Jess could be Mary, and I was reluctant, remembering the one some years ago that I considered to be a farce. Clare began telling me what she had planned. I cut her short with "Will it be reverent, Clare?" Yes, she assured me it would be. Then she could ask Jess with my blessing, I said.

The walk started at the Central Station where we had to assume Mary and Joseph (played by John, a server) arrived in Newcastle by train, looking for somewhere for her to give birth. I had to chaperone her there (I think John was over 18 and did not need chaperoning) and arrive in good time so we were not seen by our hoped-for public. First we had to go to an office and ask for one of the managers, David Keech, who would sign us in. It was very important, in case of fire, that the station staff knew who would be in the station. Trains would be arriving all the time disgorging passengers who would not be known to be on the station, but ours not to reason why. David greeted us kindly with the standard Geordie greeting "Yrite?" He filled in some paperwork for us, then he led us across the bridge to the First Class waiting room. Wow! As we walked he told us there was no fire drill planned and if we heard a fire alarm we should make straight for the far end of the carpark. The waiting room was locked, but David talked to a nice lady in red who produced a key and let us in. We felt very special by now! I gave Jess the bag containing her BVM outfit and she was directed to a disabled toilet to change. She ceremoniously shut the door in my face. John, who did not need to remove any intimate garments, pro-ceeded to change in the waiting area. Jess had never seen her outfit so I wondered if she would manage OK on her own, but she did. David and the nice railway lady hovered and were very protective of us. Would we like a cup of tea? Sadly there was no time to accept.

Over the past week I had tried to make an outfit as easily, cheaply and convincingly as I could. It was dark, so there would be no risk of close scrutiny. I had made a long sack-dress with blue lining material, sewn up the sides but rough cut at the neck and hemline, with a matching sash to hold it all together. Under this she wore a white jumper and a cushion held on with tapes, and over it a cream pashmina. She managed to get it all on stylishly, and was soon ready. John had similar gear that made him look very Joseph-like. In the waiting room a man with a microphone, who was from Premier Christian

Radio, a local religious radio station I had never heard of, asked them what the journey had been like so far. Joseph and Mary were not expecting this, but they did creditably. We set off to walk back across the bridge to the portico, Mary holding Joseph's arm and me walking behind them. My job was not only to chaperone Mary (who didn't need me now she had Joseph) but to answer any questions from passers-by or protect them from mischief-makers. In the event I was surplus to requirements. David escorted them over, and took great care of them.

In the portico a great many people were gathered, more than I expected and I don't know where Clare had got them from. They were in a sort of enclosure made from display boards, and everyone had either a little lantern or an electric nightlight. I understood they came from IKEA. No doubt Clare had squeezed a budget from our officially impoverished Cathedral. She had a big illuminated star on the end of a flexible wand, and we all had to follow the star. It suited her. She had a portable sound system on a trolley, and the engineers had disguised it as a donkey which was very cute. She introduced the event, the choir sang a carol, and off we went.

First we stopped at the Royal Station Hotel next door. The Star asked for a room for Mary and Joseph. The manager told her that it was indeed a hotel, and a bit about its history, but that they were sorry they hadn't got a room to spare tonight. Oh dear. However some of the hotel staff joined our processions and went on with us.

We stopped at the Mining Institute on the next corner. We needed some shepherds. Were there any there? No, the miners told us. No shepherds, only miners. Would miners do? The Star thought that was a very good idea, and two miners, having told us all a wee bit about the Mining Institute, joined us with a lovely dog called Sasha.

Next we came to the Lit&Phil. Now the Star was looking for wise men. Surely there must be lots of wise men, and wise women, at the Lit&Phil? Yes, indeed there were! One of them told us a bit about the Lit&Phil. They had no accommodation for Mary, but they had been reading prophecies about this event and had been looking out for it. Some of them joined us and walked on with us. As we walked along we sang several carols.

Now we had to cross a busy road, and the Star had arranged wardens in safety jackets to see us all safely across. It wasn't very busy, but it was best to be careful. Across the road was the Castle where the Star hoped someone would be able to help Mary. Alas, no. The two Roman centurions who greeted us told us the Castle was now closed for the night. They were just going off duty themselves. Oh dear – the BVM was getting desperate. What could anyone do to help? The kindly centurions said there was a sort of church just up the road. We might try there. They came with us to see.

The Star led us to the Cathedral west door. This is where planning came in. Normally the Cathedral would have been tightly shut for the night, and no one would have responded to our urgent knocking. But the Dean had been primed, and was expecting us. He opened the door and warm light flooded out. "Come in! Come in! You must be frozen!" he said.

Somewhere between the west door and the crossing dais Mary gave birth to a doll. She put it in a manger and sang a carol to it. Then we all sang a few carols before being regaled with Gregg's mince pies and hot chocolate. And that was the Walking Nativity.

It may or may not have been Clare's finest hour, but it was all brilliantly executed. She seemed to have thought of everything, and had inspired the enthusiastic participation of many people who had formerly been strangers. And it had indeed been reverent. It was a great success.

On Christmas Eve we spent the night at Sleeperz, a different hotel that seemed better suited to our needs. This time we had Sarah with us as her family had similar logistical problems to us – one parent playing the organ for services at Cullercoats and the other looking after young children. This was lovely for Jess, and indeed for us too. I had taken Scrabble to play in any spare time we had between services, but we found the time was fully occupied eating our three-course supper in the dining room. I had to go along to the Cathedral with the girls as I had been asked to stand in for Emily at Midnight Mass, and she had given gave me a list of all the girls' parents' telephone numbers in case any of them should take ill. I tried to find an unobtrusive spot in the Thomlinson Room and sat and read my Kindle (*Things Can Only Get Worse* by John O'Farrell). On the notice board I read a lovely typed letter from Father Christmas to the Choristers. It said that he and the Chief Elf had been looking over their "naughty and nice" list, and they could see that the choristers had all been very nice, so they got a present, etc. When they went down to the nave to rehearse I followed them and sat not far away with my back to them. The Head Chorister came across and said I didn't need to sit so close, but I assured her Mr Roberts had told me to be wherever the girls were, and she accepted that. As well as being an emergency person in case of sickness I suppose I was also required to be able to testify that any subsequently alleged hanky-panky had definitely not occurred.

When the choir went out to start the service I followed behind, but not too closely so I was not seen. At the bottom of the stairs I stayed in the Song School hallway till I heard all their feet go past, then I waited a few seconds. I opened the door very quietly (bleep-bleep-bleep-bleep - CREEEEAK) and stuck my head out, only to see that they were still lined up in the Eastern Chapels for prayer. I shut the door (CREEEAK) enough to hide me but not quite closed by the big magnet so I didn't have to bleep again. I waited, heard all the feet go by, then tried to sneak out again. All was quiet in the south Quire aisle and I could see the choir and clergy processing down the central Quire aisle (how did they get there?). This was a bit unusual but I assumed they were going straight down the central aisle to the font. Maybe they did for all I know, but when I got to the nave the servers were processing to their seats and my path crossed theirs. Gosh – should I dive ahead or hang back? Thinking they would be followed by the entire assembly I decided to dive through quickly. It was most embarrassing, but I doubt if anyone knew or cared. The servers, who could easily have trampled me into oblivion, were not fazed by my unseemly antics. I found Roger and shrank into my place. Emily, who is neurotypical, would never have behaved like that.

In the earlier service I had managed to drip lots of candle wax down the only pair of trousers I had with me, and was determined not to have a candle tonight, but I was offered a tea-light in a little glass holder which was much more practical. The Dean, who had not quite left for Peterborough, preached. He illustrated his sermon with an anecdote about his daughter Georgie who was nannying in the USA. Apparently she had told her five-year-old charge that not everybody believed Jesus was the Son of God, to which he replied, "They don't believe in Jesus? That's rude!" Just before The Peace Clare asked us all to blow our candles out before we rushed round kissing each other, in case of accidents. She also told us the bells had just rung for midnight, so it was Christmas Day. I wished Roger a happy birthday.

After all too short a night we were back for Christmas Festal Eucharist. This time Bishop Mark preached, and he preached from the floor because, he said, it was

Christmas. That was a nice touch. Afterwards there was no coffee, because it is generally assumed people have other things they want to rush off and do. Well, some do, some don't, but we don't have coffee anyway. I could have done with some, and the biscuit that always goes with it. All the choristers had been given a decent-sized chocolate Santa. Our Christmas taxi driver, Ronnie Kay of Westerhope, was waiting for us outside. It was good to see him. I think our cat Robyn, who stays home alone on Christmas Eve, was probably glad to see us too, but she pretended not to have noticed we had been out.

The year ended with MYC singing services at St Paul's Cathedral on the Saturday and Sunday, 30th and 31st. We felt it was Roger's turn to chaperone as I had been to St Paul's recently. He was not sure if he had ever been at all. They set off at 6.45 on the Saturday morning and were in London by 10.45. The country was currently under snow, so that was pretty good going.

In the days leading up to this event we had been sent information about what was required. Among this was an embargo on heels more than an inch high, and any luggage larger than given dimensions (a very small rucksack) as there was nowhere to put it. This was very inconvenient to Jess as she was going on to stay with her cousins and needed at least a small suitcase. Happily when I put in a special request it was granted. No food would be provided during the daytime, so choristers must bring packed lunches or make their own arrangements for the 45 minute lunch break. Well, packed lunches that have been travelling for six or seven hours lose their appeal, and it is likely to be very difficult to find quick food in a busy city on a Saturday lunchtime, so the message seemed to be "Suffer, starve and sing." But it is undoubtedly a tremendous privilege to sing in St Paul's Cathedral, so we did not complain. We are so grateful to the RSCM for this and many other opportunities. Roger was not allowed into the Cathedral free until Evensong so he stumped up his entry fee which would entitle him to go every day for a year if he should happen to be passing. He found sustenance in the Crypt cafe where he enjoyed afternoon tea. His opinion of the Cathedral generally was similar to mine, but like me he was glad of the opportunity to see it, and to hear Jess sing there. After Evensong he came home. Later Jess told us that St Paul's was her favourite place in the whole world (except for home, she added charitably). She said Simon Johnson, the St Paul's organist, had told Adrian that they had been a pleasure to work with. "And organists *never* say that!" said Adrian.

On Sunday, January 7th, we had a farewell Evensong for the Dean. He took the service and gave the homily. Towards the end there were tributes to him from Geoff Miller (who is to succeed him in an acting capacity), Tim Wigglesworth for the congregation, the Lord Lieutenant for the County and the Lord Mayor for the City. I think they all gave him something. The Bishop wound up the proceedings by saying a prayer over his head, and that, short of a very long procession, was that. There was a very good congregation. Afterwards there was wine or orange juice (perhaps because the choir were involved) and decent nibbles which lasted well. The main reason they lasted was that on these occasions a lot of people load their plates and then stand chatting in front of the table so that no one else can get in. It's surprising how some quite cultured people have no manners when it comes to buffets. Roger spent a long time queuing to say goodbye to the Dean. I did not. I sat and read *Fire and Fury* by Michael Wolf, which was not on sale in the UK till tomorrow, but thanks to the miracles of modern science was available on Kindle yesterday.

At the end of January there was a special ceremony for Gordon who was retiring. He was given two engraved whisky tumblers, but we understood there would be something further for him on Wednesday night which was his last official day. Instead of coffee we had a large celebration cake, rather like a wedding cake but with no decoration. I wasn't chaperoning till Jess's organ lesson and I'm not sure why I was there without her, but I had the rare opportunity of hearing the boys' choir sing. I rarely heard them without at least some of the girls and they were very good and much better than I expected. All round, the music at that service was beautiful. During the organ lesson I was eating a snack, and Gordon passed me. I assured him I was not making a mess, but he said I needn't worry, there was lots of mess in the south transept where coffee had been served and there was squashed cake all over the floor. What a backhanded compliment to Gordon, making him clean up his own squashed celebration cake. I had had a piece myself earlier, but I ate it up tidily. If I had dropped any I would have picked it up, not left it to be trodden on.

In the evening we had a lovely Epiphany carol service, and the music throughout was really inspiring. At one point we were invited to go to the front and take a candle, one per household, and light it. I didn't, because "one per household" sounded a bit mean and I didn't want to rob them of their candles. Gordon and Alan were both there, and Gordon led the procession. I wondered if he was just working for sentiment and Alan was really the one on duty? It would not be like the Cathedral to be paying two vergers at once.

In *The Link* which was just published there was a nice picture of Geoff, our new Acting Dean, demonstrating the use of the "Tap and Pay" machine that had just been set up at the back of the Cathedral for visitors who felt inspired to give a bigger donation than they had enough change for. Every tap of a credit card gave £5. Geoff was asked to repeat the process several times for the photographer, without considering the consequences, and he found later that he had unwittingly donated £20!

When I got to the Cathedral on Wednesday evening Gordon was showing some visitors round. That is something he will miss, and we shall miss him doing it. He is a mine of information about the Cathedral and what goes on in it. When Evensong began Father Steven started off by announcing prayerfully that this Evensong marked the retirement of Gordon Scott our Head Verger, and Gordon had chosen much of the music. Afterwards Gordon would be pleased if we would all join him in the Refectory. Amen. It was a very good turnout and most of the Quire seats were occupied. The choir excelled themselves and all the music went well. We sang *O Jesus I have promised,* and at the end Kris played *Crown Imperial* as a recessional. At the end of the service we all clapped which is unusual but sometimes happens. I think everyone loved Gordon.

As we scoffed refreshment later I didn't know what had happened to Jess and I phoned her. She said she was walking up to Monument with Sarah. Could she come back? Yes, but it would mean leaving Sarah. I gather they were now near enough to the Metro for her to consider it safe to leave Sarah, and she came back. I asked why the other choristers had not come down? Oh, they were having Theory. Couldn't they miss Theory for such a special occasion? No, their parents would be expecting them to be under Ian's care at Theory. Quite right too, but it seemed a shame. She checked with Ian (and I suppose Gordon) that she could take some nibbles up for the choristers, and she disappeared. It seemed sad to me that the choir had been singing for Gordon (and God but that's another story) and were not allowed to come to his binge. They would all be sure to be starving. Healthy children always are.

Steven did a very nice little send-off speech and presented Gordon with a framed picture of the floodlit Cathedral and a "very generous cheque" (said Gordon). We all clapped for a long time. We said goodbye to him, confident that it would not be long before we saw him again. I thanked him for being so kind and friendly to me over my chaperoning years, and he thanked me for my sympathy on occasions when I had commiserated with him for the burden he was under. He kissed me and Jessica, but not Roger. Well, there must be limits.

One Monday night in early February a special meeting was held after Evensong for any interested members of the congregation who wanted to talk about what sort of Dean we were now looking for. This was not a chaperoning matter, indeed Jess went home on her own, but I thought it would be very interesting. In its way, it was. About a dozen of us, certainly no more, were ushered into the Eastern Chapels where it was no warmer than it ought to be, and directed to a row of chairs that had been put out. The Dean of Bradford was there, with a man who was a layman on the commissioning body. I sat next to Marjorie Wood. Clare started off by telling us to get into three groups of four. We were given coloured Post-It notes and first we had to discuss the challenges that faced the Cathedral. We wrote these challenges on the Post-It notes, a spokesperson told everybody what we had put, then we stuck the Post-It notes on a flipchart board. After that we had to discuss the qualities a Dean would need in order to face those challenges, and write them on a Post-It note of a different colour (I am truly not being sponsored by Post-It notes). Clare said she hoped we would be finished by 7 o'clock (only 45 minutes to discuss something we had been assured was very important). Helen Wright was our group's spokesperson, and she kept us focussed. We discussed such issues as money, the civic life of the Cathedral, getting more young families into the church, etc, etc – in short, all the things we wanted someone else to do for us. The Dean of Bradford wound up by saying it had been enormously helpful and that we should keep praying as he knew we were doing. He briefly outlined the selection process which began with advertising and then making a short list of applicants. I was shocked. Did they have to apply? I thought they were supposed to be called by God! Where did God come into it? I had naively imagined some senior clerics sat around (possibly praying, possibly not) and saying, as the spirit moved them, "What about old Ginger Higginbottom? He's a good bloke!" Afterwards I asked Marjorie if I had heard right and she said oh yes, they applied. Did bishops apply too, I asked incredulously? Oh yes, everybody applied. (You can imagine: "George dear, can we have a new dishwasher?" "Well, Agatha dear, money's a bit tight at present, but I see Bath and Wells is up for grabs. Shall I apply? If God called me there, we'd have a palace!" Meanwhile, as we were to discover, God was quietly getting on with the matter without our Post-It notes.

A week or two later the Acting Dean announced one Sunday morning that the owner of the Dog Leap Cafe was having a financial struggle and had decided to wind down the business. A very small groan greeted this. Most of the congregation probably never used the café, but quite a few did, including a lot of staff, and recently Dean had begun opening for booked lunches on certain Sundays. As a gesture of support I tried to book lunch after the service. I was, rather reluctantly I felt, booked in. I knew there was little chance of any replacement, and I was sorry. Every Cathedral should have somewhere that visitors can get at least a hot drink. I went in again the following day when I was in the Cathedral for the organ recital, and Sheila Cavanagh, his second in command, told me Wednesday February 27th would be Dean's last day. He was selling off some of his merchandise, and I bought a mug and a teatowel. The end of another era.

At the beginning of March two very exciting things happened. The first was that we had snow, driven by an American visitor called Storm Emma, and the second was that Ian had been invited to take his choirs to The Sage to sing with the Sinfonia Chorus in James Macmillan's *St Luke's Passion* on Saturday 3rd. The first rehearsal was at The Sage on Friday evening after school. It was quite obvious that this was going to present a logistical challenge. The chaperone put on her thinking cap. Jess would probably not be able to get to work on Saturday morning as the A1 was closed by snow, which would be a blessing in disguise, and we should have to take quite a few taxis as bus services would be sure to be disrupted. The wind became very strong, and on Thursday night we sat by the gas-fire thinking of all the brave people who had to work out in the dark and cold to keep our essential services running.

On the Friday morning there was an email from Ian. Oh good, I thought, he's being very sensible and cancelling. Not so! Commuting between Gosforth and Newcastle Ian probably hardly knew it was winter. The letter was all about what was going to happen at The Sage. He hoped to see everyone, except anyone whose safety would be at risk, of course. Well, Jess's would, but he couldn't do without her. There were lots of warnings on the news to stay at home, but if the buses were running it would seem a bit feeble not to go. But what about coming home in the dark, across ten miles or so of open country, and the emergency services stretched to their utmost and beyond? I decided to book us into Sleeperz for two nights, and I did. We could travel to Newcastle in daylight, and come home on Sunday in daylight, hopefully by bus. Roger would stay at home with the cat.

We set off about 2 o'clock on Friday, taking a taxi the short distance to the bus station to avoid dragging our suitcase through all the slush. Our room at Sleeperz overlooked the station carpark, and it was an eerie, silent scene, quite deserted except for a few cars whose owners had abandoned them because they could not get home. Many of the people staying in the hotel were trying to get north and had given up. No trains were running. Jess entertained herself by phoning her friends and I read. It seemed a pity to have to go out in the cold, but that's what we were there for! We had to be at The Sage by 6.15 for a 6.30 start. L.A. taxis came for us within seconds of us calling them, and got us to the Sage in about four minutes. Jess took some photos of the river scenery under snow.

I got myself a cup of cocoa and found a table in the Sage café and got stuck into a crossword. The café-bar is expensive and rather slow and seems only to be open at peak hours when it is heavily oversubscribed. I was lucky to get a table early on. My cocoa was nice but rather pricey at £2.90, and not at all hot. I made it last as long as I could. Happily no one came to sit with me. My table for four was up against a wall and not conducive to sharing with strangers. There were two events on: one at 7.30 and one at 8. A pianist sat down at a grand piano and entertained us with music, but it sounded like trills and scales and arpeggios all rolled up together, with little recognisable music. But it was pleasant. He was ignored and never clapped, but he never stopped trilling long enough to be clapped anyway. As the 7.30 people left to go to the auditorium the 8 o'clock people arrived for drinks, but by 8 the bar was deserted again. Oh goody, I thought, I would have some more cocoa and maybe a bite to eat. No, they were closing now.

Soon after 8 o'clock I happened to be in the toilets when a gang of noisy girls came in squealing and giggling in top doh. I recognised Jess's voice so I lay low till they had gone out. After three minutes of meaningless hysteria they bunked off and all was peaceful again. The rehearsal ended at 9 and Andrew Reid arrived for Sarah. He met me in the concourse and asked if Jess and I would like a lift back across the river. I gratefully accepted. The girls looked sober and tired when they came out. You would never have guessed they were the same as the rowdy mob in the toilets. Back in our room we assembled a scratch supper from left over tea snacks and made drinks with sachets.

Next morning we had several hours to spend before we met at the Sage again. I left Jess sleeping while I had breakfast then when she woke up I went down with her and had some more coffee while she breakfasted. I popped out to do some shopping, and found a beggar sitting outside the station portico looking very cold. I gave him some chocolate and asked him if he knew the Cathedral was open all morning and he could get warm there. Yes, he knew, but of course sitting on the street in the worst weather is more lucrative – people are more likely to give money if only from guilt, as I know myself. It takes a very hard man to ignore a starving beggar in the snow, and most Newcastle people are very generous. In the Cathedral he would have been warm but nobody would have given him money.

Jess found out from Twitter that the Cathedral had in fact been open all night for the relief of the homeless. Someone who was not a member of the Cathedral community had had the idea of opening it and asking people through social media to provide food and bedding. The clergy supported the idea and the response had been overwhelming. It had been a great success. However it was not repeated for a second night. I was later told that the insurers had not approved, and had insisted that there must be a certain number of paid staff on duty. This was not possible to arrange. At least the coldest night had been covered. Jess and I went to the Lit&Phil where to our surprise we met Roger. We all sat and read and enjoyed their excellent refreshments. I popped out to get food for Jess's mandatory packed lunch from Sainsbury's on the station, and a sandwich for myself in case the Sage bar was closed when I needed it. We stayed there till we were thrown out when they closed at 1 o'clock, and got a taxi to the Sage. There she soon met up with friends and I left her to it.

For this session I was a parent-helper and although there was nothing for me to do I suppose I was necessary for legal reasons. I joined the party in the Barbour Room upstairs and did another crossword. Eventually Ian led us to the stage where I sat in a rather unnervingly vertiginous seat and waited. The Sinfonia and their Chorus arrived, and I listened to the rehearsal. I have to say it wasn't my kind of music and I didn't like it much. I made myself useful twice: taking one little girl to the toilet and I was asked to take another to get her finger dressed but I had a suitable plaster in my bag. I was told she had been chewing her finger till it bled. Maybe she had forgotten her packed lunch. Later, back in the Barbour Room for lunch/tea, I was required to count heads on a group toilet visit. Such fun.

Time drifted by. There was supposed to be a pre-concert lecture by James Macmillan, but a message came to say he was stuck at Dublin airport. It seemed a very long time till they all went down at 7.15, but the choristers seemed to be enjoying being together, and Ian and Kris were in very good spirits and kept everyone happily occupied. Ian had given me a ticket, and I made for the auditorium. As I tried to get into Hall One a steward told me kindly that rucksacks were not allowed in if they were bigger than a piece of paper he had in his hand. Yes, mine was bigger. Sorry, but it couldn't be allowed. I must take it to the coat desk where it would be looked after. Curses! Ian and Kris, who I bumped into in the corridor, fell about laughing at this, which wasn't kind. I had once suggested that Kris's haircut made him look like a certain dictator, and now I was being treated like a terrorist which was I suppose he felt was poetic justice. Anyway, if my little rucksack had had a bomb in it, it would have blown up the cloakroom and still done quite a bit of damage, not least to the nice cloakroom attendant. I had been carrying it all day, so why did it suddenly become a security risk at 7.30? Back at Hall One I was kindly allowed in and shown to a seat. I needed to change my reading specs for my distance ones, but they were in my rucksack. I felt thirsty, but my water bottle was in my rucksack. Oh sugar!

The concert was quite good in the end. It lasted about an hour. I was at the back of the stalls where there were few patrons. The whole floor was about half full, but this might simply reflect the bad weather. The upper levels were not being used at all. Ian had told the choir to watch Jess carefully and stand up and sit down when she did, and they did and it was very good. They sang very well, but if they made any mistakes no one would have known. That's one of the beauties of modern music: no one knows what to expect. Shirley Wilkinson was a few seats away from me with a friend and she greeted me warmly. Later she sent Jess a kind email of compliments which was encouraging as Jess had not felt comfortable with the piece at first.

Andrew kindly gave us a lift "home" again. It was too late for supper at Sleeperz, so I asked Jess if she would like to go to one of the nearby restaurants for a meal but she said she would rather send out for pizza. What is it about pizzas? I get to hate the sight of them (which is unfair to pizzas). It was now well after 10. By the time we got it, there was little hope of digesting it. We were awake most of the night. Next morning I think Jess would have liked to go on sleeping for hours, but we had to be out of our room by 11 and we both needed breakfast. The Scottish refugees in the hotel seemed to be thinking they might start trying to get home today. We got a taxi up to Haymarket, and a bus home. We had seen so much snow and ice, and had had to navigate so many slippery surfaces that I shall always think of that weekend as our skiing holiday.

A Saturday in mid-March presented more logistical challenges. First Jess went on her own to the King's Hall at Newcastle University where she was to rehearse for a production of *Carmina Burana* that evening. This was a school choir event, but between the afternoon and the evening she had to be at Durham Cathedral with the Cathedral choir to sing for their Patronal Festival evensong. I was not needed in the morning, and I arranged to meet her out at 3. This presented me with a slight problem because although the King's Hall had not moved since I was last there, several new buildings had sprung up around it and I could no longer find it. I don't know what its local nickname might be, but whenever I asked anyone where the King's Hall was they didn't seem to know, even if they worked there. Eventually, after a nice young clerk had looked it up on a map, I seemed to be on the right track when I saw Jess coming towards me. She had finished early and decided to look for me at the nearest taxi rank. It seemed not to occur to her that I was looking for her, not waiting for a taxi. But God was looking after us, and brought us together without even waiting to be asked.

By now it was very cold with gritty snow in the wind. Jess phoned for a taxi which came within a minute and took us to Durham in style. The driver said he could not take us up to the Cathedral, which we felt sure was not true, but he dropped us off in town and we walked up. Jess was in a hurry and took what she thought was a short cut, but it wasn't and I got to the other end of it before she did. She hurried on up the hill and disappeared. I continued at greater leisure and made straight for the Undercroft Restaurant. They were only serving coffee and cake now, but that was better than nothing. I asked for decaf coffee, hot chocolate (no problem there) and a cheese scone. Oh no, sorry, cheese scones were off. I could have some chocolate cake. I didn't really fancy chocolate cake with hot chocolate, but I was desperate. I sat in an obscure corner and remembered I had an M&S

sandwich which I surreptitiously ate with the coffee. Well, they hadn't got a sandwich to sell me! I wrapped the cake up in serviettes to take away. I carry a plastic drinks cover (cut from the cover of a WHS exercise book, and not yet patented) to keep drinks warm, and it came in useful. It didn't keep the hot chocolate very hot, but I suspect it had not been very hot to start with. It was warm and wet and calorific.

By now it was time to find a seat for Evensong. I was able to sit on the front row by permission of a sidesperson who I asked for a padded seat. Durham has only a very few pew cushions. They only seem to deal with hardy-bottomed worshippers. For some time I sat in glorious isolation, then a party of people came. One of them told me I was about to be surrounded by visitors from Canvey Island. I knew that Canvey Island was not in the South Seas but in Essex, and largely filled with oil refineries. I asked one of them what had brought them to Durham. It seems one of their number was a keen fan of St Cuthbert and had organised (or arranged to join) a walking pilgrimage from Chester-le-Street. They must be a tough breed in Canvey Island because it was a terrible day for walking, with cold winds and sometimes blinding snow. The visiting preacher had also done the walk, and was still in good enough shape to preach. As usual it was a lovely service and a privilege to be sharing it.

By arrangement we went back to Newcastle with the choir on their mini-coach. I gave Emily a contribution of £10 for my ride. She was reluctant to take it, and so was Ian when he knew, but I assured them that we used to be charged that in Michael's time (I did not mention that Michael had, on advice, stopped taking parents and hangers-on). After all, they had saved me a taxi. We got off at the Cathedral and Jess took her cassock in, then we walked to the station to pick up a taxi back to the King's Hall. The concert had already started, but *Carmina Burana* was not till later. Mr Forbes, the KEVI Head of

Music, knew Jess had a full schedule with a scattered audience, and he made allowances. She disappeared. I collected my ticket from the desk, and as there was only one ticket in the envelope I knew Roger must be already there. Phew – we had packed it all in, and now it didn't much matter what happened for the rest of the night. Though I might just squeeze in the irrelevant information that *Carmina Burana* was very, very good!

April 24th was the Annual Congregational Meeting. We met in the Refectory, currently called the Cathedral Hall, after Eucharist. I noticed from the minutes for last year that the meeting had ended with the Grace, but this year the (Acting) Dean both began and ended with thoughtful prayers that would have been worth God listening to. That was an encouraging start. The meeting proceeded fairly briskly (well, we were all getting hungry) but Marjorie Wood brought up the matter of her grief that we no longer had a café. Geoff explained what the current options were, and how none of them could be afforded. Leila McDermott stood up and said she wanted to second what Marjorie had said. As a welcomer she found it very embarrassing to tell visitors that we could not offer them a cup of coffee. Another lady asked if we couldn't at least have a hot drinks vending machine, but Geoff seemed anxious to leave that topic (I expect he was getting hungry too). At the end when we were saying goodbye I told the Dean that I also felt strongly about the café issue, and I thought we should do something voluntary and minimal. He seemed to agree. I said if five ladies could be found to do one day a week each, I would be one of them. Maybe that was foolish, but what I had in mind would not be very demanding. I envisaged one lady at a time, or two if available, being in the Refectory and serving tea, cocoa or instant coffee, chocolate biscuits and love to anyone who came in. During the summer we have many visitors. They might not be ready for a meal (holiday makers often restrict their eating to breakfast and dinner for economy) but would presumably like a sit and a warm drink – and maybe a chat. Geoff seemed to agree.

I went to sit in the nave where I could read and carry on with chaperoning Jess's organ lesson which was in progress. Clare came by and had a chat. I had recently written to her about my worries for the homeless when the Cathedral pews and radiators were removed, as there would be nowhere for them to sit/lie and get warm. She said they were taking the matter very seriously and giving it a lot of thought. I had also raised the matter of the café and she was concerned about that too but had different views from mine. She said there were so many eateries in the city that we should need to offer something really special to compete. I said I disagreed, and I knew what people wanted in a Cathedral because I had been to so many. Mainly visitors want a rest, a drink, a biscuit and a feeling of love. She agreed about the love. I repeated my offer to do one day a week for a minimal, non-profit-making coffee spot, and I thought it ought to be funded by donations to avoid one level of accounting with its necessary complications and legalities. Clare said she would think about it. And she did.

In mid-May I heard that a new Head Verger had been appointed. She was a lady, with a doctorate. I wondered what good a doctorate would be to a verger. I just hoped she had good muscles. I also hoped she was good on high ladders, putting little purple bags over crosses. The following Sunday a short paragraph in the Notices told us that Dr Carys Underdown had been appointed as our new Verger. I was told she was a Doctor of Celtic Theology. That would not be much use to her when the boiler broke down or she had to move dozens of heavy benches around between services, but maybe it appealed to the appointing body as a useful attribute when, as happened not so very infrequently, the Verger had to take weeknight Evensong. Slipped into each copy of the Notices was a little card inviting the congregation to pray about the appointment of a new Dean. I wondered why we had not been similarly invited to pray about the appointment of the new Verger. It's a much more important office. We can manage, and have done, for weeks at a time without a Dean, but we are lost when the Verger is off sick.

In June I had an email from Jean Skinner, who was responsible for Cathedral Hospitality. She later rejoiced in the title "Canon Pastor". She asked if I would like to discuss my recent offer to make coffee for visitors. I replied that I would be glad to discuss it. I would have to add three hours to the day for travel, but it would not hurt me for a while till it got established and there were more people volunteering.

On Sunday, June 10th, it was announced before Eucharist, by a man I didn't know, that a new Dean had been appointed. He could not tell us who it was, but he could tell us that the choice had been unanimous! Their identity could not be revealed till about the end of the month because all sorts of checks have to be done (I suppose to ensure that the new Dean was telling the truth about him/herself). No give-away pronoun was used, so we didn't know the gender of the new Dean. Then on the 22nd Jess found out from Facebook, that great source of information, that Geoff Miller, formerly the Archdeacon, was to be the new Dean. Later that day the news came to my in-box as an email from the Bishop (not to me personally, you understand). This was very good news. Everyone liked Geoff.

A couple of Sundays later we had a strange ceremony after Eucharist. After the Benediction Clare took centre stage and called Carys, the newly appointed Verger, to come and stand opposite her. She asked Carys a lot of questions about what she promised to do in her job, and Carys replied to each in a deep and confident voice: "I will, the Lord being my helper." At the end the congregation was asked if they would promise to support Carys in prayer, and everyone answered "I will!" (except Christine Hawkins who said "Maybe"). It all seemed a bit unnecessary. By now Carys was on the payroll, and it would be understood that she was contracted to do certain things, whether she promised or not.

In July Ian had a new event as part of the year-end celebrations, this being to raise money for the trip to Belgium. It was a Singathon, when the choirs assembled on a Saturday afternoon and sang people's special requests. There was no charge for listening, but for £10 you could sing with the choir (I'm not sure if anyone did), for £25 you could choose a song, and for £50 you could conduct the choir. I have no idea what level of musical expertise you needed for that, if any, but as far as I know only Christopher Reid took them up on that one.

When I went into the nave it was a bit like a Monday organ recital – just a handful of elderly people. I found myself a good seat. The system was that the choir performed two chosen pieces first (I think the patrons had to get away, both being priests) and quite a lot of practice. It all seemed very informal. I had not expected to choose a piece myself, but in the end I did. I chose Rutter's *The Lord Bless You and Keep You.* I wrote it on a piece of paper and gave it to Ian with £25. I noticed there was a small refreshment outfit in the south transept, so I got some coffee and a chocolate chip cake. Later I bought three more cakes, and later still I had another cup of coffee. The Singathon proper began at 2.30, by which time there was slightly larger audience, and went on till 4. I have no idea if Christopher conducted well or not because I am not that musical, but the choir sang in unison so I have to suppose he did. Another, much longer piece, was conducted by one of the adult singers. Ian's wife Kate (with Baby Roberts *in utero*) joined the choir and sang with them for one piece while Ian took a turn looking after Ernest and Arthur. I was peeved to discover that the Rutter piece had already been requested by someone else – I think another grand-parent. I could have saved my £25! I knew I couldn't possibly ask for it back. Towards the end Ian asked if there was anyone else in the audience who had a request. I called out, "May we have the Rutter again, please? You've had two lots of money for it!" Ian seemed to think that was fair, and they sang it again – beautifully. It made my day. At the end, apparently at John Lewis's request, due to some sort of in-joke, they sang a Howell's *Magnificat* with Ian conducting in a strange yellow suit with a bit of red at the back. It was not till he turned round to bow at the end that we realised it was a chicken costume! It certainly went down well with the choir.

On Monday, June 16th, I did my first hospitality stint at the Cathedral. I had opted for Mondays because I would be there anyway, listening to the organ recital. The south transept had been set up with three small tables, each with four chairs, and a big table for a servery. On the side there was a big (and very dangerous looking) urn of hot water. I spread out tablecloths I had taken and tried to make the outfit look as welcoming as possible. The only person in sight was David Peel, the duty chaplain for the morning. Like me, he didn't have many customers. Organ music was being played, so that was another human being in the vicinity. It was reassuring. Paul Wait, the Vestry Assistant, told me that the hospitality box (containing coffee, tea, sugar and paper cups) was under the table. I knew Paul existed, but I had hardly seen him before as he worked weekdays and daytime when I was rarely there. I wasn't very busy that first day, as few people were expecting to find refreshment, and we had very few visitors. But, as came to be the case week after week, there were one or two people who I was very glad to be there for.

The choir were getting very excited about their forth-coming trip to Belgium. An itinerary came home, with all the meals listed. Cassocks must be taken of course, and smart black shoes, which would half fill their luggage straight off. Ian also told us that the CCA in their wisdom had decreed that a jacket (a zipped hoodie called a zoodie) should be ordered that everybody could buy and wear for identification and uniform on the trip. It was a good idea, but yet another expense and was unlikely ever to be worn again. It was not exactly compulsory, but Ian said he knew everyone would want to buy one as a special souvenir that would bring back happy memories in years to come. I felt sure there would be a generous profit margin. Still, on a foreign trip the most important thing is for leaders to be constantly counting heads, and the zoodies would be a great help. We duly coughed up.

Now Jess was almost 16 and really didn't need a chaperone except when one was legally required. This summer she had to go to Salisbury for a week with the MYC, and we decided she might well go by herself. It only meant changing trains in London, which she had done a number of times already. Her friend Laura was planning to join her, so she would have company for most of the journey. I got up at dawn (why does dawn crack so loudly?) and got her to Newcastle by taxi, where she met up with Laura. I had given her a carefully worked out schedule for getting there, and she felt quite confident. I think she was relieved. Grandparents can be *so* embarrassing. After she had gone, looking cock-a-hoop at a table on an almost empty train, I looked around for somewhere to have a snack. I'd had breakfast at home, but I needed to unwind after the rush. I had a nice cup of cocoa in Gregg's and a quiet read (*Middlemarch*). It was a Bank Holiday Monday and I was doing my hospitality stint at the Cathedral. I would normally be there about 10.15, but today I was there about 8.30. There was an organ recital as usual. Ian and Kris are not deterred by little things like bank holidays, and they seemed to have the usual appreciative audience.

I have, over the years, learnt to use a fairly unsophisticated mobile phone, and I kept it by me all day in case Jess had any problems. I suppose that's called online chaperoning. My online chaperoning began quite early on when Jess sent a variety of fairly frivolous texts. All seemed to be going well at her end, but I had to discourage her from texting unnecessarily as my primitive phone battery would not last. I was not yet clued up to charging it on the hoof. She phoned me from the Underground, but the reception was so bad I had no idea what she was saying. Later she managed to tell me that they had missed their Paddington train, and consequently everything was running late. She asked me where she had to change trains, and I said it was all on her schedule, but she said the schedule was no good any more. I said there would be plenty of trains, and if she was in doubt she should ask railway staff. Once there was evidence that she was getting a bit panicky, and I was glad she had Laura for moral support. Jess was the seasoned traveller of the two, but it is always nice to have someone with you. I knew Jess had plenty of money and a tongue in her head, so I didn't worry (much). We had told Adrian that she might well be late as she had such a long way to go. Eventually she texted to say she had arrived safely in Salisbury, and I was very proud of her.

Jess celebrated her sixteenth birthday at Salisbury. I arranged with Sarah King to provide a big birthday cake for her to share, and it was made by Rik, the chef at Sarum College where the choir would be staying. Sadly Jess didn't think to take a photo of it before it was eaten up, but apparently it was a very good cake. But the icing on the cake, so to speak, was a live broadcast of Evensong on BBC Radio in the afternoon. We were able to listen to that, and we fancied that from time to time we could hear her voice. Singing on the radio with a prestigious choir is not a bad way to celebrate a milestone birthday

It had been my intention to go and collect Jess from Salisbury, if only for the pleasure of attending a couple of services and hearing her sing. I had bought my ticket, booked a hotel room for Saturday night and was all ready to go, but Jess told us there was a local rail strike and very few trains going to and from Salisbury. Laura's parents were going to fetch her, and they offered to give us a lift to Basingstoke where we could get a train with another company. I gratefully accepted, but on later consideration I decided it would be simpler all round if Jess went home with Laura and stayed there till the next day. Laura's parents were happy with that and I was very grateful to them. You may recall, or you can read in the history books, that the City of Salisbury had a bad time that summer. Losing my visit was the least of their worries.

2018-2019

Some time during the early autumn a discovery was made that caused near chaos in the Cathedral. We had asbestos in our cellars! It had probably been there for over a century, and it had been known since the 1940s that asbestos could cause cancer, but no one had ever bothered about it. I suppose it was found by someone doing assessment work for the hoped-for re-vite. The cellars were the preserve of the verging staff, and hewers of wood and drawers of water have rarely had any more consideration than they should have from their employers with respect to occupational hazard, if it could be avoided. Asbestos and coke fumes went with the job of caring for churches. At least our vergers did not have coke to contend with.

Something had to be done, and it had to be done fairly quickly because the boiler switch was in the danger zone and no one could be allowed to go and switch it on. Of course it wasn't so much a case of danger as of insurance. For several weeks the main Cathedral was without heating. The vestry and song school were on a different system and the non-verging staff were alright (Jack). As an act of enlightened self-interest I bought a couple of electric halogen heaters to keep me warm when I was doing coffee, and I always had to collect them from St George's Chapel where they had kept the worshippers (if there were any) and the priest from freezing at the 8 o'clock communion service. But the Cathedral is a big space to heat with tiny electric fires, and it was necessary to drink a lot of coffee to keep warm. Red gowns were provided for welcomers who wished to wear them, and once I was so cold I wrapped myself in one of those, but I felt and doubtless looked a fool. Our homeless visitors who came in to snuggle up to the radiators were disappointed, but they too were able to warm up with coffee, and if they wanted a nap there was a supply of donated blankets in a not-very-secret cupboard. But happily it was a warm autumn.

I don't know what happened in the end, and when I asked Alan he rightly told me to mind my own business, but after a few weeks heat was restored. Of course the removal of the asbestos could not be done with HLF grant money, even if we had the grant, and it had to be found, but the Cathedral was always strapped for cash. I don't know how they paid for it, but the good Lord seems to have provided.

In September the choir were asked to sing a requiem mass for the funeral of Ronald William Mark, who was before my time. Failing health had prevented him coming to church for a long time, and I had not heard of him before, but Ellie told me he had been a big supporter of the choir and had provided the medals the senior choristers wore to show their rank. I wonder if the choristers knew? Acquiring your first blue ribboned medal, then if you were very lucky maybe a green one, and if you were supremely lucky maybe the yellow one, was such an excitement. Most of the choristers would not have known Mr Mark, but he doubtless shares their excitement from Heaven.

For a long time Ian had felt that the "old" organ was worth restoring, and the Friends of the Cathedral kindly provided some money for it to be repaired. It was only a holding job till much more money might be available in years to come for a more thorough restoration, but it was able to be played again. It did not cost as much as might have been feared, but the process caused a lot of hassle. Eventually it was ready for Harrison and Harrison to move in and do the final work. One Monday Ian and Kris asked me how I had enjoyed that day's recital. Well, it was very good, I said (it always was). But what did I think of the restored organ? Oh dear, I hadn't known they were playing it. I am not very musical and although I love organ music, one organ sounds much like another to me. They were disappointed in me. The stopgap organ had to be kept, just in case, so the organ loft continued to house two consoles. Jess played both of them. But although I couldn't tell the difference, I was very glad that the old one had found its voice again after several years of silence. Emblazoned across the front are the words (in Latin) "Let everything that hath breath praise the Lord". Yes indeed.

One Sunday in mid-September Canon Clare announced some joyful news – Ian and Kate had a baby daughter, and had named her Iris. If Ian had any paternity leave he certainly didn't take it that week. A few days later he told the choristers that he was very tired – he had not slept for several nights! I was glad Ian had a daughter – it would ensure the survival of the girls' choir!

My Monday coffee outfit continued, but kept getting moved around. After a week or two I was told I should operate from the south-west corner of the nave. This was a bit better for me because I was more visible to potential customers, but then I was told I had to move again, to the north-west corner. I didn't like it much because there was a huge pillar between me and the welcome desk and I was not in sight-line of the other volunteers (if there were any). I asked Paul to help me move back across, but he said no, Kate (Sussams) has been very particular about it. It seems there was a new spy camera (or CCTV to be polite) high up on the wall opposite me, which covered the west and north entrances. If any of us got attacked, the CCTV would (when it was too late) reveal the identity of our assailant. Hmm. Well, if you're going to have to be careful about scratching yourself you like to be told! A number of people told me that I ought to wear a personal safety alarm like a fat, ugly wrist watch, which I could get from a cupboard in the vestry. Jean Skinner, at a safeguarding meeting, demonstrated one to us. It made rather a noise, but nobody came. I asked who should have responded, and why they hadn't done, but there seemed to be no answer to that. I didn't want one anyway. If in doubt, a good question is "What would Jesus do?" I am quite certain he would not have used a personal alarm, even if they had been invented. I believed I was serving God, and I trusted him to look after me. So far he always has done.

The last Sunday in September the CCA held their AGM in the Refectory after Eucharist. As we assembled we looked at copies of the agenda which had been left out for us by someone. I saw that the meeting was to open with prayer. It should, of course, but rarely did. There wasn't a dog-collar in sight – who would do the honours? Just at the last minute Ian arrived and sat down. He is of course Chairman of the CCA. He looked at the agenda. "The first item is a prayer, so we will have a prayer," he said. He shut his eyes (how do I know?) and offered a short and competent prayer. The rest of the meeting was short and competent too. We were glad about that, because we had a lunch date. Where?

Our new curate, Thomas Sharp, loved cooking and feeding people, and he had arranged a pilot launch of a new venture: a Sunday lunch for students. No students had been invited today, but a number of interested people were meeting over lunch to talk about it and eat their way through an experiment. Roger and I made our way to the Eastern Chapels where Thomas was serving lunch. He had specially chosen the Eastern Chapels to be more accessible to people who might come and who might not easily find their way to the Refectory. Two tables were set with cutlery and a few people were sitting down already. I found an empty chair and introduced myself to my neighbour who was called Anthony. We had previously been told that we should have a talk by a certain Newcastle University Chaplain, but he was not there so we lunched without a talk (sob). Kris and Jess, who had been trying to have an organ lesson, gave up and joined us. Whether they found our chatter disturbing or the smell of the lunch tantalising I don't know. There were about 15 of us altogether. As people were still assembling and the food was in danger of getting cold Thomas said we would start at once and say grace half way through. That seemed sensible. We thanked God for the curry we had received and the pudding we were about to receive.

I forget that first menu, but Thomas favoured vegetarian stews and curries with fresh vegetables and rice or pasta, and filling fruit or jam puddings and custard for afters. Whatever it was, it was always very good. He had no idea of the quantities he would need, so he worked on faith, and there was always enough and often seconds. He started preparing the food as far as possible the night before, and the actual cooking was done before Eucharist or afterwards, and was usually all ready to serve by 12. At the end a plate was passed round for contributions according to what we felt able to give. As time went by we started using a teapot instead, which had the advantage that the money, if paper, did not blow way, and anybody who didn't want their contribution to be seen could drop it in discreetly. Thomas started calling it the Teapot of Mammon. Naturally the food had to be paid for, and again Thomas worked on faith. He told us how much the meal had cost, how much had already been given towards it, and how much each of us needed to give, if we could, to break even. Usually it was much less than £1. Some gave less if they were hard up, and those of us who could give more presumably did. Thomas generally seemed to get the amount he needed. He had other sources of money. One was an obscure order of sisters who used to have convents but no longer do (well, you can't get the nuns) and had some resources to share with worthy causes. At the end Thomas asked for a limited number of people to help with the washing up (limited so we didn't overcrowd the kitchen), and he usually got enough. He once said the camaraderie around the sink was the best bit. It all seemed to be a great success, and it was decided to do it on a regular basis. As Roger and I were generally waiting for Jess between choir activities we decided we would always stay too. It was a very long time since we had been students, but some non-students were obviously needed for gravitas (and welcoming).

I once asked Thomas how much trouble he had had selling his idea to the powers that be. I know that the minutiae of such a project can be debated forever and often abandoned because of perceived difficulties, but apparently Canon Clare had told him to "just do it". Hooray for Clare.

When the lunches started in earnest for students we had quite a few, though some of them were already attached to the Cathedral. Several of them came early and helped Thomas with the cooking, and several – an overlapping several – stayed to help wash up. A number of the congregation stayed too, as it was just right for people who lived alone. Homeless people who might be around dropped in too and were welcome, and the lunch was always announced from the lectern before the service, usually by Clare, and everyone was invited. It was perhaps a good thing that everyone didn't stay! Clare generally stayed herself and was often joined by her husband Lyndon. That first week we had two kinds of curry with prawns, herbs and brown rice, and chocolate sponge and custard for pudding. Mmmm.

One of my self-appointed jobs was to give everyone a sticky label with their name on, to help us to get to know each other. After some weeks an irritable congregant said "I think we all know each other's names by now!" but of course if there was just one person who was a stranger, and there always was, they needed to know people's names. One homeless person who joined us for lunch came into the Cathedral next day when I was doing coffee, and greeted me by name which was so nice.

"Hello Christine!" he said. "Hello – it's Jack, isn't it?" I replied. Yes, it was worth a lot of labels.

There was only one improvement that could be desired – the church was very cold! Even when there was heating on, not much of it seemed to accumulate in the Eastern Chapels which were open-ended and draughty. There was no means of heating the plates either, and hot food is not so good eaten off cold plates. I usually snuck into the ladies with my plate and warmed it under the hot tap! But the food was very good. Thomas worked on the assumption that everyone was vegan, and added a few things for omnivores – bowls of grated cheese, soured cream and an optional jug of what we called "cow custard" for those who were not impressed with plant-milk custard (though when it was coconut milk custard it was delicious!). A short digestion break came half way through the meal when Thomas went to retrieve the pudding from the oven. They were always very nourishing puddings, often what we called stodge at school but far superior. Once there was a polite debate about what Spotted Dick might mean, no one daring to believe it was what it sounded like. But of course it was. Thomas asked us to bring any spare disposable containers we had so that he could give left-overs to anyone who would like them. There always seemed to be plenty left over. Thomas loved cooking, and he put his talent to his Master's service

It was not just food he was offering, but love. One week there were not many of us, and it was suggested facetiously that Thomas should go out into the highways and byways and compel them to come in. He did just that! He walked up to Monument, inviting people who were sitting on the pavement begging. He came back with a few, and some of them came frequently after that. I don't think I have it in me to do that, but Thomas does. Thank God for Thomas.

The choir were now getting ready to go to Belgium at half term. Lots of money had to be raised, and naturally by the choir and their parents. There were cake sales and all manner of small money-spinners, and one night a very good concert was held in Morpeth at St George's URC. The choristers were paying for themselves, but the lay clerks, who could not be expected to dip into their pockets, were paid for by the Cathedral. Jess brought her cassock home to be washed. A menu came round for us to approve, and the choristers were asked to choose what they would like out of the available choices. One form asked if they would like adult or children's size portions! To me there was only one sensible answer. Anyone who couldn't manage to eat up an adult portion would be sure to find a hungry pal who would finish it up for them! And for a healthy child on a hard-working foreign trip, without benefit of the home biscuit tin, any portion would look pretty small at the end of a busy day!

Saturday, October 29th, was an important day for the Cathedral. Geoff Miller was to be installed as our new Dean at 4 pm. A highlight of the installation, of course, would be the singing by the choir. On the same day, at Doncaster Minster, YOST were having an assembly for organ scholars and their parents. Jess had missed out on a number of YOST events for one reason or another, and it seemed such a shame she should miss this one. I worked out that if we left very early and took taxis at strategic points, and if we asked permission to leave Doncaster very early, we could go. Kris, who could not afford to be late for the installation himself, would have liked to go but could not risk it. He was sceptical about my plans, but I promised I would have Jess at the Cathedral in good time even if I had to take a taxi all the way from Doncaster. He helped her to prepare a party-piece to play. It was a modern piece: *Paean* by Philip Moore. As I listened to her practising it I was horrified that she seemed to make one mistake after another. Kris, however, said she had played it very well and if it had been an exam she would have got at least a merit. Well, it has always been my impression that a lot of modern music sounds like nothing more than a string of mistakes. I won't say the piece ever grew on me, but as I listened to her practising it several times it began to sound a little bit more like music. And of course if Kris said it was music, it must be. I have every confidence in Kris.

We left Morpeth station at 8.18 and travelled directly to Doncaster. We took a taxi to the Minster and were there well before 11. I had already contacted Chris Cowell to let him know we were pressed for time and would have to leave very early. In the Minster Jess was warmly welcomed by a lady called Ellie May (or Ellie-May), who knew all about her having to leave early, and she disappeared. I looked round for somewhere to sit.

I was approached almost immediately by a lady who asked me if I wanted to go to the toilet. She was accompanied by a man who looked interested to hear my answer. I was naturally taken aback. The man explained apologetically that when anybody wanted to go someone had to unlock the south door, lock it again, take the person to the adjacent Church House, unlock it, wait till the person had been to the loo, lock up again, unlock the south door and let them back into the church, then lock up again. Quite a palaver! I said I didn't want to go at the moment but soon would, then it occurred to me I had better go now. The nice man took me through, and handed me over to a nice lady who was in charge of operations in Church House. I had to stand chatting to her till other people had finished so we could all be shepherded back together. Apparently the church gets quite a lot of naughty people breaking in, not for a quick prayer but for a quick thieve. It seems there is plenty to steal – not silver, as in days of yore, but electronics!

Chris Cowell welcomed us all, and urged us, if we hadn't done so, to help ourselves from a groaning board of a big assortment of lovely cakes. I got some coffee and shortbread and set up a pew for myself. It was lovely home-made shortbread and I ended up having three pieces. Jess got a cup of coffee but only drank half of it before going off to socialise. Chris Cowell said the Newcastle scholar had to play and dash, so they would hear her do her piece first, but that was to come later. First we had an interesting talk by their Director of Music, Darren Williams, about organs in general and theirs in particular. Then we resumed socialising (and scoffing) and Jess got the organ set up for her. She was astonished and somewhat overawed to find that the composer, Philip Moore, was present and at the organ to help her and set her up! This must have made her nervous, though he was apparently very encouraging. She also met the wife of her scholarship sponsor, whose identity she had not known.

I was urged to have another cup of coffee but declined for practical reasons. I was told, however, that another toilet safari was about to begin so I joined it. What a carry on! Then I had another cup of coffee and a piece of lovely lemon drizzle cake. Jess played her piece confidently and I really couldn't tell whether she played it well or not, but the audience seemed to think she did and gave her hearty applause. At 12.30 I found her and reminded her that we had to go in fifteen minutes. At 12.40 I told her to say goodbye to anyone she needed to say goodbye to, and join me at the west door in five minutes. Oddly enough the west door was kept open. Goodness – a person might have snuck out and gone round to the loo without an escort! But for all their funny little ways, Doncaster Minster was a hospitable and inspiring place.

We walked to the station by a route our taxi driver had recommended, and found our way quite easily. We got there with twenty minutes to spare, and I gave Jess two Minster cakes that I had purloined for her. Our train, bound for Edinburgh, was on time, and we had a nice, calming ride to Newcastle. Jess scuttled off to the Cathedral for a rehearsal at 3 for the service at 4, and I followed at leisure, stopping off for a light lunch. I have no doubt Ian and Kris were relieved to see Jess.

I found a seat on one of the plastic stacking chairs at the back of the nave. It was already pretty full, and I didn't know whether Roger was there or not. The Bishop took the service, of course, and we each had a very smart order of service on heavy paper with lots of colour and I gather they had cost £2 each. They will be a very nice souvenir. It was a delight to see Gordon in the procession. I had hoped he would be back from time to time. Geoff gave a very good sermon. I think it was at that point that he reminded us that, although he was the new boy, he had in fact been associated with the Cathedral longer than any of the other clergy! The choir sang beautifully and Jess had several solo parts and sounded good though she was by now having trouble with her voice due to a persistent cold. Afterwards there were of course refreshments, and I had the great pleasure of giving Iris a cuddle while Kate took the boys to choose canapés. I never got near the buffet table, but I was able to get two canapés off a tray being carried round by a lad I didn't know. They were tiny pancakes topped with smoked salmon and red stuff. It was the first time I ever knew refreshments to be carried round at a Cathedral binge, and the lad deserved to be immortalised in literature. I'm only sorry I didn't know his name. I found Roger, then Jess, and we had supper at Ben & Jerry's in the Eldon Square Grey's Quarter. It had been a long and busy day for Jess, and she was not well, so I was proud of her for her stamina.

Next day Thomas was doing Sunday lunch again but he had not been able to get into the kitchen the previous evening because of the catering. He stayed up most of the night preparing lunch, and only had four hours sleep on a friend's sofa. As a supplement to a lovely ginger sponge pudding he served the left over canapés from last night: cream scones, tiffin and strawberries dipped in white chocolate. It is said that there are eight spiders in every pound of chocolate, so we must hope that the strict vegans among us took no risks with the strawberries. At 5pm there was another pre-Belgium fund-raiser concert, and Jess was to sing a solo in it. Kris, who had been due to play an organ solo, had to rush off to Kent where his father was ill. Ian asked Jess if she would play her party-piece again. When he introduced her organ solo he told us all that she had played it yesterday at Doncaster and her page-turner had been none other than the composer. The audience seemed duly impressed. When she finished she got very good applause. Mike and Liz Kelly served hot drinks and shortbread during the interval, which was very welcome and cheering. At the end, in her role as Head Chorister, Jess stood by the west door thanking people for coming. It had been a brilliant concert all round, and I found myself putting £20 in the basket, and although I got to the basket pretty sharpish, mine was not the first £20 note. The choir had put so much into it, they deserved to do well. I told Ian afterwards that I had never enjoyed a concert more. I have enjoyed quite a few as much, but none more.

Next day, when I arrived to do my coffee stint, there were lots of important-looking people gathered around the west end of the nave. My immediate reaction was to go out again, then I thought that was ridiculous and I went back in. I was told they were having a service to celebrate Trafalgar Day. A lady smiled at me and said "Hello Christine!" but I couldn't guess who it was. It looked like my Methodist friend Nigel Collingwood's wife Lindsay, but what would she be doing at the Cathedral? It transpired a few minutes later that they were there together for the service, being members of the Collingwood Society. It is generally assumed that Nelson won the Battle of Trafalgar, but it was really Collingwood because Nelson was dead. The Collingwoods and other civic dignitaries were ready for coffee, but not for mine. They had theirs elegantly in the Refectory, probably served by Ellie with shortbread. Admiral Lord Collingwood's ostentatious memorial, near the north door, is passed and ignored over and over all the year round and it is nice to think that on this one day of the year he is remembered, and that English text-book history should be closely connected with the life of the Cathedral.

At last the choir were off to Belgium, and Roger and I had a week's holiday from chaperoning. We went to the Cathedral as usual on the Sunday morning (to support Thomas's lunch, of course) and we were interested to hear Father Steven, at the end of the service, tell the congregation that the choir were in Belgium and ask for our prayers for them, and thank the visiting choir who had come to sing for us today. I had a nasty suspicion that, if it hadn't been for thanking the visiting choir, he might have forgotten all about our own choir. We do not very often get asked to pray for specific people.

Christmas was soon upon us. In the south transept we always have a very tall tree, which is adorned with lights and festoons of lilac net. Gordon had always risked life and limb setting it up from a tall ladder. Now someone else had done it – perhaps Alan. I first saw it this year when I came to do coffee on Monday the 10th. Mella Brooks, the welcomer, wondered why the lights were not on, and we both thought they ought to be. I didn't know how they were switched on, so I asked Alan Walton, who was also welcoming, if he could do it, and he obligingly did. The tree looked very cheerful and festive. A few minutes later they were switched off. Carys was in evidence, and I asked her if she had put them off. Yes, she had. Couldn't they go on again? No, they couldn't. It was not Christmas, she said, it was Advent. They would be switched on on December 25th. That was that. We were sad.

We had a Christmas Extravaganza concert on a Friday in mid-December. It was to be given by the Cathedral Choir and the Tyneside Orchestra. It sounded good. Jess had been quite unwell for several days, and was finding it difficult to keep going, but she would not even take time off school. She insisted on going to this concert – goodness, she had a solo! We asked Emily to be kind to her – quite unnecessarily because Emily was always kind. The concert began well with a few words of welcome and a prayer from the Dean. I was glad. Deans do not always know when a prayer is appropriate and don't always offer one, but Geoff knows that prayer is always appropriate in God's house. He gave the pulpit over to a youngish woman called – well, I'll call her Betty Bloggs – who I gathered worked for a local radio station. She was a sort of link person, introducing everything that we already knew about from the programme and then telling us how fantastic it had been which we knew. Some of us, quite a few in fact, tried to keep the clapping going for a very long time to thwart her, but it didn't. She just stood there yelling "Fantastic!" over the clapping. She made lots of corny comments comparing what was happening with her own childhood experience, as if it had been a hundred years ago. I made a mental note to tell Ian that I didn't think the choir needed a cheerleader, but someone later told me that it was Betty's concert. She had apparently organised the event and got a lay-clerk friend to fix the Cathedral Choir to take part and presumably another friend fixed the Tyneside Orchestra. She clearly enjoyed herself. I suppose as she was a local personality she was considered to be a crowd-puller, but good ale needs no bush and the Cathedral Choir and the Tyneside Orchestra need no Betty.

The best bit of the concert, for us and maybe for one or two others, was Jess's solo rendering of *There were Shepherds abiding in the Fields*. In spite of being poorly she sang beautifully. That was Christmas for me. I understood that Ian was hoping to produce a whole

Messiah next year and I hoped he would. I always feel, when I've heard *Messiah*, that I've had my Christmas.

The festive season was not without its downside. Next time I arrived for my Monday coffee stint I found I had been banished to the west end at the foot of a pillar. My usual corner was not available because the last inches of the nave had been packed with extra chairs so that the impoverished Cathedral could make as much money as possible by selling as many tickets as possible for Christmas events. My small serving table had been put in a dark, draughty spot, and as there was no room for me to sit behind it I had to sit in front of it. I was subject to a howling gale every time the doors opened. Naturally there was nowhere for anyone to sit to drink coffee. I was told this was on the Dean's orders, but I hardly believed that. I didn't serve much coffee. I think some of my usual clients must have felt an air of inhospitable bustle as they opened the door to case the joint, and retreated.

Clare did a re-run of her walking Nativity, and asked me if I would chaperone Jess as she and "Joseph" walked to the station from the Cathedral. I knew Jess was having a sleep-over with a friend that night and would not be coming home afterwards, and Roger and I had planned a private celebration of our emerald wedding. That's fifty-five years, and if you've never heard of an emerald wedding, as I hadn't, it's because they are relatively rare. I told Clare why I shouldn't be there and that I was confident Mary would be safe with Joseph. Clare sent us a lovely message of congratulations.

As usual the choir gave a very good performance over Christmas. One special item, much hyped, was a "first modern day performance" of a carol somebody found in a Cambridge library which had not been seen since the C15th. Somebody had edited it. Later we heard the BBC had recorded the choir singing it and it would be on the radio. I don't remember it being musically memorable (we certainly didn't go out whistling it), but it was a nice link with the past, and an example to the choristers of the long tradition of church music of which they could be proud to be a living part. Sarah came to Sleeperz with us again, and she was good company. The remaining night between Midnight Mass and Eucharist rehearsal was very short. Few people realise how hard Cathedral choristers work, especially at Christmas.

As Roger and I made our way to the Cathedral we saw a beggar sitting on his sleeping bag in the cold. I gave him a cereal bar and a chocolate angel and said, "Come and get warm in the Cathedral!" but he said "I'm not allowed in the Cathedral." I said yes he was. People were always allowed in the Cathedral. If they behaved very badly they might get thrown out, but that was only till next time. If they behaved they were always welcome. No, he said, he was not. Who said so? The Police. Oh! He told me he was the lad who had the article written about him in the Journal last year when the Cathedral was open to the homeless on a snowy night. He had gone round telling people about it so they knew, and he had an axe put through his shoulder. He showed me the scar. I knew nothing about this as we do not take the Journal. I urged him to come back, but he wouldn't. Later I told Thomas about this, and he said yes, the police did sometimes tell people they could not go into public places, and the Cathedral was a public place. It was affected by all sorts of laws concerning safeguarding etc, and the lad was probably right. It was such a shame. He looked a nice lad, and was certainly sober then. It was awful to think that, while the Cathedral does its best to welcome and tolerate anyone, other authorities can overrule us and forbid them entry.

The Dean preached that morning. It was a good sermon and I remember it, which is unusual! It was about ordinariness, and he started off by asking "Did you know that Jesus was a painter and decorator in Bethlehem?"

No, we didn't, and we perked up with interest. It seems there are five Bethlehems in the world and in each of them there is at least one person called Jesus (or Joshua which has the same linguistic root). This painter and decorator lived in a Bethlehem in South America. Another was a postmaster in a Welsh Bethlehem. It was colourful and a change of approach.

Our Christmas was nicely rounded off with a special Christmas lunch provided by Thomas. He had planned it weeks before in the hope of inviting some Durham students. I had asked if we three could go, and Thomas as usual seemed very happy to include anyone. Both the Bishop and the Dean dropped by to greet us all as we were settling down to scoff, and both expressed themselves only too sorry that they couldn't stay (you have to believe Bishops and Deans, don't you). The Bishop singled us out, seeing our name labels bore the same names as hers and her husband's. They too are Christine and Roger. How long had we been together, she asked? Fifty-five years. Oh goodness, we had beaten her by seven years, she said. She and her Roger had been married for 48 years. Later, with the aid of Wikipedia, we worked out that our Bishop had been practically a child bride, and was now 67 or 68. We thought it was time she retired and made room for some poor unemployed person to be Bishop. I have no doubt she thinks so too. But meanwhile she's doing a great job.

Thomas had set the lunch table beautifully, this time with tablecloths and crackers. It looked lovely. It seemed eighteen people were expected. He served a lovely lentil bake, lots of nice vegetables (carrots, parsnips and sprouts), roast potatoes and two sorts of gravy. I seem to remember he added a few treats such as pigs-in-blankets for the omnivores among us. For pudding there was a flamed Christmas pudding, cake or cheesecake. No alcohol was served, for which I was glad, but some was used to flame the pudding. Before he flamed it Thomas thoughtfully asked if anyone would rather have theirs served first. No one objected. I don't drink alcohol, but I sometimes eat it. We had two birthday boys, Roger and Peter Day, and they were invited to light the brandy round the pudding and we sang to them. We finished with tea or coffee which we don't usually have. It was an occasion of much spiritual warmth, and we hardly noticed the physical cold. One of the two or three homeless people who came was telling Roger how he had slept the previous night outside the portico of Central Station. He had been so cold (it had been down to -1°) and had shivered all night. He had worried in case the shivering stopped, because he knew the next stage was death. Clare was planning to try to get this man and the others into a refuge for the night, but there are so many homeless, so many nights, and so much cold weather yet to come. It was very sobering. But it was a very happy Christmas lunch and I think we were all really grateful to Thomas.

Now Jess was sixteen I was finding my chaperoning services less often required, but in February she started having private singing lessons with a young man called Toby Ward who we didn't know. The lessons would be after Evensong, and it seemed to me that it was proper for me to be present. Jess was horrified at the idea. She knew that Toby taught in a girls' school, had a DBS and would not need her to be chaperoned. I recognised that it might be embarrassing for us all, but I still thought it was proper. I phoned Ian to ask him what he thought about it. He hesitated. It was grey area, he said. It wasn't absolutely vital for me to be there because he and the lay clerks would still be rehearsing in the Song School above, and the Thomlinson Room had a glass door so anyone passing would be able to see in. I reluctantly said I would not go. Later I remembered I had to go to Newcastle anyway to return an item to a shop before it closed, and I decided to ease my conscience by going to Jess's lesson after all. I met her, and we went up to the

Thomlinson Rom after the service. It was, as usual, teeming with life, but it thinned out as people departed. Eventually it became obvious which of the throng was Toby. He looked very young, I suppose in the same way that policemen look very young to old ladies. He approached me as if to ask me to leave but I said I was Jess's chaperone. Oh, he said, he had a DBS and worked in an all-girls school and was used to teaching girls, and there was no need for a chaperone. I replied, in my Aspergic way, "Oh, a DBS just means you haven't been caught!" This is perfectly true, and it would be better if more people remembered it, but it did sound rude and Toby was naturally taken aback. He said I could stay if I wanted, but the lesson would go better if I didn't. I quite understood that. A relationship has to be forged between teacher and pupil, and the presence of a third party does not help. OK, I said, I would sit on the staircase. In fact someone had kindly left a comfy chair on the little landing. It was not for me but to prop the Song School door open, but it was just right and I gratefully sat on it. I could see through the door window, but I tried not to look. I spent my 40 minutes sitting on the landing, and it wasn't cold. The trouble was that I had forgotten to bring my Kindle, and I had nothing to read. Jess had lent me a Philosophy text-book, but it was not riveting. But I managed. I ate my salad sandwich and drank my Yazoo and listened to the lay clerks rehearsing, which was very pleasant. It had all been embarrassing for me, but Jess had enjoyed her lesson very much and was full of praise for her new teacher.

The passing of the great Christian festivals was sometimes memorable in surprising ways. That Lent was memorable for an issue over chocolate (the eighth deadly sin during Lent). I had taken to putting little bowls of individually wrapped solid milk chocolate eggs on my Monday coffee tables. I found them going cheap in my excellent local Yorkshire Trading Company shop, and bought a good supply. By each little bowl I put a notice that said "Please help yourself to an Easter egg, to remind you that Jesus rose from the dead and is alive and with you forever!" It was one of my small ways of spreading the Gospel. One Monday towards the end of March Clare came briefly into the Cathedral to introduce the visiting organist, as she often did. She came over to my coffee counter and, with a winning smile, said she wished I wasn't doing Easter eggs in Lent. It was not yet time for Easter eggs. We would make a big thing of eggs and chocolate at Easter, and this would help to emphasise the glory of Easter, etc. I said I disagreed and I should continue to put eggs out unless she expressly forbade it. Well, she said firmly, she forbade it. I knew I was beaten. Clare is Canon for Liturgy and says what goes on in the Cathedral. I was left to clear up my eggs and (metaphorically) cry on the shoulders of my fellow welcomers. Roger Styring said he would take the eggs with him. I had no doubt he would do something worthy with them.

The Church of England seems to like to use Lent to pretend that God is dead, so they can produce him like a rabbit out of a hat at Easter and have us all shouting "Hallelujah!" (which we are not allowed to say during Lent). God has never died, in spite of our attempts to kill him. Jesus was only dead for about 36 hours, not for the six weeks the church likes to stretch out his agony. He died on the Friday afternoon, leaving just enough time for his followers to deal decently with his body before the Sabbath began at sundown, and he rose so early on the Sunday morning that no one ever knew how early. The way the death and resurrection of Jesus fits in so neatly with Sabbath observance has always amazed me. Although far away geographically, I always think of the line of the hymn *O Sabbath rest by Galilee.* Dead or not, and I believe he was, Jesus was certainly resting. But God wasn't. I feel the Church of England overdo liturgy and underdo evangelism.

Towards the end of March, when I was beginning to feel my chaperoning days were almost over, Jess and I had a nice surprise. Ian sent us an email saying Jess (as Head Chorister) and Gabe (shortly to be boys' Head Chorister) had been chosen (by him) to represent the Cathedral at a Diamond Trust event run by Friends of Cathedral Music in Liverpool later in the year. A chaperone was needed so I should have to go with her. He wanted a quick reply. I replied directly to say that Jess was not there to be asked, but if it was OK with her it certainly was with us. In fact, of course, she was delighted. The icing on the cake was that our expenses would be paid – mine too as I was necessary! Even if Liverpool isn't my favourite cathedral, I was very grateful for Jess having the privilege of being invited to sing there. We looked forward to it.

Each Lent the canons set up a series of lunchtime meetings (once with lunch but no longer) on various topics. Once they each talked about a favourite poem. Another time a favourite word. This time the series was called "Canons in Conversation" and each canon in turn was "interviewed" by Canon Clare, probably along pre-determined lines so that she only asked the questions they wanted to answer. I was not usually free on Thursday mornings, but sometimes a kind friend took on my Thursday duties so that I could go to the Cathedral. The talks were often quite interesting, though not necessarily memorable as intended. Father John's talk one year was memorable for his terrible cough, though he persevered. Dean Dalliston read an impressive poem about my least favourite insect, and I asked him for a copy in the hope that it would help me to love that insect better. Dean Miller, encouraged by Clare, spilt some fascinating beans about his private life. Father Steven told us about some of the people who had influenced him in his religious life. He was born in an East Anglian coastal village where we had sometimes taken our sons to paddle. He did not spill any beans at all. He told us he had been an ordained priest for thirty-four years but had never been a vicar. Until he came to the Cathedral he had spent his life in Education.

On one of these occasions I was glad to notice that one of the other welcomers was doing the coffee stall in the nave. She had a man sitting with her who I didn't know. He was scribbling intently, and did not look up. Assuming he was supposed to be part of the welcoming team I eventually said I was Christine and what was his name? He told me he was Steve Forster from Together Newcastle (of whom I had never heard) and he was working with the Dean to see what ought to be, or could be, done about homeless people. They wanted to think of another word to describe homeless people (I suppose they think "homeless" sounds rude, like some people think Senior Citizens sounds better because "old" is rude). I said, "What about 'people'?" I'm not sure if he got the message. One question they were trying to address, he said, was how to help homeless people who had spiritual problems. I said well, I usually started off giving people a big smile. This seemed to impress him and he wrote it down. I said I also carried Alpha booklets called *Why Jesus?* in case I thought they might help anyone. He wrote that down too. He also wrote my full name down, so maybe he was going to report back to the Dean. He continued to sit and make notes. He was there to observe, not to chat. Once or twice I went over to visitors who were sitting in the pews to ask them if they would like a hot drink. I didn't know whether they were homeless or not, but I knew they were probably cold. I wondered if Steve might have a spiritual problem, but I didn't give him a booklet. He was the wrong side of the counter.

This reminds me, however, of a homeless visitor who occasionally came in with spiritual problems. He may or may not have been homeless, but he declared himself to be. I'll call him Ezra. He came in one Monday when I was doing coffee, and said he needed to speak to a priest about an urgent spiritual problem. Now if I know anything about spiritual problems it is that they are rarely urgent. Maybe a person might wonder if he should recant before they lit the faggots, but that was not Ezra's current situation. I took him to the vestry which seemed to be full of women chattering. Was there a priest on duty, I asked? No, not at present, but Canon Clare would be coming in to take Evensong at 5. Ezra said no, not Clare. He did not get on with her. The Verger and the Operations Manager came to the door and gawped. There is really no other word to describe what they were doing. I felt cross. "Are either of you ladies in a position to give urgent spiritual help to our friend?" I asked. They both shook their heads and continued gawping. "Would you like to talk to *me*?" I asked Ezra. He looked keen. "Well, do you do occult theology?" he asked eagerly. No, I said, I didn't. Oh dear, then I would not do. He told us he had recently had an argument with Clare and had called her a *******. "That was very rude!" I said firmly, completely forgetting all the advice I had been given in numerous safeguarding training sessions. Yes, he knew, and he had apologised to God many times for it. "Have you apologised to *Clare*?" asked the Director of Operations (also forgetting her safeguarding training). As Ezra and I walked back to the nave I suddenly remembered that there was a chaplain on duty. Goodness, I had forgotten him! It was Roger Styring. I handed Ezra over to him, and they proceeded to have a private spiritual discussion. I hope it helped Ezra. He needed attention, and he got it. I think it was Simone de Beauvoir who, in her memoirs, admitted making up colourful sins to confess to the very handsome priest at her Catholic boarding school – so colourful he felt obliged to report the matter to the headmistress. Maybe she and Ezra shared a need.

The Cathedral was getting very excited about the forth-coming decision by the Heritage Lottery Fund as to whether we deserved a grant for renovations or not.

Posters and displays appeared everywhere telling us what wonderful things were planned to make the Cathedral fit for "C21st worship". I was sceptical. As the time drew near the Dean announced that he planned to spend a whole day in prayer in St George's Chapel, and he warmly invited anybody to join him as their time allowed. I would have joined him with pleasure, but I didn't think he would like me to if he had known how I would be praying.

Monday, May 13th, was the big day when the decision of the Heritage Lottery Fund would be publicly announced. We knew already what it would be. Weeks ago Geoff had told us that he knew something that he was not allowed to tell us, but we might notice that he and his staff were smiling! In the service yesterday he told us that he still could not tell us anything, but that tomorrow would be a very significant day for the Cathedral. When I got there on the Monday morning a lot of important-looking people were beginning to gather. Some might have been from the HLF, but a lot were from the media. Geoff looked so excited. The other big news of the day was that Carys the Verger had left. She and the Cathedral had proved incompatible. We stood at the beginning of a new era.

We were told that life would continue much as normal till the end of the year, then in January all Cathedral activities would be confined to the east of the rood screen. The nave would be screened off and no one allowed in. The choir, of course, functioned mainly at that end of the church so they would not be badly affected. It was felt they might have to sing from the Eastern Chapels to leave more room in the Quire and side aisles for congregants. I was now involved in the Junior Church, assistant wardening and welcoming, and I was happy to continue in those roles, but I knew my chaperoning time was drawing to an end. Jess had decided she would do one more Christmas and then leave, in order to revise for her A-levels. It was still months away, and seemed light-years. Tomorrow never comes, and surely, surely next January wouldn't. I rather regretted her decision, because I knew how much she would miss choir, but in view of our distance from Newcastle and her dependence on public transport she was having to spend too much of her time travelling there and back

Roger and I were among those who volunteered to be interviewed by Safeguarding Auditors. This was a commission that was enquiring into every English cathedral to see how safeguarding was going. There were seven of us parents, and two auditors called Lucy and Sally. We had to talk about how we saw safeguarding working, or not working, for our children. We had a very interesting chat for about half an hour. Then we adults went out and the girls came in, six or more, and Jess was one of them. We were allowed to wait in the next room. Kate Sussams was doing the honours, and she produced a very good snack for the girls and took it in – store sandwiches, crisps and juice in cartons. There was nothing for us, but we were in control of our own lives while the girls had been starving at school all day. When I say girls, one of them was Evan. It had been a very positive meeting as far as we were concerned, and I gather the session with the choristers was also positive (it sounded it through the wall). We had the odd critical comment, but in general we were all very pleased with the way our children were looked after. Ian and Kris and their assistant Emily Stolting took great care of them.

This month we lost Father Steven, who was taking what must have been early retirement, and he would be sadly missed. Canon Clare installed three new choristers – Angela, Maggie and Melody – and promoted Sarah Reid to be a Lead Chorister (a new position to replace the former Senior Chorister because, as Ian said, promotion was to do with responsibility, not age). We were pleased to think that Sarah might be Head Chorister before very long.

Towards the end of May a training day was held for welcomers and others who have to do with visitors to the Cathedral. There were twenty four of us and I hardly knew any of the others except David Peel. It is a common complaint of Cathedral volunteers that they do not know each other, so this was a good opportunity to meet and mix. After a very welcome coffee and biscuit we were taken on a tour of the Cathedral by Pam Walker who is a mine of information about the windows and monuments. She is very interesting. I knew I would not be able to remember much of what she said, and I wished she had written a book. Someone asked her how she knew so much. "Well, I was born and brought up here," she said. Pam, of course, was the person who put the poster in Smail's window, so we owe her a lot.

After a very good sandwich lunch, and more coffee served by Ellie, we spent the afternoon session being talked to by two ladies from HAC (Housing Advice Centre). It was supposed to be all about what we could do for the homeless people who might come into the Cathedral asking for help, and in the fine tradition of churches it seems we should tell them where they could go. We already have a list of relief agencies to refer people to, and we all know about it, but in most cases the agencies only operate five days a week, if that, and from 9 to 5, if that. The dejected, hopeless and desperate come to us, and we just send them on somewhere else. On one occasion I remember having to tell a man that he should hurry to the place I was recommending as they closed for the weekend in an hour. It was as though I was saying, "Hurry up and go." Perhaps this is inevitable, but it is sad. Our job, as welcomers or whatever, should not be to tell them where to go (they usually know) but to do something for them then and there – a smile, a kind word, a cup of tea and an invitation to come as often as they like and make themselves as comfortable as they can. To talk and to listen, and to be friends to them. And to recognise that many of them prefer living on the street to the hostels and bleak accommodation they may be offered by cold officialdom. But that was not on our agenda.

People are not homeless just because they have nowhere to live, any more than people are sick because they don't take medicine. People are not born homeless, and if they end up homeless it is usually either because family relationships have broken down or because the family they had let them down a long time ago. Some were ejected from the family home by their mother's new partner. Others were brought up in care, and have graduated from it. Others have left prison after a long spell, and no longer have anyone to care about them. They want a home, but a home is so much more than the cold, empty flat they might be allocated if they are very lucky. One young man, after being given a flat and living in it for a few weeks, told me he was thinking of going back on the streets. It was lonely in his flat, and he missed the camaraderie of the streets.

One Wednesday morning in June Jess and I set off for our expenses-paid trip to Liverpool. We did not have to present ourselves till 4pm, but Jess had managed to book a tour of Liverpool University in the early afternoon which was very useful. We checked into Moorfield Premier Inn, where we were too early to have our room but were able to leave our luggage. We were only there for two nights, but a chorister's luggage is substantial! We found a nearby pub called the Railway Hotel and had a nice early lunch. Their speciality was scouse which was an excellent slow-cooked beef'n'vegetable stew with potato in, served with pickled red cabbage and bread. I didn't want the bread (it was crusty and dentally challenging) but I buttered it and wrapped it in a serviette so as not to offend them. The scouse was very good. On our way back to the Premier Inn in pouring rain we passed a homeless person sheltering under an arcade. I gave him my little parcel of bread-and-butter with apologies, and he was very pleased.

This trip I was carrying a bundle of copies of Greta Thunberg's recently published little book *No One is Too Small to Make a Difference*, and I was leaving them around where I thought they might get read. I did not give one to this chap as I felt his carbon footprint would be very, very small as he had so little to pollute the planet with. I gave one to our next taxi driver who drove us to the university. He was an eastern European immigrant, and he told us he had been a student of Hope University and had a PhD. So far it hadn't done him a lot of good, but an education is never wasted.

At the University we were given a short talk in a lecture theatre by a member of staff, then a fourth-year student took us for a walk round some of the adjacent buildings and showed us a typical student bedroom. It wasn't terribly interesting, but what impressed me most was her excitement in showing us a small triangle of grass, a green space in a fenced area where students could sit and sun themselves in summer. I thought of the magnificent gardens that so many of the Oxbridge colleges have, and decided to cross Liverpool off my mental list. So did Jess.

At 4pm we had to present ourselves in the crypt of the Metropolitan Cathedral. We knew where it was, but we had great difficulty getting in to it. The Cathedral is built on a mound, and we had to climb about fifty or more stone steps which was taxing to me both physically and nervously because the huge, circular, crown-shaped Cathedral was looming over us at the top. I don't know how funeral corteges, for instance, get up there. There was a lift to the car park below and we took it down, but we still got lost. We found the café and the shop and had a snack, and Jess bought herself a pencil because she had left hers in her suitcase. Eventually we found a man in a security uniform who showed us the street-level entrance to the crypt. It was most impressive. It seemed to be subterranean, but in at least one place there were windows. It was presumably the foundations of the Cathedral, and in my humble opinion far more beautiful. It was built entirely of brick, and seemed to consist of two large long halls with no evidence of purpose, and between them a very good concert hall with fan-vaulted brick walls and roof. The acoustics were wonderful.

Our reception was very good indeed. A welcoming committee had provided excellent refreshments of generous sandwiches and squash for the visitors – yes, parents as well. I met Gabe, Newcastle's other representative, and his mum. I left Jess to it and rootled round for somewhere I could sit unobtrusively and read in comfort. Other parents gathered at the back, but eventually drifted off to look for more fun. Most of the rehearsal was done sitting, which was maybe not the best singing position but was fine in all other respects. After her tiring trek round the University Jess was probably glad to sit down. The singing sounded really amazing. I recalled the Battle of Jericho and hoped the vibrations would not dislodge the bricks above our heads and bring the Cathedral crashing down. The rehearsal went on for a couple of hours, then we were dismissed, knowing we should not be returning to the Crypt. I was so glad to have seen it. Jess phoned for a taxi to take us back to our digs. She always did this now, and was getting very good at it. All I had to do was pay! After supper in the restaurant (thank you, sponsors) we had a good night's sleep which was welcome after our long day and Jess's energetic singing.

Next day, Thursday, was the big day. After a good hotel breakfast we took a taxi to the Anglican Cathedral for 10 o'clock. We were directed down to a suite of rooms on the floor below, not the choir school where we went on a previous occasion. As the choristers arrived they were welcomed and checked off, then taken to the nave to rehearse. Parents were now redundant till lunchtime. I had a mooch round their excellent gift shop, trying to convince myself that they had nothing I needed. I collected my ticket for tonight's concert. I read my Kindle, had some coffee and listened to the rehearsal. The singing was most enjoyable to hear, but the acoustics were not as good as the Metropolitan Crypt! I booked a table in the restaurant for 12.15, where Jess eventually met me. They too were serving scouse and I had some, but it was not quite as good as the Railway Hotel had served. For one thing I only got a small teaspoonful of pickled red cabbage! I didn't have pudding because there was only cake, and I felt I would be better off without it. Maybe later.

We now had an afternoon to spend, and we had thought of doing The Beatles Experience or going for a ride on an open-topped tour bus, but when we went to the door it was raining heavily and we stayed put. We explored the Cathedral for a while, then we chanced to bump into a girl Jess had met on a previous choir adventure, and they spent the rest of the afternoon catching up with each other. Later, after another snack in the café, Jess said she would like to go for a walk, so we went out to see what offered. By now the rain had subsided to a light drizzle. A tour bus came along, and we asked the driver how long it would be before he got back to the same spot, but he said he wouldn't be coming back. It was his last trip. It did not occur to me in time to go as far as the bus went and get a taxi back. We just walked, but did not find anywhere very inspiring.

Eventually it was time to take our seats for the concert. I had a posh, £30 free ticket for the front block, though the chairs were of a modest metal-and-plywood stacking sort. It was a super concert, with many pieces of music that by now I knew, and I enjoyed it very much. What I did not enjoy was the several women near me who were leaping about with their iPhones videoing the proceedings. I knew this was forbidden, but it seemed these woman, all of them, had special dispensations to make nuisances of themselves. The Duchess of Gloucester was there as the special guest, and Jess was lucky enough to have a chat with her in the interval, but she had to hurry away before the second half because her helicopter had broken down and she had to go home by train, and there were not many trains. She gave a very gracious short speech. The other special guest was John Rutter who gave a little talk begging for money for the FCM so they could help poor choristers whose mummies and daddies couldn't afford the expense of choir. I had never met any, but I can well believe there may be some in the world. It was certainly entertaining.

At the end, as usual at such events, the choristers took ages saying goodbye to each other till they were forced out by the closure of the Cathedral. This was especially emotional for Jess who knew that she would have few chances to meet many of them again. I tried to reassure her that although choir might be coming to an end, they were all musical and the chance of them meeting up again in life was high. When we got back to the Premier Inn we found to our dismay that the restaurant had closed for the night. Goodness – was it really so late? Jess suggested phoning out for an Indian takeaway, which she did, but of course we were not able to finish it and there was the inevitable waste. If the Inn had a bird table we had no access to it. Jess remembered that one of the *Messiah* pieces she had shortly to sing at Newcastle had a difficult bit, and she rehearsed it in our room. I hoped the guests in the adjacent rooms liked Handel! As far as we knew no complaints were made. It had been a wonderful experience for Jess, and she had enjoyed it. I believe she was a credit to her Cathedral, and I was very grateful to Ian for giving her the opportunity.

Choristers don't get a lot of rest. Jess had to get off the train in Newcastle and go straight to the Cathedral for a rehearsal of *Messiah* which was to be performed the following evening. I would have liked to go and listen, but she felt she had endured my company for long enough. I took the luggage and went home.

For all J's choir years we had hoped that *Messiah* would be staged, and now finally Ian had decided to do it. Jess had another rehearsal in the early afternoon of Saturday, then she and some of the other bigger girls went for a binge together to a nearby ice cream parlour. There were no imported singers: it was entirely the girls' choir, lay clerks and scholars, with a small imported baroque orchestra. The solos were shared out, and Jess had one soprano sequence. It was a super performance and we thoroughly enjoyed every minute of it. What the choir lacked in professionals it made up for in professionalism. Afterwards Marjorie Wood, one of the Cathedral Readers, told us she had been going to *Messiah* all her life and this was the best she had ever heard! Indeed, I think listening to my granddaughter singing my favourite oratorio that night was the highlight of my chaperoning career. I hope Ian was pleased with them all. I think he must have been.

At the end of June there was an ordination service, and I was one of the wardening team to escort the Bishop. At the end she thanked us most graciously, as though we had been protecting her from dangers inconceivable. On reflection, I suppose that is what we were there for, and why we had to walk in front of her with ceremonial staffs. If anyone dared to assault, or threaten to assault, the Bishop, the wardens' duty would be to beat the assailant round the head (or wherever), till they desisted. Quite a thought. Maybe wardens should have lessons in combat, just in case. Such events are usually peaceful nowadays, but one of William Bell Scott's paintings at Wallington shows the sort of thing that could and did happen in a church in days gone by.

The last treat of the year was a Three Choirs Festival at Hexham. Jess went ahead on her own, and Roger and I turned up at the Abbey in time to hear the last rehearsal. We sat in the empty nave at the end of a row. Almost immediately a group of four people came in and sat next to us. In an empty nave they had to sit next to us – why? The row was meant to fit five people, and these four made it six which was too many. The gentleman (?) of the party sat next to me and it was all very close and personal. Our arms were rubbing together. I felt I needed a chaperone myself. Roger was unaware of my situation, so I just wriggled past him and decamped. He followed me, somewhat disgruntled at having to gather up his bits and bobs. I was very disgruntled because I had lost the good view I'd had.

The choirs sang one piece together, then each choir sang a block of songs, and at the end they joined together again for the finale. It was very good, and worth the £10 we were charged. I gathered Jess had had quite a good time, though the girls in one of the three choirs had been distinctly less friendly than the others! They had had a very big tea with lots of pizza that apparently "just kept coming"! It suited us to travel home on the same train as the choir, but we kept to the other end of the train in order not to be embarrassing.

On the last choir Sunday of the year we had a very good pot-luck lunch in the Refectory, and Ian made his end-of-year speech in which he thanked everybody it was possible to thank. He paid a glowing tribute to Kris, and also to Jess for being such a supportive Head Chorister, being so kind to the younger ones and generally being like a "mother hen". In the evening service we had a sad farewell blessing to four choristers who were leaving – Hannah, John, Clare and Paul. Megan was also leaving, but she was away on holiday. After the clergy had recessed the choir sang, invisibly and unaccompanied from the Eastern Chapels, Tennyson's poem *Sunset and Evening Star* which is a favourite of mine. It was very beautiful. Jess was not leaving of course, but she had a feeling as if she was. It was an emotional occasion. She had told Ian she planned to leave the following January, but he persuaded her to stay on a little longer than that because he was planning to make a choir CD. The previous CD had been made just before Jess joined the choir, and she was always hoping there would be another. Now she was hoping very much to be part of this one.

Now it was time for all chaperones to have their summer break, but as Ian was continuing with his organ recitals throughout the year I duly turned up to man a coffee stall on Mondays. We still got some homeless people coming in, but now the weather was warm they often found it more lucrative to stay out on their pitches. We had more tourists too, but many of them came in with iPhones glued to their faces, walked round quickly photographing as they went, then left. They'd "been there, done that" and were off to see the next tourist attraction. Few of them wanted coffee. Of course, many of them would have had big hotel breakfasts with big hotel dinners to look forward to, and when they were ready for coffee they would probably prefer a café with a more exciting menu. Even when trade was slack, I still valued the opportunity because there was nearly always someone I was glad to be there for.

Later in July the Cathedral held interviews for a new canon to replace Father Steven. I was among a privileged number who were invited to help with this. I seem to remember that I was invited, rather than invited to volunteer. Before Sunday Evensong we all met in the Refectory where the two candidates, a lady and a gentleman, were introduced to us. We were divided into four groups, and the first two groups took turns to invite the candidate to grill us, while the other two groups got lost. We all said a few words about ourselves, rather like a group ice-breaker but more appropriate because the candidate really did want to know who we all were and where we all fitted into things. We were not allowed to ask questions – the Dean had been most specific about that, but the candidates could ask us any questions they liked to find out what made the Cathedral tick. After about half an hour the candidates swapped over and grilled the other group. Then we broke up for Evensong, and after that the other two groups took a turn. It seemed to me to be a very good system. At the end of it all we had an excellent fork supper in the Refectory, and carried on chatting. It was quite an evening! The interviews took place the next day, and I understood that they were conducted by a panel in the Education Suite and each candidate had to preach a sermon. Poor dears, they would not have the benefit of a pulpit to hide behind. I remembered the agonies of supervisors' visits at teaching practices, and my supervisors were never Bishops or Deans. But presumably the candidates had been this way before, and they survived the ordeal. And that was how Father Peter Dobson came to be our Canon for Outreach and Discipleship. His predecessor, Father Steven, had been Canon for Education. Oh well, a rose by any other name …

This year the MYC spent their week at Norwich, staying in UEA accommodation and commuting. I was not required, but I wanted to go down and hear them sing. We had lived in Norfolk many years before, and had worshipped at Norwich Cathedral for a treat every Christmas Day. I went down on the Saturday afternoon and spent the night in some very peculiar digs. The room was excellent, but was in the roof and accessed by a very narrow, steep and winding staircase with an inadequate handrail. The swivel window was only able to be opened for about two inches before it collided with a door frame, so I tried not to think about what would happen in the event of F-re. I had some food with me, so I stayed put till morning. Leaving in the morning was worse than arriving. I'd had to go upstairs on tippy-toes because of the narrowness of the treads, but I couldn't do tippy-heels coming down. I debated shuffling down on my posterior, but that seemed even more risky. It was a relief to be out. The area seemed oddly devoid of cafes where I could get some breakfast, but I had had coffee and chocolate biscuits in my room so I expected to survive.

Norwich Cathedral had a holiday gimmick (perhaps not a word they would have used). They had hired a fairground helter-skelter so that visitors could see the Cathedral from a different angle. It was huge and filled the west end. It certainly attracted visitors who were passing, and maybe some who weren't, but as far as I could see it did not attract people to join in services. It was of course free, which it would not normally have been at a fairground. I explored where I could. The visitor centre with its café was not open yet, but happily the toilets were. Unhappily they had a leak and I found myself having to wade through a large expanse of half an inch of water. There was no one around, but I found a stray cleric and asked him if the leak was known about. He looked as if he didn't really want know (understandably) but felt perhaps he should investigate. The result was that the toilets were closed for the rest of the morning and visitors and congregation had to queue patiently outside one loo for the disabled. A kind verger had already shown me where the vestry facilities were so I was OK!

I went back to the nave and sat in an unobtrusive place listening to the choir rehearsing. I had not told Jess I was going to be there, but I texted her to say that there was a woman sitting at the back who looked very like me. She was amazed when she saw me. She came to have a word, but after the service I didn't see her again because of the general crush. I went to the café for a snack, but there was a long queue and I am allergic to queuing. During the whole of my time in the Cathedral not one person had greeted me, except for a lady canon who smiled and said hello as she rushed past. Another young lady, standing protectively over the offertory box, thanked me graciously when I put £10 in it. Maybe it was my fault for arriving early and before the welcomers got cracking, if indeed there were any. I retraced my steps to the station, still finding nowhere to eat, and picked up overpriced snacks as I went. It had been a short and not entirely satisfactory visit, and I think it was the last I was to make for that purpose, but it had been good to see Norwich Cathedral again and to hear the MYC singing beautifully as ever. I was glad to get home and have a proper meal at last.

Next day, as I did my Monday stint, I had several interesting visitors. A couple of homeless men, with a little white terrier called Lucky, came to enquire about where they could get food, and how they could get to London. Where was the station? One of them had a very loud voice, and had to be hushed from time to time. After giving them coffee and biscuits, and a bowl of water for Lucky, I went outside with them to show them the way to the station. The one with the loud voice asked me to go closer and talk to him, but I remembered my safeguarding training and didn't get too close, but near enough to hear him. "I won't hurt you," he said, reinforcing my feeling that it was time I got back to the safety of my coffee stall. He asked, in a low voice, why some people had always been nasty to him? I said that was just the way of life. But this was his own family, he said! Yes, how true, for so many people. I waved them off on their travels. As I went back into the nave I saw a little group of people huddled near the Welcome desk, staring at me and chuntering. It was the chaplain, the welcomer and another volunteer. One of them said "That sounded like a difference of opinion! Were you all right?" I said if they had had any worries about me it was a pity they had not come out to see if I needed rescuing!

A Chinese student, here on an English Literature course, spotted my little Chinese saucer that I use for wet teabags. She told me the character in the middle of it meant Longevity. Hmm – for me I hope! Then she asked about the difference between Anglicans and Protestants. It sounded a bit like an exam question: "Anglicans are Protestants. Discuss." It's like saying a cat is an animal, but not all animals are cats. I hope I enlightened her a wee bit, but it is a question that sometimes occurs to me. I think it depends on the Anglicans!

A young black man (well, he was) sat quietly in a pew by himself for a long time. He didn't look homeless, but he looked lonely. I went over and asked him, as I do, if he would like some tea or coffee – no charge. He looked up very gratefully and said he would love some coffee. Tears gathered in his eyes. "Oh dear, are you unhappy?" I asked and he said yes. Unhappiness is the chaplain's province when there is one on duty (and mine when there isn't). I asked Roger Styring to come over and have a chat, and he did, and I took coffee and biscuits. Later, when I went to offer a fill-up, he had gone, so I suppose Roger must have been able to help him. It's a great privilege to be able to offer even such small comfort to a person in distress.

Another visitor did sketching. She asked if she could sketch me, but I said I wouldn't be able to pose as I was busy here and there. She did a quick sketch, then she told me she was so impressed because she went to lots of cathedrals (touring them like Roger and I have done over the years) and had never seen a refreshment facility for the homeless. Indeed she had not often seen homeless people being welcomed. She cited one Cathedral (I forget which) where she had been chatting to a welcomer and a scruffy man came in. The welcomer had whispered, "Oh, he comes in every day. I wish he wouldn't!" I think secretly one or two of our welcomers might share that attitude, but the Dean and Chapter have made it very clear that the poor are to be welcomed. After all, they are only Jesus in disguise.

At the end of August the choir had another treat. This year it was called *Choristers' Camp Stays at Home* (a somewhat Blytonesque title). On Tuesday, Wednesday and Thursday, August 27-29, there were "three fun days" at the Cathedral, doing singing practice in the morning, having a packed lunch and spending the afternoon having different exciting larks. The first afternoon they went bowling, the second afternoon they went to see *Lion King* at a cinema in Gateshead, and the third afternoon they went to Laser Quest. The third day was Jess's 17th birthday, and I had already given Emily a nice M&S cake with candles so they could celebrate it. It wasn't very big for a crowd, so I told Jess to buy some Colin Caterpillar cakes on the way, as a supplement. Colin Caterpillar is an M&S character, and he lends himself to Swiss-roll type cakes with bright Smartie spots on. In the event one of the little choirboys also had a birthday but had nothing to celebrate with. Jess very nobly gave him one of her Colin Caterpillar cakes, and let him have second use of some of her candles, so they were able to sing that song to him too. (No, I swear Marks and Spencer are not paying me to advertise their cakes.) Other things happened in Jess's life that day, but when she got home she said it had been a super day, and I think spending a lot of it with the choir had been a great joy to her.

2019-2020

At the beginning of October the Dean held a special meeting to find out what we think underpins our planning for the "new" Cathedral. I understood it was for volunteers. For whatever reason it had been decreed that the Cathedral should be closed to visitors that morning, which I felt was quite unnecessary but mine not to reason why. When I got there the main doors were locked. I banged on the door with my very wet umbrella, rather like a bishop does at his enthronement or Black Rod does at the House of Commons, but there was no response. I remembered the side door would probably be open, and it was. I hung my brolly and raincoat up in the ladies, then went to the Refectory for the meeting, I hoped I had not missed coffee, and I hadn't. Ellie was serving coffee, small croissants and *pain au chocolat*. I am not a pastry person but I had one to encourage the Cathedral to keep up such provision!

The room was laid out with tables to seat eight. At first it looked like a wedding, but the finery was just glasses and jugs of water, paper and pencils and bumf. On each table was a list of who was to sit there, with the name of the facilitator. My table was allocated to me, Shaun Cutler who I didn't know, Chris Sayers likewise, Neringa, Kris and Geoff. Eventually we all sat down, but Geoff did not join us. He sat at the front near Canon X (I didn't catch his name) who was a visitor brought in to lead us. Geoff spoke briefly once or twice, and was much more lively, relevant and entertaining than Canon X.

No, we did not begin with prayer. We were told to discuss, in turn, three elements: inspiring worship, welcome and empowering worth. After each element we had a short plenary session and our facilitator Shaun read out an anonymous selection of our contributions. Nobody was very sure what "empowering worth" meant, but we got by. It was mainly anecdotes, some mine. Later in the morning we broke for more coffee, this time with slices of cake. There was also lots of prepared fruit – melon, grapes, pineapple etc – on each table. Most of us hung back for whatever reason, but Kris ate his way purposefully through ours. He suddenly let out a fierce sneeze, and we all urged him to eat more fruit to top up his Vitamin C.

The meeting was much better than I expected. Most of the assembled company were not volunteers but paid staff and hangers-on, and quite a few of them probably made no pretence of being Christians, but they were all human and seemed to want to provide a welcome to the marginalised. At the end, packing us off, Canon X added, "… and if you are that way inclined, do pray about it." I fear too many of us are not "that way inclined", and we should be. You can't run a Cathedral with people who are not "that way inclined". Presumably the lack of prayers was because those who were not "that way inclined" might have been offended/embarrassed. Well, tough. But the Heritage Lottery Fund are presumably not that way inclined, and they just want their money to be spent well. They have ordered us to acquire a hundred more volunteers. Maybe none of them will be that way inclined – who knows?

At one point in his remarks Geoff told us that some of the embroidery ladies had expressed horror at the Great Unwashed being allowed to use the hassocks to sleep on. These hassocks had been lovingly worked by ladies long gone but affectionately remembered, they said, and they didn't want them to get dirty. Geoff said it presented him with a dilemma. He knew what was right, but also felt some sympathy with the embroiderers. I fear I didn't. Who were they making the hassocks for? Of course hassocks were intended to be put on the floor to kneel on, and would soon be dirty. Many of the homeless who come into the Cathedral have been awake much of the night, trying to protect their scanty possessions from vandalism, or perhaps too cold to sleep. The pews offered a safe and protected place to sleep for a few hours, but pews are very hard. A row of hassocks can make a big difference. Perhaps if the embroiderers had been more aware of the situation they would have been proud to have provided even such limited comfort. As we left I was delighted to see that the Cathedral was now open to visitors and obviously had been for some time. I know several people had been distressed that it should be closed.

Last Night of the Proms seems to have become a favourite, and was repeated in October, the choir being joined by Dunstan Silver band. Kris's mum was there, up from the deep south. The Dean gave us all a warm welcome, and asked if we would indulge him in having a short prayer. God must get sick of short prayers – why are we always in such a hurry when we talk to him? Enough people joined in with the Amen to suggest that many of us did not mind at all. This was one of the last occasions we were likely to hear Jess singing in a concert with the choir, and she and Christopher Reid shared the solo lines of *Salutaris Hostia* by Eriks Esenwalds. They sounded very good together, and I was reminded of hearing Aled Jones singing a duet with Sarah Brightman many years ago. If I say which couple I preferred, you'd only accuse me of bias.

Another treat, though not for me, was in November when the choir were invited to sing at the Sage with the Prague Symphony Orchestra. I was not needed because Emily walked the choir across the bridge and back. I gathered it had been an enjoyable experience. It's a good way for a visiting ensemble to whip up interest and ticket sales in the local community, but it is still a privilege for the children to perform with famous professionals.

A great excitement was on December 6th when Jess was asked to sing "professionally" in a concert Kris was organising at the Cathedral. It was a combined performance by Northumbria University Choir and our own two adult choirs. The first half was to be a selection of Britten songs with harp accompaniment, and the second was to be Haydn's *St Nicholas Mass*. The four soloists were to be Emma Banks, Louise Reid, Nathaniel Thomas-Atkins and Patrick Owston — quite a distinguished line-up. Sadly on the morning of the 5th Louise was ill and knew she wouldn't be able to sing. Kris was in a quandary and asked Jess if she could help out. She knew and loved the Haydn, and she was happy to accept. Roger and I arrived early and got good seats, for which we were later reprimanded. Very young soloists prefer their ancestors to hide at the back. We were very sorry to see that the concert was thinly attended, with perhaps fewer than fifty in the audience, but they were most appreciative and clearly enjoyed it. We loved it. Jess did very well and was given a special curtain call at the end for, as Kris put it, saving his bacon. Before it began he had thanked me for letting him borrow her. "She'll get £100!" he said. I said well, it was even more special to her to be thought *worth* £100, to which he gallantly replied, "Oh, Jess is worth *far* more than that, but I have a tight budget!"

Time was running out. Jess was now in her A-level year, and felt she should resign after Christmas in order to concentrate on her studies. Choir was just taking up too much time, mainly because of the time she had to spend travelling to get to and from the Cathedral. She told Ian, but he persuaded her to stay on till February half-term in order to take part in a professional recording he was having made in the new year. Meanwhile we knew that everything that happened over Christmas would be the last time for us. It was a bit sad.

On Friday 13th there was a Christmas concert by the choirs and the Tyneside Orchestra. It was similar to last year's Christmas Extravaganza, but without a cheer leader. This time there were two refreshment teams, one each side of the nave. David and Vicky Pickering and Jennifer Ross were doing coffee and shortbread one side, and the Kelly family were doing mulled wine and mince pies the other side. It was a great success, and no doubt a lucrative enterprise. I prefer a hot drink myself, and to have a choice was wonderful. It goes without saying that the concert itself was excellent. Jess had a solo, and at the end she was given a valedictory by Ian because it was probably her last public performance. A special feature of this concert was three little songs sung by the Choristarters, a group of Year 2 children who Ian was hoping would graduate into the choir in due course. At £15 per adoring parent this was a shrewd move, and it certainly added an "Aah!" quality to the evening. We look forward to hearing them again, many times.

Roger kindly took over two of my usual stints – he helped steward at the Walking Nativity (this year Sarah Reid was Mary) and stayed for the subsequent carol singing, cocoa and mince pie. Next night he nobly froze in the Castle at the carol concert. This year it was only held on one night, but in two shifts. Roger just attended one of them. It was quite as cold as usual, and the choir were very brave to endure it. He and Jess were very lucky in being given a lift all the way home. There was a Vivaldi concert on the 22nd which did not involve Jess but I had offered to do stewarding, for which I got a free ticket. Roger said he thought he would like to go to it, so I let him do my stewarding for me so that he could have the free ticket. That saved us £28! I wouldn't (much) mind paying £28 to hear Jess sing, but that pleasure was not on offer. On the 23rd he went to do a bucket-shaking stint at Sainsbury's where the choir were singing carols. Shoppers were generous in their donations and clearly loved the singing. Some of them were moved to tears. I wondered where they thought their donations were going? Maybe they weren't very bothered. I think it was a very valuable contribution to public Christmas, as so many people never hear the Gospel message of the Nativity, and so many children think Christmas is all about Santa, reindeer and snowmen. And the choristers looked so angelic!

Christmas, our last as a choir family, proceeded much as usual. Jess attended the Crib Service to encourage the younger girls who would not be singing at Midnight Mass. The Bishop took the service of Nine Lessons and Carols and all the music was wonderful. Sarah joined us at Sleeperz for the last time, and we enjoyed her company. The Dean and the Bishop of Berwick shared Midnight Mass between them, the Dean preaching. I told him I remembered his sermon from last year (because I thought he would like to know that someone had been listening). He said he had a similar theme tonight, but with a different illustration. It couldn't have been quite so good because I had forgotten it by morning. Then at Christmas Day Eucharist everyone was hugging each other (if they were that way inclined) and wishing each other a happy Christmas. The most surprising treat was coffee and mince pies, which does not usually happen on Christmas Day because it is generally assumed people want to rush home to prevent their turkey burning. I was very grateful for a hot drink. We did not have a turkey burning, as we were staying for lunch.

This, although only the second, would be the last of Thomas's Christmas Lunches. After the service we sat around and read till lunch was ready. There was nothing to do because Thomas had done it all in advance. Again the tables were most attractively laid with pretty red cloths, this time for eighteen. There were tiny Nativity sets, oranges, chocolates and coloured lights, and it all looked very festive and welcoming. No one seemed to appear except the people who were involved, and I assumed that, as often happens on Sundays, people would turn up at the last minute from wherever they had been hiding, but no one did. The hot food was put on the serving table, and I went trotting off to see if there was anybody still around who might like to join us. When we sat down there were ten of us. Ten people in a family home might seem a lot, but in the Cathedral it didn't look quite so many, and I knew Thomas had been hoping for more. I went down the nave twice looking for hopefuls, and asked two separate ladies who declined politely. Later a man and a little boy appeared but the man also politely declined. It is a bit unexpected to be suddenly approached by a strange woman and offered a free Christmas dinner! The little boy looked sad, but accepted a chocolate gold coin that Jessica pressed on him. People who are sitting or mooching around in an empty church at 12.15 on Christmas Day are sure to be in need of a dinner, but might not like to admit it. One or two of our regulars normally came on public transport which of course was not running today, and most students had gone home. I think we all felt very sad for poor Thomas who had put such a lot of time and trouble and love into it. Sadly those of us who attended were, for the main part, not a bundle of fun, and we lacked a catalyst for merriment. Thomas and Peter did their best, but they had to work hard to keep everyone's spirits up. Of course, the main consideration was that as few people as possible should be lonely at Christmas, and maybe Crisis and other organisations had mopped everyone up this year. Crisis are a much better option because they are warmer and provide a whole day of celebration, whereas we have to clear out afterwards and can only offer a limited amount of creature comfort. But I would like Thomas to know how much we appreciated his efforts, both years. Those who came might not generally be considered needy, but had needs of their own. There is a general belief that at Christmas everyone has a happy family to celebrate with, but it is not always so.

There was lots of food left over, and I took home sprouts, parsnips and potato, and we had a very good cheese'n'vegetable pie for tea. I found a big polybag of trifle too. I don't know how I got it and I may have picked up a bag belonging to someone else, but it was very good. I can confirm that trifle from a polybag tastes just as good as from a cut-glass bowl. Maybe it was the love that had gone into the making of it.

We knew that 2020 was going to be a challenging year for the Cathedral. The workmen were starting work in January, and all worship activities would be in the Quire. The choir would sing from the Eastern Chapels and the Quire stalls would be for worshippers, supplemented by chairs in the side aisles. The Dean called the Warden team together to discuss how this could best be done with dignity and decorum. Who would do exactly what, where, and how? Would there be too many people to fill the available space (well, we can dream). The tower bells would be rung as usual, but the communion bell would have to be given a holiday as there would be no access to the rope. What about special church occasions like ordinations? Oh, arrangements had already been made with another church to host them. The entrance to the Song School would have to be used as one of the two general thoroughfares – would this put the choristers at risk? I volunteered to take my trusty Kindle and sit and freeze in the hall when the children were arriving and leaving (an offer that was never taken up). Canon Care said kindly that I would not need to freeze as there would still be heating in that part of the building! There was scope for a lot of worrying to be done by those who like to worry. Oh well, we should see how things turned out. As it happened, all these considerations were to be the least of our worries.

I knew I could not do a refreshment stall for the Monday organ recitals any more, and I offered to be a welcomer instead. I was offered Friday afternoons, and told I would have to stand (or sit) in the very draughty hallway outside the Refectory. No, I could not make coffee for anyone in the Refectory. That would create problems.

I had wondered what the homeless people would do now they could not come into the nave and hug a radiator. There were radiators in the Quire – would the homeless find their way there and feel able to make free with such comfort as was possible? The first time I attended Evensong in the Quire I was delighted to see a young man asleep in his sleeping bag in the corner by the Ascension Chapel altar, on a shakedown mattress of the big cushions from the former children's chapel, and with an empty mug from a hot drink one of the verging staff had made him. When I say I was delighted, I naturally wished he had a better lot in life, but he had come to the Cathedral for comfort and found a bit. He sounded drunk and looked depressed, but we smiled at each other and exchanged a friendly word. Within the hour the Cathedral would have had to close and he would be on the street again, but we had been there for him for that short time, and it may be that few other people were ever there for him.

One Friday afternoon two visitors came out of the Quire looking very worried. One of them said, "Excuse me, there is a man asleep in the church!" I said yes, there often was, and we knew that homeless people often came in wanting a sleep and we welcomed them. "We think it's what Jesus would do," I said. They were clearly astonished, and left deep in thought.

One exciting morning in mid-January Jess was tele-phoned with the offer of a provisional place at Trinity College, Cambridge. She couldn't wait to share her news with everyone, and that afternoon she set off for choir rehearsal with a big drum of chocolates to celebrate with. First she told Emily, to explain why she had brought chocolates, and Emily was so pleased for her. She had a phone call from Ian, and passed the phone to Jess so she could tell him herself. Then Kris came in, and Emily asked him if he had heard Jess's news. No, he hadn't! When she told him he chided her for not having told him at once because, he said, "You're the nearest I've got to a daughter!" For eight years the choir had been like an extended family to her, and she probably felt it very keenly that night when they all rejoiced with her. But it had its down side: now she had to work very hard to get the required A-level grades of A*AA, which would mean a lot of brain slog and, as Jess saw it, giving up choir for revision. But all good things come to an end. There would be other choirs, and at Newcastle another little girl was waiting to be Head Chorister!

Since Christmas we had been hearing increasingly about a new virus that had reared its ugly head in a town called Wuhan in China. There was no known cure for it, and it was causing concern in medical circles. Naturally it's a small world and diseases spread quickly by jet airplane, and before long it was identified in the west. The illness, called Covid 19, was actually only slight for most people, but it could be very nasty and perhaps fatal for older people and those who were clinically vulnerable. One morning I was amused to see some Chinese students shopping in M&S in face masks! Were they trying to protect themselves or other people? I felt they must be overreacting. Little did I guess that within a few weeks we should all be wearing face masks!

Towards the end of January, as I was packing up after a welcoming session, a young Chinese gentleman came in. He looked anxious. He told me he was from Wuhan, and he was very worried about his family and friends there. He wanted to pray for them. He was *almost* a Christian, he said. I asked him if he would like to talk to a priest, but he did not seem to understand me. I asked him to follow me, and led him to the vestry where I knew Father Peter would be because he had just come in to get ready for Evensong. I told him my name, and he told me his. Yes, there was Father Peter, and I left the young man in his capable hands. They were still talking when I packed up and left, and I could tell the young man was being helped.

As days went by we heard a lot about the new illness on the news. It was called Coronavirus. Gradually it took over in importance from Brexit, which had for many months been the main topic of everyone's conversation. Everyone expected the Government to do something about it, and they duly did. Their main concern was to keep the NHS supported so that anyone who got sick would be able to have hospital treatment if necessary. It began to look as if the excellent and much maligned system might be overwhelmed and unable to cope unless drastic action was taken. The Prime Minister and his team took advice from the top scientists, and made frequent TV appearances to inform the population what we must do. Right from the start the advice was to wash our hands as often as we could, and to keep at a good distance (two metres) from everyone else. The slogan was "Stay at home. Protect the NHS. Save Lives."

On Sunday, February 2nd, Ian asked the choir to stay behind for half an hour after Evensong. Canon Clare had specially requested that they should make a recording of the National Anthem, with a change of pronoun, for such time as it might be needed. The Queen was 94 and in excellent health, but it could only be a matter of time before we had to sing "Send *him* victorious." I got the impression Clare was hoping to corner the market for recordings when a demand was created. A professional recording company was called in, and the choir sang their way through three different settings, from which Ian could make a choice at greater leisure. We sat quietly and listened, and it was a most un- nerving experience. I was ten years old when the pronoun had last been changed, and of the assembled company I think Roger and I were the only ones who had ever experienced a male monarch.

The building work was going on apace. So far it had mainly involved exploratory work, but from March 9th we were told there would be no heating in the church for eight weeks. That was bad news! March is not a very warm month, and we were not all as young as we used to be. But we had been warned. I knew there were small portable heaters I could use on Friday afternoons, and I could take a little one of my own to supplement them.

The recording of the long-planned choir CD could clearly no longer happen in the Cathedral. It was more complicated than the National Anthem recording and could not be accomplished in half an hour, so it was decided to hold it in St George's Church, Cullercoats by their courtesy. On February 22nd the choristers went there for a full day's rehearsal. Jess was given a lift both ways, and I clearly was neither needed nor wanted. We very much looked forward to having a nice recording in due course, as a permanent memento of Jess's choir years and a nice gift for her family and friends.

Jess told me Kris had asked her to sing with the Cathedral Youth Choir who meet on Tuesday nights, practise for half an hour and then sing for Evensong. That will be nice for her, keeping her hand in at the Cathedral and having a serious regular sing. After so many years of disciplined singing, suddenly being limited to singing in the bath is very hard.

Well, dear patient Reader, the story ended on Sunday, March 1st, 2020. We took our last taxi to the Cathedral, and Roger and I had our last breakfast in the Vermont. It was comforting to reflect briefly that we should be saving quite a bit in future! I had to eat up quickly because I was wardening with David Dunscombe. There is not much to do under the new system, but of course if any unexpected problem arises the wardens have to deal with it. Happily today no problem did. At the end of the service I stood by the south Quire gate to watch Jess being de-commissioned. Geoff and Ian went up to the

High Altar followed by Jess and Rachel. First Ian presented Rachel to the Dean and asked that she should be installed as the new Head Chorister, which seemed the wrong way round, then, as the order of service expressed it, the Dean "presided over Jessica Hawkins laying down her office as Head Chorister". He said a prayer over her, then he presented her with the usual copy of *Messiah.* I'm not given to crying so I didn't, but I felt very emotional. Up in the Thomlinson Room she had a tearful farewell with the other choristers, and was given some generous presents. Best of all was a lovely scrap book Rachel had organised for her, with loving messages from many people including Michael Stoddart. It was the end of an era for her. So many good people had made the framework of Jessica's life, and they had all moved on. When she left choir only John Lewis was still there of all of them.

It was also the end of an era for the Cathedral. Not only were services confined to the Quire area, but after a few weeks they had to stop altogether. By the end of March the whole country was in lockdown. Over the coming months churches were sometimes closed, sometimes open for private prayer only, and sometimes services were allowed with a maximum of 30 worshippers including the clergy. The 30 worshippers had to have a distance of two metres between each of them, and after a time it just got too difficult to organise, and too few people wanted to take advantage of the permitted facilities. After the following Christmas Geoff decided to close the Cathedral, and wisely.

Meanwhile, however, a great deal of work went on behind the scenes to maintain a spiritual life online. The Music Department pulled out all the stops to enable the choir to continue singing, with online rehearsals and sometimes, when circumstances permitted, real ones. An email came round telling choir parents about the safety measures Ian, Kris and Emily had taken to ensure the choristers were safe from infection when they met. They would work in small groups, would each have their own chair, carefully measured to be at least two metres from the next one, and would stay by that chair throughout with no mingling. On each chair, Ian said, there would be a wrapped chocolate biscuit such as a Penguin or Club. How nice! A year or two ago Ian had set up toasters, bread, margarine and jam in the Thomlinson Room for anyone who was peckish, as of course all choristers are after a day at school, but this facility could no longer be used because of the necessity of distancing. A chocolate biscuit would help to ameliorate this deprivation.

Now, in anticipation of Jess leaving, we had told Ian months ago that we would like to make a thank-you gift to the Music Department, and we had hoped that it could be something that would increase the comfort of the younger choristers. Ian told us he would think it over and let us know, but so far he had not done so. Maybe it was difficult. Well, it occurred to us, on reading this email, that chocolate biscuits were going to make a big hole in either Ian's pocket or the Cathedral's dwindling resources, so we suggested setting up a Jessica Hawkins Chocolate Biscuit Fund. Ian liked the idea (and so did Jessica), and so it came about. We could not afford to do it in perpetuity, much as we would have liked to, but for the coming year and the foreseeable future.

Hopefully the Cathedral will re-open sometime in 2021, but it will never be quite the same again. Ellie is retiring in the autumn, and a new voice will be heard on the end of the telephone. The Bishop and Dean will be retiring in the not too distant future and passing on the mantle to someone else. Hopefully Clare and Peter, Ian and Kris will still be part of a new team, including people in the office who the congregation rarely or never see. The Lord giveth, and the Lord taketh away. Blessed be the name of the Lord.

And we may be sure there will be fundraising for a new organ! There will always be something exciting going on. I don't need to go to the Cathedral any more, but of course I shall do. It has become part of me, and I want to continue to be involved. I have met some lovely people on my chaperoning journey, and I know I shall meet lots more. Being a choir parent is a huge commitment of time, but very well repaid by the joy of hearing so much lovely music, and often knowing that our little tykes have inspired some people to the point of tears. Some of the choristers admit that they do not believe in God. More than one or two have been bribed and cajoled by ambitious parents. Most of them are tired at the end of a school day and would probably prefer to go home to relax. Yet their combined performance is often evocative of the Heavenly Choir. Truly, God works in a mysterious way!

"Let everything that hath breath praise the Lord!"